Hasidic Responses to the Holocaust in the Light of Hasidic Thought

Hasidic Responses to the Holocaust in the Light of Hasidic Thought

Pesach Schindler

KTAV PUBLISHING HOUSE, INC.
HOBOKEN, NEW JERSEY
1990

Library of Congress Cataloging-in-Publication Data

Schindler, Pesach.
Hasidic responses to the Holocaust : in the light of Hasidic thought / by Pesach Schindler.
p. cm.
Includes bibliographical references and index.
ISBN 0-88125-310-3
1. Holocaust (Jewish theology) 2. Hasidism. I. Title.
BM645.H6S25 1990
296.3'11—dc20 90-47102
CIP

Manufactured in the United States of America

To my dear wife Shulamith
and my children
Chaya, Geeta, Meyer, Nechama, Avi

Contents

Introduction

Among the victims of the destruction of European Jewry from 1939 to 1945 were thousands of Hasidim and their spiritual leaders, the Rebbeim or Zadikim. These Jews represented a tradition originating in the religious-mystical-revivalist movement founded by Rabbi Israel Ba'al Shem Tov (1700–1760) in Eastern Europe.

The purpose of this study is twofold: first, to determine how Hasidic leaders and ordinary Hasidim conducted themselves during the Holocaust, and how they understood the terrible events they were witnessing and living through; and second, to show the relationship between their responses to the Holocaust and certain basic concepts of Hasidic thought.[1] Specifically, we seek to determine the underpinnings in traditional Hasidic thought for Holocaust responses related to the problem of evil and suffering, the dynamics of national redemption, *Kiddush Hashem* (the Sanctification of God's Name), the unique interaction of the *Rebbe*, Hasid, and Hasidic confraternity, and resistance activities.

An introduction provides the historical and ideological context for the study, devoted in particular to Hasidic doctrine and tradition. The Holocaust responses, gathered from primary and secondary sources, are classified and examined in accordance with accepted methods of historical research. These are correlated with aspects of Hasidic doctrine, drawn especially from the major eighteenth- and nineteenth-century Hasidic masters.

FINDINGS

Hasidim sought to justify God's role during the Holocaust by denying that there was any theological distinction between *din* (retribution) and *rahamim* (compassion) and between good and evil. All that emanates from God is *hesed* (goodness, kindness), though it may be hidden *(nistar)* from man's finite perspective. Suffering must therefore be accepted with love *(kabbalah be'ahavah)* and *mesirat nefesh* (personal sacrifice) on the basis of faith *(emunah)* and unquestioning trust *(bitahon)* in God's ultimate justice. Responses also focused on the phenomenon of *Hevle Mashiah* (the pangs of suffering prior to the coming of the Messiah), the prerequisites for Jewish redemption, the debilitating character of *Galut* (exile), and the centrality of Eretz Yisrael (the land of Israel) in the redemption process. Responses were reflected in the concept of *Kiddush Hashem* (sanctifying God's Name in martyrdom) and the emphasis on *Kiddush Hahayim* (sanctifying God's Name in life) in defiance of the enemy's objective to degrade and terminate life. In this aspect of the work I focus on the special relationship of the Rebbe to the Hasid and the refusal of the Zaddik to abandon his community in a supreme act of *Ahavat Yisrael* (love for fellow Jews). Hasidim, in turn, derived comfort from the Rebbe, who provided encouragement *(hithazkut)* during the terrible ordeal. Responses of physical resistance were sparse and were correlated with the Hasidic tendency to spiritualize references to violence and warfare. The study documents incidents of significant passive and spiritual resistance. These include violations of edicts against religious activity, especially in its Hasidic form, often within the framework of illegal underground Hasidic cells operating in the ghettos.

These responses were correlated with aspects of Hasidic thought. Correlative Hasidic elements evident throughout include the symbiotic interaction of man and God, the manner in which the initial action of man *(etaruta deletata)* has an impact upon the upper regions *(etaruta dele'ela)*, and the tension between the activist and quietist schools in Hasidism.

CONCLUSION

The study indicated that Hasidism responded to the trauma of the Holocaust within the framework of Hasidic tradition. This response pattern provided the Hasid with the means that enabled him to confront and overcome the trials of the Holocaust with dignity and moral integrity.

ACKNOWLEDGMENTS

I am pleased to express my appreciation to those who have guided and assisted me in this study. I am particularly grateful to Professor David Rudavsky, the chairman of my committee, for his deep concern, encouragement, and good advice from the very conception of this project to its culmination. I am indebted to Professor Nathan H. Winter at whose urging the researcher resumed the post graduate studies that ultimately led to this project. Acknowledgment is also made to Professor Lee A. Belford for his counsel and interest. Among my teachers at New York University, I must also single out Professors Janice L. Gorn and Paul M. Mattingly, who helped me considerably during the initial stages of the research.

I was fortunate to benefit as well from the inspiration and assistance of Professor Abraham Joshua Heschel, a master of Hasidic literature. Acknowledgment is also made to the staffs of the Judaica Division of the New York Public Library and the Toronto Jewish Public Library, and Dr. Israel Frankel, head librarian.

Acknowledgment is made of the generosity of the Memorial Foundation for Jewish Culture and the Hebrew Culture Foundation for doctoral study and research grants. I am also indebted to Dr. Morton Siegel for his encouragement and understanding. These fine people can only have enhanced and improved this work. It is this researcher who bears the responsibility for any of its shortcomings.

Finally, to my dear wife Shulamith I am deeply indebted for her patience, devotion, and deep inspiration. To my children Chaya, Geeta, Meyer, Nechama, and Avraham, I leave this work as a gift of love and affection.

CHAPTER 1

The Problem

FACTORS IN THE EVOLUTION OF THE PROBLEM

Autobiographical

I arrived in the United States on February 22, 1940, on one of the last civilian vessels to leave Rotterdam at the onset of World War II. Having experienced neither the ghetto nor the concentration camp, I do not qualify as a "survivor" of the Holocaust, but for some time I was considered a refugee on official documents, and the impact of those momentous years left a permanent mark.

It is recorded of Simon Dubnow, the noted Jewish historian, that prior to his death at the hands of the Nazis in 1941, his last plea was in the form of a mandate to the survivors to record accurately all the tragic details of the Holocaust. Dubnow's entreaty may have been related to the biblical injunction "Thou shalt not forget,"[1] aimed at Amalek and his spiritual descendants. If a certain sense of compulsion is considered helpful in scholarly research, I may claim to have obtained it from Dubnow and the biblical guidelines.

The Problem of the Holocaust

The Holocaust has raised serious questions for people of all faiths and ideologies. Man's response to the inequities of life is part of the Jewish tradition. The challenges to God posed by Abraham, the psalmist, and Job,[2] within the framework of faith, are the eternal questions of mankind.[3]

THE HASIDIC PHENOMENON

In seeking to study responses to radical crisis, I sought a subject concerned with more than physical survival. The Hasidic-mystic tradition had achieved significant stature in the Jewish communities of Eastern Europe by the end of the nineteenth century. It had to contend with immense opposition both in rationalistic-talmudic circles and in the secular camp. Hasidism was not to remain only a system of thought. By its own definition, Hasidism permeated every moment of a genuine adherent's life. By 1939 cohesive Hasidic confraternities and rabbinic dynasties were prominent in every community in Eastern Europe. The Holocaust endangered the physical existence of the Hasid; it also tested his devotion and fidelity to the Hasidic way of life.

As mentioned in the introduction, the purpose of this study was to examine the available documented responses to the Holocaust of Hasidic leaders and their Hasidim in an attempt to discern the correlation between their responses and certain basic Hasidic concepts. These concepts included the relationship of God to man and the Jewish people, and the related problem of suffering and evil, the messianic idea and redemption, *Kiddush Hashem*, the mutual bond of Hasidic fellowship, and the relationship of the ordinary Hasid and the Zadik or Rebbe. Aside from these topics, I centered my investigation on the resistance—physical, spiritual, and moral—of Hasidim to the Nazi onslaught. Since there was little physical resistance of a documented nature, I attempted to determine whether the relative absence of resistance was consistent with the totality of Hasidic thought and its response to the Holocaust.[4]

In regard to the problem of theodicy, I singled out the following issues for more detailed study: Hasidic interpretations which justify God's actions and relate events to God's attributes; interpretations which attempt to focus on man's attitude to God, in particular, the acceptance of one's fate; questioning of God's actions and attributes in the light of the experience of the Holocaust; the beneficial and detrimental consequences of suffering.

Related to this is the complex of messianic ideas which are in part the common heritage of all Jewish thought and in part particularly Hasidic. These include the concept of *Hevle Mashiah*, the period of suffering which is to usher in the messianic era, the prerequisites for redemption, the nature of exile and the Diaspora, and the role of Eretz Yisrael.

Finally, I examined the effect the Holocaust had on the Rebbe-Hasid relationship. In the main, Rebbes remained with their Hasidim in order to comfort and encourage them, assist and organize rescue operations. They continued to hold the fraternal Hasidic meal, the "tish," under adverse circumstances. In return, the Hasidim maintained their loyalty to their Rebbes; in the process, both Rebbe and Hasid maintained the value of *Ahavat Yisrael,* love and compassion for fellow-Jews.

DEFINITIONS

Before we proceed any further, several key terms will be defined for the convenience of readers.

Hasidism is a revivalist and mystical religious movement that originated in Eastern Europe in the middle of the eighteenth century. It was founded by Rabbi Israel Ba'al Shem Tov (1700–1760), also known as the Besht.

The Zadik (lit., "the righteous one") is the central religious figure in Hasidism. The first Zadik was Rabbi Dov Ber of Mezritch (1710–1772), a disciple of the Besht. Each Hasidic group or branch is headed by a Zadik. By way of charismatic personality and personal piety, and sometimes but not always through intellectual attainments, the Zadik is the model and source of religious inspiration and guidance for his followers. The Zadik is also often referred to as the Rebbe.[5]

Holocaust is the usual designation for the destruction of European Jewry by the Nazis during World War II (1939–1945).[6] The Hebrew terms *Shoah* (devastation, ruin) and *Hurban* (destruction, catastrophe) are also commonly employed.[7]

Kiddush Hashem literally means, "Sanctification of the (Holy) Name," as opposed to *Hillul Hashem,* "Profanation of the Name." As developed in the Bible, this concept appears general and abstract.[8] *Kiddush Hashem* was specified and concretized in Rabbinic Judaism, directing the Jew to dedicate his daily routine acts to the service of God. Man's behavior is expected to reflect positively on God's purpose in creating him. The role of the human being in the universe is perceived as one of partnership in creation. In time, the ultimate form of *Kiddush Hashem* was expressed in the Jew's "readiness to suffer martyrdom, [in which] a man brings home to others an awareness of God."[9]

WHY THIS STUDY IS IMPORTANT

The Holocaust is considered *sui generis* in Jewish history, and possibly in the history of all mankind. Martin Buber, Jacob Robinson, and Salo

Baron emphasize its historical uniqueness.[10] Elie Wiesel notes the "terrifying theological implications" of the realization that the Covenant between the Jewish people and their God had been broken for "the first time in our history.[11]

Though traditionally observant Jewry made up a large portion of the Jews caught in the Holocaust, the *religious* response to this unparalleled disaster is only beginning to be studied with the care that other aspects of the subject have received. Thus, we know more about resistance, atrocities, biographical data of the victims, concentration camp routine, rescue, attempts at secular cultural life, self-government in the ghetto, the fate of the children, and the fate of the women than about religious responses.[12]

Among the assumptions of this study is the internalization of major aspects of Hasidic-mystical thought into the realities of the daily life of the Hasid.[13] "Classical Hasidism was not the product of some theory or other, not even of a Kabbalistic doctrine, but of direct, spontaneous religious experience."[14]

The special significance of the study may be denoted in the rephrasing of the problem statement as follows: How did Hasidic leaders and Hasidim respond in the wake of a deep crisis which exposed the Hasidic life and thought pattern to a critical test? Were these responses in any way related to aspects of Hasidic thought?

CHAPTER 2

Related Literature

THE BIBLIOGRAPHY OF HOLOCAUST LITERATURE

The largest of the institutes and archives devoted to Holocaust research, Yad Vashem in Jerusalem, in partnership with Yivo in New York, has prepared and published a comprehensive ten-volume bibliography of Holocaust literature, including the Yiddish and Hebrew press and periodicals, eyewitness accounts, diaries and letters, war trial documents, and the works of the illegal documentation centers which operated in the ghettos and camps.[1] Though the index to the bibliographies is not refined and does not necessarily focus on the specific area of our study, a comprehensive review of this literature did reveal isolated sources, especially eyewitness accounts of Hasidic responses. This literature proved essential in providing the general context for this study and an appreciation of the conditions prevailing during the Holocaust.

THE MEMORIAL VOLUME PROJECTS

A second important source of Holocaust literature is the substantial body of memorial volumes dedicated to specific communities, prepared and published by the survivors following World War II. Typically, a volume of this kind traces the history of a community from its inception through its destruction. A survey of these volumes reveals brief references to religious life before and during the Holocaust. Hasidic aspects are dealt with in a sketchy fashion, often limited to a listing of Hasidic leaders who perished. Justifying the need for his volume on the religious history of Lvov, Fischer-Schein attributes the lack of material depicting relgious life and experiences to the failure of Orthodox Jews to document the activities of their communities and their role in the Holocaust.[2] Even where aspects of the Holocaust related to religious life were recorded, they are not adequately represented in the memorial volumes.[3]

UNDERGROUND PRESS, GHETTO AND CAMP DIARIES, CORRESPONDENCE

The relatively sparse treatment of religious activities, and specifically of Hasidic activities, is equally reflected in the underground press, of which there were 170 editions in the Yiddish language alone.[4] This is to be understood in the light of the fact that the great majority of illegal publishing activities in the ghettos were carried on by secular movements such as Hashomer Hazair, Poale Zion, and other "anti-fascist" groups.[5] The reason why the Hasidic groups did not illegally publish their own organs will be considered in the chapters devoted to an interpretation of Hasidic responses.

The diaries and letters which have been published are in the main devoted to secular concerns, especially those whose authors were associated with resistance and partisan elements. The diary of Hillel Seidman and the notes of Shimon Huberband document religious life, and the pertinent sections will be treated as sources.[6] The diary of sixteen-year-old Moshe Flinker reflects a profoundly sensitive and philosophical outlook of devout religious thought on the Holocaust background, but provides no evidence of specifically Hasidic orientation.[7] The notes of Emanuel Ringelblum and the diary of Chaim Kaplan deal in the main with general ghetto life during the liquidation of the Warsaw Ghetto.[8]

HASIDIC LITERATURE AND THE HOLOCAUST

Primary Documents

Two major Hasidic documents written during the Holocaust have come to light. These are considered most significant for the present study. In both cases the authors were distinguished Hasidic personalities who employed Hasidic sources in order to support (or refute) opinion or valuations relevant to Holocaust events; in consequence, the opinions or valuations propounded in the documents are considered "responses" as previously defined.

Esh Kodesh

The Piazesner Rebbe, Rabbi Kalonymos Kalmish Shapiro, was a descendant of a renowned Hasidic dynasty originating with Rabbi Elimelech of Lizensk (d. 1786), Rabbi Israel, the Magid of Koznitz (d. 1814), and the Seer of Lublin (d. 1815). His wife's family was rooted in the Karliner dynasty. For thirty-five years he guided the Hasidic *hoif* ("court") in Piazesne, a small community approximately 15 kilometers south of Warsaw. Thousands of Polish Hasidim were his adherents, including hundreds of young Hasidim who were full-time students in the Yeshiva that he founded in Piazesne. During the period from September 1940 to the summer of 1943, the Rebbe recorded the discourses he delivered on the Sabbath and holidays.[9] Prior to the destruction and final liquidation of the Warsaw Ghetto in the spring of 1943, the manuscripts were hidden in a jug and buried underground. In his last letter to his followers, the Rebbe requests that the manuscripts, if discovered, be sent to his brother, Rabbi Yeshaya Shapiro, in Tel Aviv. The Rebbe was killed in the fall of 1943. An exhaustive search in the Jewish Historical Institute of Warsaw by Baruch Duvdevani a Hasid of the Rebbe, revealed the letter and subsequently the jug with the manuscript was accidentally discovered by workmen digging a foundation for a new apartment building. The discourses were subsequently published in Israel under the title *Esh Kodesh* ("Holy Fire").[10]

Em Habanim Semehah

The other Hasidic primary document is *Em Habanim Semehah* ("A Happy Mother of Children"), by Rabbi Yissachar Shlomo Teichthal, a Hasid of the Munkacher Rebbe, head of the rabbinic court in Kustolan and Pishtshan.[11] He began writing it in Budapest in January of 1943, and it was published in December 1943, before the formal German occupation of Budapest on 19 March 1944. The author was subsequently transported to Auschwitz along with most of Hungarian Jewry.[12] He met his death on a train carrying inmates from Auschwitz to Bergen-Belsen on 24 January 1945.

Em Habanim Semehah passionately urges observant Jews to evacuate their communities in the Diaspora and rebuild Eretz Yisrael as a necessary prelude to the *Geulah Shelemah* (final redemption). The author accuses the leaders of Orthodox Jewry of opposing settlement in Palestine, especially during the pre–World War II period, therefore unwittingly contributing to the mass murder of the millions of Jews trapped in hostile Europe. Thus the Orthodox authorities, among them Hasidic Rebbes, share the responsibility for the Holocaust in progress.[13]

Secondary Documents

Among the few who have devoted research to the Hasidic communities during the Holocaust is Moshe Prager, who describes the Hasid's steadfast trust and confidence in God's ways. In Prager's journalistic accounts, evidently compiled from eyewitness reports but not always documented, the Hasid seems able to confront the tribulations and tests of the moment with confidence, hope and fortitude and without flinching from "pure faith." He ignites the dark environment about him with "Hasidic fervor."[14] In another work, Prager describes in detail an underground complex of young Hasidic followers of the Rebbe from Gur with partial eyewitness documentation.[15] The heroism of these young Hasidim is not manifested in the form of physical resistance but in the manner that they continue to dress in Hasidic garb, conduct illegal study cells, and carry out dangerous humanitarian missions. Writing under the pen name of Moshe Yehezke'eli, Prager also devoted a modest volume each to a detailed description of the perilous escape of the Gerer Rebbe from Warsaw in the spring of 1940 and of the Belzer Rebbe from Budapest in 1944.[16] Eyewitness reports and supporting primary sources document the extreme devotion of Hasidim to their Rebbe, the Rebbe's unquestioning acceptance of the martyrdom of his own kinfolk, and his messages of comfort, hope, and optimism regarding the redemption that would emerge from the funeral pyres of a martyred people.[17]

Menashe Unger devotes an extensive volume to sixty-four leaders of Hasidic dynasties who perished in the Holocaust.[18] Reports of their final days appear as partially documented eyewitness reports. The major Hasidic responses in Unger's work may be classified as follows: (1) The unbending faith of the Hasidic Rebbe and the manner in which he accepted his own fate with "love," even as he hoped and prayed for "imminent salvation." (2) The unceasing efforts of the Rebbe to comfort his flock and to provide spiritual solace and encouragement in the Hasidic tradition of *Ahavat Yisrael*. Numerous opportunities for escape were often turned down by Rebbes who refused to abandon their Hasidim during the crisis.

In addition, three anthologies devoted to the religious response by

Isaac Levin and Mordechai Eliav contain Hasidic material, including eye-witness documentation. These volumes served as keys to primary sources though they do not always meet the standards of rigorous historic research.[19]

CHAPTER 3

Hasidic Doctrine

HISTORICAL BACKGROUND

The Sabbatian "heresy" of the seventeenth century left Jewry in spiritual disarray. The charismatic Sabbatai Zevi (1625–1676), a young mystic from Smyrna, stunned and captivated the Jews everywhere with his messianic claims, but his conversion to Islam shocked the masses of Eastern European Jews who were being ground down under relentless physical, social, and economic persecutions. The Chmielnicki Cossack massacres of 1648–49 had devastated entire Jewish communities. The years 1648 to 1795 also witnessed the disintegration of the Polish empire, which had represented an element of stability and security. As a result, the insecurity of Eastern European Jewish life increased rapidly.

A response was forthcoming in the form of a mystical-revivalist movement which began to evolve under Rabbi Israel the son of Eliezer, known as the Ba'al Shem Tov or Besht, and his devout circle of disciples. Clusters of intimate mystical groups known as *Hevrah Hasidim* and *Haburah Kadisha* were already active as the Besht emerged.[1] Their activities were characterized by ecstatic forms of prayer following the style and guidelines of the kabbalistic mystical circles of 16th-century Safed in Palestine and subsequently also in Sabbatian groups. The prayers were often accompanied by outbursts of joy, song, and dance. Religious fellowship among Hasidim was also characterized by the fraternal meal, especially on the Sabbath and festivals, which served as an opportunity for Hasidic discourses. In all their activities the Hasidim sought to achieve the state of *devekut*, i.e., the sublime religious experience of "cleaving" to the divine.[2]

In the initial stages, the Hasidic groups were bound to the sole leadership of the Besht. Following his death (1760), and under the influence of his leading disciple, Rabbi Dov Ber of Mezritch (d. 1773), the institution of Zadikism evolved. The Zadik, the venerable master, would now relate in a unique way to his own circle of Hasidim, and they, in turn, would see in their master a model to be emulated and a source of guidance and inspiration for their spiritual and material concerns.

In the eighteenth century, Hasidism spread rapidly in economically depressed areas, especially in the outlying regions of the Ukraine, such as Podolia. The movement then expanded into Volhynia, Galicia, central Poland, and eventually Romania and Hungary.

Hasidism introduced major new concepts into Jewish life. It represented a continuation of the mystical-kabbalistic tradition,[3] drawing from the major kabbalistic work, the *Zohar*, and the teachings of the great sixteenth-century master, Rabbi Isaac Luria of Safed (Ari) (1534–1572). Hasidism's massive contribution was to articulate mystical Jewish experience, especially Lurianic Kabbalah, in such a manner and form that the esoteric and concealed became the way of life for a majority of Jews in Eastern Europe during the late eighteenth and nineteenth centuries. Indeed, under Hasidism, the "kabbalistic heritage" was "popularized."[4] New significance was infused into standard mystical concepts and practices. Hasidism thereby bridged the stark realities of life for the Jews in Eastern Europe by endowing them with religious meaning. It strove to provide a satisfactory response not only for the learned and pious scholars, whose learned activities maintained their morale, but also for the simple and ignorant Jew who most often felt spiritually isolated and deprived during the catastrophic events about him. The Hasidic movement restored a measure of human dignity to the average Jew and provided him with a mode of communal experience in which life took on a new meaning.

As background for our treatment of the Holocaust, the highlights of Hasidic doctrines will be grouped under the following major headings: (1.) experiencing God; (2.) the purpose of man; (3.) the role of the Zadik.

EXPERIENCING GOD

How does one experience God, the essence of transcendence and goodness, amidst the mundane and evil? One of the major creative contributions of Hasidism, and underlying the substrata of Hasidic thought, was its response to this question in the formulation of *Avodah Begashmiut*.[5] This concept directed man to serve and experience God *within* the mundane,[6] the imperfect, and even the immoral realm forever; there will the divine spark be found. This paradox was realized by denying that matter and evil existed independently. Evil is conceived as either a perversion or as a "stepstool" of good,[7] rooted in the divine. "It is merely the lowest rung of the absolute good."[8] Divinity emanates from and flows into *all* reality, existence, and being, even into what man may perceive as suffering. The struggle between evil and good is merely a product of human psychology and thus irrelevant to cosmic events as the Kabbalah sees them. "The fire of the 'holy' has consumed the substance of good and evil."[9] This produces a distinctly quietistic strain in Hasidic doctrine where suffering becomes irrelevant, and the subjective distinctions between God as Judge and God as a source of compassion dissolve into a supreme religious experience where all that is, is God, and all that is God is good.[10] By fulfilling God's will and purpose and conducting one's whole life in accordance with the *mitzvot* (divine commandments), man merges the mundane with the holy. He serves as a bridge across which the divine sparks may return to their origin. In this process, however, man is not merely an inconsequential instrument for larger purposes. In striving for *devekut* (i.e., cleaving to God), man is privileged to climb to the pinnacle of religious experience and thereby achieve a worth greater than himself.

Though *devekut* is central to all of Jewish mysticism, Hasidism rescued this experience from the esoteric, austere, and ascetic confines of kabbalistic mysticism and made it directly accessible to every Jew who sought it out. Simple and sincere prayer uttered with purposeful concentration and intention (*kavanah*) became the most effective means for achieving *devekut*.[11] Descriptions of *devekut* vary. They assume the passive form of meditation. This permits the Hasid to absorb the divine emanations in an unobstrusive and quietist manner. The *devekut* mood may, however, shift to ecstatic joy *(hitlahavut)* during the peak of the experience that allows the frail human being to unite with God *(hitahdut)* as he intensely senses a love for the divine *(Ahavat Elohim)*.[12] During the height of the *devekut* experience man is able to dissolve or release the egoistic forces operating within him *(hitpashtut hagashmiut)*,[13] making it possible for the soul to reunite with its divine source.

Hasidism appealed to the downtrodden masses, since it convinced the common man, bereft of the opportunity for religious study and intellectual pursuits, that he too was endowed with the capacity to serve God and experience Him.[14]

THE NATURE AND FUNCTION OF MAN

Hasidism, like many major religious movements, was fascinated by the paradoxical interrelationship of man's body and soul. The soul was clearly accepted as an integral component of the divine essence. As for man's corporeal and physical aspect, Hasidism posited two conflicting views. On the one hand, the body is the abode of the "evil inclination," and it remains the task of man to disengage himself from material concerns. A variant theme directs man to elevate matter from its pristine roots. In the first instance, man is engaged in a life-and-death struggle with the negative forces in his environment. In the second instance, he is involved in a rehabilitative process whereby the body, and all matter, is exploited as a valuable resource to elevate him to a higher state of existence.

In either case, Hasidisim adapted and laid new stress on the kabbalistic interrelationship between the upper and lower worlds. The acts of man in this world affect the cosmos as a whole.[15] Man's task, by fulfilling the divine will through purposeful religious acts, serves to abolish the disorder and discord in the universe. Man becomes an indispensable force in returning the universe to its primordial harmony. This perfect state is characterized by the expression *Ayin,* i.e., that which is devoid of any substance save for the original divine presence, which cannot be described, except for its nothingness.[16] Man's purposeful action is referred to as "raising" (or returning) the *Mahshavot Zarot* (the alien thoughts and ideas) to their divine source. Man serves God by "rescuing" the divine sparks temporarily imprisoned in the materialistic realm. Whereas Kabbalah's emphasis, however, was on the *tikkun* (rehabilitation) of God, Hasidism focused on the *tikkun* of man.[17]

As long as godly sparks were as yet unredeemed, both God and man were in a state of suffering and Galut (alienation and exile). Hasidism yearned for the Messiah and strove to hasten his coming, despite initial attempts to neutralize and cool messianic fervor in the wake of the Sabbatian debacle. The centrality of Eretz Yisrael (the land of Israel) for the Jew, and, indeed, the cosmos, was unquestioned by Hasidism.[18] Eretz Yisrael was equated with God's presence.[19] He who settles in the Holy Land hastens salvation. Hasidic tradition is saturated with the legends about the unsuccessful efforts of the Ba'al Shem Tov to settle in the land of Israel. His *aliyah* ("going up" to the Holy Land) would have summoned the Messiah. The Heavens decreed otherwise. The time was not yet ripe for Israel's redemption.[20] Subsequently Hasidic groups settled in Palestine in order to hasten God's return from Galut and to benefit from "God's holy spirit."[21] Others felt that prior to any national redemption, each man must redeem himself from his limitations, his personal Galut.

It is in this context that the unique Hasidic attitude to joy is best understood. Dejection, depression, and regret for past actions represented an alien element in man and in the universe.[22] Joy, unbridled enthusiasm, and *hitlahavut* (ecstasy) in the worship of God, and operating as well in man's mundane affairs, allowed him to achieve *devekut* with God, even as it represents a harmonizing force in the discordant cosmos.[23] Hasidism's focus on *tikkun* in this world directed the Hasid to achieve a state of *Ahavat Yisrael* (love for fellow Jews). A unique fraternal bond tied fellow Hasidim *(anshe shlomenu)* to a common communal framework. A mutual sense of responsibility was already evidenced as the small and undeveloped Hasidic circles closed ranks during bitter struggles with their violent opponents, the Mitnagdim, during the eighteenth century. This fraternal tradition was sustained throughout the history of the Hasidic movement and was radically tested during World War II.

The Hasidic confraternity was also enhanced by the emphasis on the traditional Jewish value of *anivut* (humility) and beyond this, *hishtavut* (stoic nonchalance),[24] and *hitvatlut* (the dissolution of the self).[25] Especially in the teachings of Rabbi Dov Ber of Mezritch and his disciples, man is asked to dissolve the *Ani* (the "I") in order to achieve the divine state of *Ayin* (nothingness).[26] This mood of submission was at first directed at achieving *devekut* with God, i.e., *yeridah tzorekh aliyah* (lowering oneself in order to rise). This quietistic strain, however, fostered the loyalty and commitment of the individual, who was more inclined to subdue his self-interest to the group.

Related to the characteristic of self-effacement is the perceived difference in the degree of emphasis Hasidism gives to man's utter reliance on unquestioning trust *(bitahon)*, in contrast to the utilization and development of his intellectual facilities. Recent studies deny that such a polarity ever existed, i.e., the schools of Rabbi Nahman of Brazlav and Rabbi Menahem Mendel of Vitebsk vs. Rabbi Shneur Zalman of Liadi. Such extremes are noted only when citing statements out of context, which at times is the case in Hasidic studies.[27] Closer to reality is an understanding of Hasidism as attempting to balance the elements of pure faith *with* study and observance of the *mitzvot*. Hasidism *was* reacting to the disproportionate focus on talmudic study that left much of eighteenth-century Jewry religiously isolated and spiritually barren. Ignorance, however, was never proclaimed as a virtue.[28]

In challenging the Hasid to reach the ultimate within the framework of his own intellectual and spiritual potential, he was provided with a model and source of support and inspiration. The elevation of the Zadik was one of the major achievements of Hasidism.

THE ZADIK

Assuming center stage in Hasidic life is the Zadik, literally, "the righteous personality." In Hasidism this term indicates the master or leader of a Hasidic community. He is endowed with supreme spiritual virtues which enable him to serve as a bridge between man and God, between this world and the cosmos. The Zadik is not a free agent. His responsibilities are massive and grave as he engages in the constant struggle to remove the blemishes within society and retrieve the godly sparks to their origin. He reaches heights of religious experience unknown and unavailable to the average man. Yet he must maintain contact with the here and now, the mundane and the corrupt, in order to bring about their transformation and ultimate return to good and God.[29] What is redeemed in this world has a positive effect upon redemptive agents in the total cosmos.

How the Zadik actually implements his leadership functions has varied greatly during the course of Hasidic history. The Besht seemed to incorporate both the "practical" *(tzadikut ma'asit)* as well as the "spiritual" *(tzadikut ruhanit)* aspect and mode of the Zadik's functions. The former included concern for the Hasid's personal well-being, the acceptance of and responding to individual petitions *(kvittelach)*, the performing of miraculous acts, assisting in the healing of the sick, and blessing the Hasidic community. To the Hasid the Zadik is able to issue or avert divine decrees with God's sanction. Spiritual leadership was provided when the Zadik focused on cultivating his own spiritual and ethical refinement, so that he could serve as a more desirable and efficacious model of religious behavior. Teaching and guidance were his primary concerns. Great importance was attached to the Hasid's periodic visit to his Rebbe and, on occasion, the Rebbe's visit to his Hasidim. The purpose of such contacts was to stimulate and strengthen the mutual bond of affection, loyalty, and dedication between Zadik and Hasid. The visit, which routinely took place on a Sabbath or holiday, would involve multitudes of Hasidim, and according to Hasidic teaching would also serve to blunt and diminish the egocentric forces operating within the Hasid.[30] For the mainstream of Hasidism, unquestioning faith in the Zadik as a bridge between man and the divine facilitated the Hasid's own quest for *devekut*.[31] Some Zadikim such as Rabbi Menahem Mendel of Kotzk (ca. 1787–1859), eventually "abandoned" their followers and went into seclusion, pointing to the desirability of the Hasid's eventual independence from the Zadik, so that there would be no separation between man and God. Ordinarily, however, the mantle of Zadikite leadership passed down from father to son. When this was not possible, the foremost disciple of the Zadik or a male member of the Zadik's family would continue the tradition of the lineage.[32] The Hasidic dynasty, thus perpetuated, usually assumed the name of the home community of the dynasty's founder. It is generally acknowledged that the proliferation of Rebbeim in the mid-nineteenth century led to a waning in the spiritual quality of Hasidic leadership.

The period of World War II witnessed the annihilation of the great majority of the Hasidic leaders and their adherents. As this study will seek to indicate, the Zadik in the main, and consistent with Hasidic tradition, would refuse to be separated from his flock. He served as a source of strength, comfort, and faith during a crisis which shook the foundations of the Hasid's physical and spiritual existence. The remaining Hasidic communities were transplanted to the United States and Israel.

CHAPTER 4

Suffering and Evil

What responses of Hasidic leaders and Hasidim emerged during the Holocaust concerning God's relationship to man and the Jewish people and the related problem of suffering and evil? Is there any correlation between these responses and the basic concepts of Hasidic thought?

The major source for this pattern of responses was *Esh Kodesh,* the work by the Piaczner Rebbe noted above.

The primary and secondary sources related to this response pattern revealed four major themes:

1. *Justification:* interpretations which justify God's action in relation to God's attributes.
2. *Man's relationship to God during crisis:* interpretations which define man's desired relationship and attitude to God, especially the acceptance of one's fate.
3. *Questioning the Holocaust events:* scrutiny, inquiry, and challenge, at times related to God's attributes, which question the purpose of the Holocaust.
4. *The purpose and consequences of suffering:* interpretations of the purpose of suffering; beneficial and detrimental consequences of suffering are indicated.

JUSTIFICATION

The justifying of God's role in the Holocaust encompasses a broad range of responses. The Zaloshizer Rebbe, Rabbi Shem Klinberg, conducting the "third meal"[1] in the death camp of Plashow, utilizes Psalms 72:17 with a Hasidic exegetic interpretation,[2] and presents the classical "defensive" justification. God's ways and the present Holocaust are incomprehensible to man.[3] With the coming of the Messiah,

God's manner of dealing with man will be revealed to man.[4] In accepting suffering with love one does not speculate on the motives of God's decrees.

God's prerogative to issue and implement decrees *(gezerot)* is articulated in the dramatic confrontation in the Bochnia Ghetto between the Belzer Rebbe (Rabbi Ahron Rokeach) and a leading Belzer Hasid. When the latter pleadingly urged for the Zadik to intervene with God to terminate the mass destruction, the Rebbe's repeated response was: "A decree from heaven!"[5]

Retribution for various types of iniquities appears as a minor motive for justifying God's action. The Piazesner Rebbe, in his *Esh Kodesh,* attributes the death of his only son, his daughter-in-law, and his mother, all killed in a German bombing attack on Warsaw at the outset of the war, to his *own* sins.[6] The "hands of Esau" prevail over the "voice of Jacob" when the Jew is not occupied with the study of Torah and does not provide proper Torah education for his children.[7] The *umipne hata'enu* ("on account of our sins") motive, however, seems muted, by and large.

Rabbinic tradition identifies God's severe attribute of *Din* (retributive judgment) as being tempered by the attribute of *Rahamim* (mercy).[8] The Piazesner Rebbe, however, is at pains to distinguish between man's finite view of *Din* and *Rahamim;* to wit, the notion of severity and harshness in contrast to tolerance and compassion. This is but man's limited, fragmented, and therefore distorted interpretation of these attributes. In reality, *Din* contains a positive component on a level higher than that offered by *Rahamim.*[9] What can that component be? The current *Hurban* (destruction) serves as a *tikkun* (restoration, rehabilitation), a kind of redemptive safety valve, which God has provided in order to avert another catastrophic *shevirat hakelim*[10] in the cosmos.[11]

"Justifying" God's action by obliterating any distinction between "positive" and "negative" attributes is also evident in the interpretation given to *hester panim.*[12] *Esh Kodesh* suggests that *hester* is in reality a *tovah* (favor) for the Jew, though it may not appear so. Unflinching *emunah* (belief) combined with its primary concomitant, *mesirat nefesh* (sacrificial devotion, lit. "giving over one's soul"), provides man with the inner resources to perceive the true nature of *hester.*[13] The Rabbi of Bilgurei (Rabbi Mordechai Rokeach, the brother of the Belzer) saw the Holocaust as both a manifestation of *hester panim* and a miraculous revelation of God's presence,[14] indicating the interdependence of these seemingly paradoxical attributes which contain within themselves elements of commonality rather than conflict.

Justification, however, moves beyond the "positivizing" of *Din*. It is the ultimate vindication of God's *Rahamim* (compassion) which appears central in the justification motive. *Esh Kodesh* cites a rabbinic tradition holding that God initially created the world with *Rahamim*, since it represented the prerequisite for all creation and its ultimate foundation.[15] Furthermore, God's compassion operates at its maximal potency precisely when the Jew stands at the brink of alienation from God, enmeshed in torment and suffering. The inclination *(yetzer)* in man is to abandon the divine. Yet within this very *yetzer* are embodied God's protective and redemptive forces of compassion.[16] Relatedly, all that emanates from God is *emet vetzedek* (truth and righteousness). God's justice cannot, therefore, be questioned.[17] All emanates from one God. Evil and suffering have their origin in good and thus can be, and ultimately will be, "returned" to good.[18]

MAN'S RELATIONSHIP TO GOD DURING CRISIS

Recognizing God as Father and King of all mankind, Hasidic leaders urged their followers to accept suffering and, if necessary, death with love.[19] Eyewitness reports of the executions of the Mezibezer Rebbe (Rabbi Abraham Joshua Heschel) in Tarnopol and the Strier-Sambover Rebbe (Rabbi Yeshiah Asher Yoles) document the final pleas of these Rebbeim to their fellow Jews to accept the divine decree with love and thus be strengthened in the process.[20]

When questioned as to how he could possibly continue the Hasidic routine in the turmoil of the Sambover Ghetto, the Komarner Rebbe (Rabbi Baruch Safrin) responded with the following exegesis of a passage from the concluding liturgical prayer recited on Yom Kippur.[21] "In these terrible times, the head has become disengaged from its body,[22] since the mind cannot possibly grasp the meaning of it all . . . and yet man must continue to seek Thy presence."[23]

"Accepting with love" is not a rational process. In a Hasidic exegesis of a liturgical selection from the Sabbath and Festival morning service,[24] the Piasezner Rebbe asserts: "Although nothing shall remain of me but bones [separated from the total body], they will still continue to proclaim: 'Lord, who is like unto Thee!' "[25] The unqualified and faithful acceptance of "Amalakite events"[26] with love is asserted in his interpretation of Exodus 17. Though Moses' hands are at his sides, Amalek has the upper hand and salvation is not in sight, Israel's fate must be accepted with love, and thus will God's justice *(Din)* be transformed into mercy *(Rahamim).*[27]

The relationship-to-God-in-crisis responses prominently include *bitahon* (trust and confidence) and *emunah* (faith, belief) in the pending and imminent salvation. It is this very relationship which hastens the yearned-for salvation.[28] Thus, when the Jewish people displayed supreme *emunah* and *bitahon* during the Exodus from Egypt, the sea opened before them as a result of their confidence in God.[29] The process of *emunah* and *bitahon* is also beyond man's ken and his "self." Faith and complete trust demand the dissolution of the self *(bittul hayesh),* which permits the "beyond man" to operate.[30] Furthermore, while *Ahavat Hashem* (love of God) is an ideal achieved by means of individual service, *Emunat Hashem* (faith in God) operates outside the frame of man's ego and permits man to respond to God in the context of Klal Yisrael (the totality of the people of Israel). During a period when Klal Yisrael seeks salvation, *Emunat Hashem* must be considered a higher form of service.[31]

The Razvirter Rebbe (Rabbi Shalom Eliezer Halberstam) invoked the principle of *Emunat Hashem* in response to fellow Jews who complained of their fate during the Holocaust. Quoting his father, the Sanzer Rebbe, he defined *emunah* as the act which defines man's limitations. God's actions are beyond question. The theological probing of thinkers like Judah Halevi (1086–1141), the great Spanish Jewish poet and philosopher, and Joseph Albo (d. 1444), the fifteenth-century theologian, known for his three fundamental principles of the Jewish faith, was rhetorical in nature and functioning *within* the frame of *emunah.* These men were cognizant of the response to their "probing" before they posed their questions.[32]

A fascinating kabbalistic transfer of the traditional principle of *imitatio dei*[33] is reflected in the Piasezner Rebbe's application of the *tzimtzum* concept to the Holocaust.[34] In emulating the divine, the Jew must also limit his own inclinations in the face of God's terrible manifestation of *Din.* The implication seems clear. Just as the primordial act of *tzimtzum* represented a divine act of grace for man by making room for the world, man was now expected to respond with his own form of *tzimtzum,* as a manifestation of human grace directed toward God![35] The implied partnership of God and man is further enhanced when human suffering provides man with the opportunity to isolate and highlight the divine image and component within himself. This process, in turn, provides man with spiritual resources that enable him to assume the terrible burden of suffering with dignity.

Time and again the discussion touches upon the various degrees of *emunah* that determine the particular relationship of man to God during crisis. *Esh Kodesh* employs a talmudic statement that stresses the extremity of *emunah,*[36] even when violating the biblical commandment "Thou shall not steal."[37]

Expressions of radical *emunah* were evident during final testaments of faith exclaimed at the time of death. The Razvirter Rebbe is quoted at the site of a mass grave: "With my entire soul and heart do I believe that the Creator of the universe exists and there is a *Hashgahah Elyonah* (Divine Providence, lit. "supervision on high").[38]

The central Hasidic doctrine of joy *(simhah)* in the face of extreme adversity is a major factor in the strengthening of *emunah.* Despair chokes the inner resources of faith.[39] However, when responding to suffering with joy, man can reach the stage of prophecy.[40] The desired state of *hitvatlut* (dissolution or obliteration of the self) is enhanced by adversity, which, in turn, permits man to draw closer to God and unite with Him.[41] This form of *devekut* (cleaving to God) releases hidden and pent-up sources of joy, triggering another cycle of *emunah* and *bitahon.*

THE HASID QUESTIONS THE HOLOCAUST

Despite (and possibly due to) the confidence and trust of the Hasid in God's benevolence, reponses which challenge and question appear alongside those which justify Holocaust events.

Among the most dramatic outbursts in *Esh Kodesh* is the exhortation to God to return the world to chaos. The author reminds God of His threat to destroy the world when His justice was challenged in the instance of the ten martyrs *(Asarah Haruge Malkhut)* who were cruelly executed during the Jewish revolt against Rome.[42] Surely the horror of the Holocaust surpasses that of the Roman period. Surely the angels in heaven are now joined by the multitude of protesting Jewish souls in paradise. Why does God not intervene and destroy His world?[43] In a remarkably similar pattern of questioning, Aaron Rapoport, a Hasid of the Ostrowzer Rebbe, Rabbi Yechezkel Halstik, confronts his Rebbe hiding under miserable conditions and asks: "Is this the Torah and this its reward? What is happening here?" The

Rebbe answers that man may be able to probe the soul of his fellow man but not the ways of God. "I was very bitter and refused to ask any more questions."[44]

Consistent with the Hasidic tendency to allegorize biblical and rabbinic commandments,[45] the Piazesner Rebbe compares the Jewish people in exile to a lost object. God is its owner. According to rabbinic law the owner of a lost object is required to fulfill the biblical commandment to search for it.[46]

The Piazesner challenges God to observe His own commandments, pointing to the laws of *pikuah nefesh* (laws relating to situations when life is at stake), which suspend all other precepts in the Torah. Should not God now suspend the normal course of events in order to save even one life?[47]

The questioning motif encompasses the classic problem of the suffering of the innocent and helpless, but is posited in a kabbalistic frame. Referring to the *Zohar,*[48] which speaks of the anguish of all departed Jewish souls when there is suffering in the world below, the Piazesner Rebbe points to the massive cosmic suffering engendered by the Holocaust, in which the victims include innocent souls completely outside the sphere of conflict.[49] The implication is that the martyrs of the past should not again be subjected to suffering. Does not traditional theodicy maintain that the suffering of the righteous in this world is justified in order to make possible a blissful existence beyond?[50]

Critical questioning is also concerned with another kind of innocent victim. In a Hasidic interpretation of the verse "Through those near to Me, I show Myself holy and I will be glorified *(ekaved)* before all the people,"[51] the Komarnr Rebbe (Rabbi Baruch Safrin) expresses concern for the simple and unlearned individual (unlike "those near to Me"—the man of learning or deep religious faith), who may not possess the spiritual fortitude to comprehend the meaning of the Holocaust. *He* will "burden" *(kbd)* God with questions.[52]

An instance of assuming a critical stance regarding God's role in the Holocaust *within* accepted Jewish-mystical theology is evident in the Piazesner Rebbe's exegesis of (1) the first two words in the concluding portion of Deuteronomy (*Vezot haberakhah,* "This is the blessing");[53] (2) the last three words of the concluding chapter of Deuteronomy (*le'ene kol Yisrael,* "before the eyes of all Israel");[54] and (3) the first word of Genesis (*Bereshit,* "In the beginning").[55] He now draws upon this material in developing the divine attributes of *Hesed*

Nigleh (revealed and apparent kindness) and *Hesed Nistar* (hidden kindness). Though the Holocaust may be a manifestation of *Hesed Nistar,* should not God *first*[56] expose the Jewish people to *Hesed Nigleh?*[57] The defenseless and simple Jew may not be able to tolerate *Hesed Nistar* without the encouraging stimulus of *Hesed Nigleh.*[58]

Hasidic Holocaust sources operate within the frame of traditional theology. They seek and see the hand of God in the Holocaust. Challenging the Holocaust, therefore, often is a matter of questioning God's strategy rather than His ultimate purpose. Thus the question is formulated: Does not a tragedy of these proportions go counter to God's own interest, and is it not self-defeating? Is it possible that the purpose of suffering is to strengthen faith? What meaning has suffering if faith is destroyed in the process?[59] Is the purpose of the Holocaust to bring about repentance? Is repentance indeed possible under Holocaust conditions?[60] If the massive destruction is aimed at the enemies of Israel, why then does God employ the attribute of *Gevurah* (strength),[61] whereby the powerful forces of warfare destroy the victim along with the oppressor? Should not God battle the enemy with the attribute of *Hesed* (kindness), which would result in selective destruction?[62] Do we not learn the lesson of the consequences of excess suffering from the Torah?[63] What possible consolation can the Holocaust offer when lives are snuffed out and the victims have barely lived at all? Such tragedy is utterly irreversible![64] Finally, the Holocaust's self-defeating character includes man's inability to serve God properly. One can and should serve God with the physical and material. This is impossible when the physical and material are being destroyed. Thus, existence becomes meaningless.[65]

THE PURPOSE AND CONSEQUENCES OF SUFFERING

The main concern of the Piazesner Rebbe's *Esh Kodesh* is the eternal problem of suffering. Though his weekly Sabbath discourses, which reflect contemporary events, are not presented systematically and consistently, the various concepts related to suffering are based on the premise that all that is emanates from God. Whatever emanates from God is just.[66] Furthermore, when man recognizes and acknowledges the hand of God in suffering, he strips away the terrible component of *hester panim.*[67] But when God is *not* acknowledged as the source of suffering and as a partner with Israel in suffering, the Jew becomes insensitive to his own godly image and the calamity is compounded by despair.[68] Since God is the source of all that is, man cannot confront the problem of suffering with rational analysis, but only by means of *bitahon*.[69] Suffering is willingly accepted. This sets the stage for numerous references to positive, though at times hidden, manifestations of suffering. Suffering is a form of *Hesed Nistar* (God's hidden kindness), which may be transformed, by prayer and study, into *Hesed Nigleh* (revealed and apparent kindness).[70] Suffering presents man with the opportunity to draw close to God.[71] *Devekut* achieved through suffering releases positive forces in the cosmic spheres whereby God withdraws decrees against man.[72] Suffering leads to a true appreciation of the state of nonsuffering.[73] Adversity also leads to a better understanding of one's Jewish heritage. As an aspect of *Hevle Mashiah,* the suffering that precedes the coming of the Messiah, suffering serves to impel the return to Eretz Yisrael.[74] Suffering should lead to a state of joy,[75] since God suffers with the Jew in the latter's calamity.

The festival of Shemini Atzeret symbolizes the mutual suffering of God and His people when the Jew is isolated from the rest of mankind.[76] The Shekhinah suffers not only with the Jewish people as a group, but with each tormented Jewish soul.[77] When the suffering of the Jewish people becomes so unbearable that God alone can bear the burden of torment, then Israel must do all it possibly can with repentance, prayer, and acts of charity, to relieve God's suffering.[78] Man derives strength from the knowledge that he does not suffer alone.[79] God's participation is a positive act that draws off the most intense suffering; without it man would be altogether unable to endure suffering.

Suffering, however, may be a two-edged sword. For the Jew who cannot grasp its positive manifestations, suffering is a physically and spiritually depressing force. To such a person, suffering is partial death[80] and of so unique a nature that although the angels in heaven may be able to sympathize with man in a state of suffering, the experience cannot be duplicated.[81] Torment may be a dehumanizing process whereby man loses his own personality and his Jewish self.[82] He is unable to find strength in the observance of Torah.[83] Suffering triggers a vicious cycle which inhibits feelings of religious inspiration and experience.[84] Thus suffering prevents man from exploiting the very resources which would make it tolerable. The ultimate consequence is the gradual drying up of the altruistic forces that operate within man and upon which he is dependent in order to resist the negative forces of his own ego. Suffering man is driven to utter self-concern, this prevents him from achieving any form of *haktanat ha'azmi* (diminution of the self), which in turn makes worship of God impossible.[85]

Suffering, however, also assures an independent objective in the form of a sacrifice to God, which is accepted with love.[86] In this instance it is not God who assists man, but rather man who assists God![87] Suffering is a continuous sacrificial process, an act of total religious dedication, begun with the Binding of Isaac,[88] which enhances God's sanctity and redeems Him.[89] Expounding the verse "to go by day and by night,"[90] the Piazesner Rebbe reemphasizes the idea of serving God not only with love, enthusiasm, and joy, implied by the term "by day," but also with suffering implied by the term "by night."[91] The Belzer Rebbe's firstborn son was burned alive in a synagogue set afire by the Germans. He expressed his loss in terms of a sacrifice to God: "It is indeed a kindness of the Almighty that I also offered a personal sacrifice."[92]

CHAPTER 5

Hasidic Concepts Related to Suffering and Evil

This chapter will seek to correlate Hasidic responses to suffering and evil during the Holocaust with the appropriate basic concepts of Hasidic thought. The general methodology employed here will also be applied in subsequent chapters.

JUSTIFICATION

When the Hasid refused to challenge God's role in man's mundane affairs, he was consistent with the quietistic and submissive strain in Hasidic thought as formulated by the Ba'al Shem Tov and Rabbi Dov Ber. "Thus [people] must abandon themselves and forget their misfortunes in order that they may enter the realm of the idea where all is equalized."[1] Material misfortune is irrelevant. With the coming of the Messiah, when the forces of alienation no longer operate in this world, God will reveal His Divine Providence, and His ultimate design will be fully comprehensible to man.[2] The Zadik's refusal to intervene in Holocaust events may be consistent with the Hasidic principle that one should not be active on one's own behalf, but must be active on behalf of God's will.[3] A "decree from heaven" is consonant with God's will.[4]

As was discussed in connection with *Din* and *Rahamim*, Hasidism was loath to correlate any of God's attributes with man's image of them. The source of God's infinite power and its by-products is good.[5] It was, therefore, not difficult to obliterate the seeming contrast between *Din* and *Rahamim*, which are humanly conceived contrasts of divine characteristics.[6] Thus, there was little compulsion for Hasidism to interpret the Holocaust as punishment, since this would isolate and distinguish *Din* from *Rahamim*. By defusing the retributive elements, Hasidism was more able to position Holocaust events in a positive context. When the Piazesner Rebbe, in *Esh Kodesh,* speaks of adversity as a safety valve to assist in the *tikkun* process, he may have been echoing Rabbi Zev Wolf of Zitomir (d. 1800), who saw in adversity the grace of God directing man to be aware of the cosmic deficiencies[7] and to pray for *tikkun elyon* (the rehabilitation or restoration of the divine cosmic elements).[8] To discover God's compassion within *Din,* according to a source attributed to the Ba'al Shem Tov, is the surest way of converting hidden goodness *(Din)* into revealed goodness *(hesed).*[9]

In summary, the underpinning of the justification motif is the *God-Source-Good* formula, which is heavily utilized in Hasidic literature. "And he shall always meditate upon, and cling to the Creator, blessed be He, with complete love, since His good exceeds all else in the universe, and all that is good is rooted in Him, blessed be He."[10] The apparent evil is merely a lower form of good, or the outer shell for the good,[11] which is transformed into absolute good through man's acts of goodness.[12]

MAN'S RELATIONSHIP TO GOD DURING CRISIS

A derivative of the *God-Source-Good* concept is the "acceptance with love" *(kabalah be'ahavah)* of all that may befall man.[13] Rabbi Yitzchak Isaac of Komarno (1766–1834) cites the following tradition in the name of the Besht: "Accept all that may befall you with love and then you will be worthy of this world and the world-to-come."[14]

Man's relationship to God with *bitahon* is also derived from this concept. Uffenheimer documents the gradual transformation of *bitahon* from the notion of general abandonment of the self *(hafkarah atzmit)* to God's will, in the teachings of Rabbi Dov Ber, to the more mundane *bitahon* related to daily cares, especially the need to earn a livelihood, in the teachings of the Magid's disciples.[15] In either case, *bitahon* is tied to *emunah* (belief, faith), which figures prominently in Holocaust responses and in Hasidic literature. "He who trusts in God will be enveloped in *hesed* [God's goodness and grace], and when he [relates to God] in the reverse, constantly fearing the punishing attribute of God, then indeed he cleaves to the attribute of *Din.*"[16] As indicated by the Piazesner Rebbe, Hasidism believed in the effect of true *bitahon* and *emunah* in achieving the objective sought.[17]

> Thus, as a result of profound *emunah* and *bitahon*, one becomes attached and attuned with one's entire thought and being to the goodness of the Creator, in whom one places one's hope and trust, and, as a result, the quest is realized without delay. This is not so when, Heaven forbid, *emunah* and *bitahon* are not complete and doubts enter one's mind, as to whether "it will be, or not be"; this [doubt] in itself is a deterrent.[18]

When the Piazesner refers to *bittul hayesh* (the dissolution of the self) as a consequence and concomitant of *emunah*,[19] he touches upon a major principle stressed by Hasidism, also related to *hitpashtut hagashmiyut* (the release or stripping of the material). True faith operates beyond the material and the "self."[20]

> . . . and when one prays he shall direct his thoughts to the Shekhinah [God's Presence], and . . . not toward oneself . . . and my teacher [the Ba'al Shem Tov] explained this as creating a division [between man and God], resulting from the intrusion of the material into the spiritual, which prevents any kind of response.[21]

Emunah, as being antithetical to theological inquiry, is reflected in the Komarner's caution: "He who engages in an investigation of the ways of the divine neither enters nor exists in peace,[22] but assimilates the aroma of heresy."[23] "Faith is not dependent upon intellectual endeavors, but rather, upon simplicity, cleaving to, and loving the only God of Israel, and the study of the *Zohar*, and the teachings of the *ARI*, but not upon speculation and cogitation."[24] As Uffenheimer indicates, in the writings of Levi Yitzchak of Berdichev (d. 1809), assume such radical proportions that the attitude of quietism is converted into one of activism, forged by the optimism inherent in radical faith.[25] Interpreting Psalms 18:4, "I shall refer to God as praised and thus will I be saved from my foes," Rabbi Levi Yitzchak indicates that when one praises God with absolute faith *prior* to salvation, then in essence one assumes the initiative in bringing about that salvation. So it was with Nahshon the son of Aminadab, who led the mass plunge into the Sea of Reeds during the Exodus from Egypt.[26]

The term *Hashgahah Elyonah* ("higher supervision," i.e., Divine Providence) in connection with *emunah* is related to the concept of *Hashgahah Pratit* ("personal supervision," i.e., divine concern for each human being), frequently referred to in Hasidic literature.[27]

Simhah (joy) as a consequence of *emunah* and *bitahon*, and *azvut* (depression) as an impediment to *emunah*, are central to Hasidic doctrine. "One should not amplify contemplation into one's every action, since it is the intent of the evil inclination to impart a sense of dread, leading to depression. Depression is a major deterrent to the worship of the Creator, blessed be He."[28] Depression is a cardinal transgression because it impairs *bitahon*.[29] *Simhah*, however, flows from complete faith in the "Shekhinah which protects him."[30] On the one hand, *emunah* is the primary cause of *simhah*. Yet there is a reciprocal relationship, since *emunah* and *bitahon* rely upon *simhah*. "*Bitahon* and *emunah* are mutually dependent upon one another, and so is *simhah*, which is fundamental—being joyful at one's lot."[31] It is precisely in suffering that one should respond with joy, since when we convert *(hithapkhut)* and dissolve *(hitbatlut)* our own desires in favor of God's wish, God is given satisfaction *(nahat ruah)*.[32] Suffering may have the effect of nullifying material reality, making possible and enhancing *devekut* and the unity of God.[33] The *devekut* experience, in turn, represents the ultimate in joy. "There exists no greater enjoyment, joy, and expansion of the mind in this world than when a Zadik cleaves to God and His teachings."[34] This then represents the cycle of *bitahon* and *emunah*.

THE HASID QUESTIONS THE HOLOCAUST

On the background of Hasidism's quietistic emphasis on *bitahon*, *emunah*, *hashgahah pratit*, *hitbatlut*, *hafkarah atzmit* and *devekut*, any activist tendency appears paradoxical and contradictory. Physical resistance, nonviolent resistance, and, in general, challenging or critically questioning the Holocaust would seem to reflect an activist stance. It is significant that Uffenheimer, in isolating the quietistic strain in Hasidism, does not deny alternative activist nuances. Admittedly, the raising of the sparks *(ha'alat hanitzotzot)*, the raising of alien thoughts *(ha'alat hamahshavot zarot)*, serving God with the material *(avodah begashmiyut)*, and the descent of the Zadik *(yeridat hazadik)* are all seemingly active aspects of Hasidism.[35] This activist-quietist dialectic may be explained in two ways. First, Hasidism did not develop into a radical quietist sect, as was the case with the Christian mystical groups inspired by Eckhart and Molinos.[35a] ". . . Conservative factors in Hasidism set limits to the quietistic tendency, since Hasidism had no wish to detach itself from the main body of Judaism or to become an antinomian sect."[36] Judaism's emphasis on praxis rather than faith put the brakes on the quietism of any group developing within the mainstream of the Jewish community.[37] Furthermore, Hasidic quietism, as distinguished from its Christian counterparts, adopted activist aspects by choice and integrated them into the quietistic framework. Hasidism's way of achieving absolute quietism was to confront and do battle against the "concrete realities, and not to circumvent them."[38] Before a human being can subject himself to the divine, he must pursue and subdue the alien elements in himself and his environment. This represents a reinterpretation of the rabbinic *yeridah letzorekh aliyah* (descent as a requisite to ascent), which was abused by the nihilist factions of the Sabbatian and Frankist heresies.[39]

The teachings of Rabbi Levi Yitzchak of Berdichev place emphasis on man's ability to actively influence the cosmic forces with good deeds, so that the "ways of those above, support themselves on the acts of those below."[40] Consistent with his own teachings, Rabbi Levi Yitzchak won legendary status by defending the case of the Jew before the heavenly court. He would use every device available to prove to God that man's positive acts justified divine reciprocity and response. It was not uncommon for Rabbi Levi to overtly challenge God's conduct. Among the numerous "advocate" and "challenge" legends, the following is not atypical. Pointing out that thousands of Jews had blown hundreds of shofar calls annually throughout the generations at God's request, he asked why God did not reciprocate and respond to man's plea for but one sounding of His shofar.[41]

Critical questioning is not limited to the teachings of Rabbi Levi. In the tradition of Rabbi Mordechai of Tchernobil (d. 1837), God is taken to task. In a daring confrontation Rabbi Mordechai accuses God of violating His own commandments. Would not the lowliest and most ignorant Jew hasten to retrieve a pair of sacred tefillin (phylacteries) which unexpectedly had fallen to the ground? Yet the people of Israel have long fallen. They are God's tefillin. Why then has God delayed in retrieving His tefillin?[42]

In general, however, challenge, questioning, and activism were not predominant in Hasidism. More often than not, the active may have served as a temporary device leading to an eventual quietistic posture, with the aim of subduing man's personal interest to that of a higher good and to the divine in man.[43]

THE PURPOSE AND CONSEQUENCES OF SUFFERING

Reflecting the mood and environment of healing into which it was born and within which it took root,[44] Hasidism responded to the problem of suffering with some care and intensity. The Besht's teachings focused sharply upon the pain of the individual, physical as well as spiritual, as documented by Ibn Shmuel.[45] Among the five ingredients deemed essential for the functioning of the universe is the dealing out and receiving of suffering, "which leads to repentance, prayer, salvation, and gratitude. Suffering is not incidental; it is an integral part of life, which may serve as the foundation of man's elevation or his fall."[46] Another Beshtian tradition defines four categories of suffering: illness, poverty, unresolved sin, and exile, of which the latter two are surely the more severe. These categories provide an opportunity to elevate alien sparks with four corresponding kinds of prayer.[47] The Piazesner Rebbe operates within the Beshtian frame that sees suffering as offering man an opportunity to rise or fall, and as scalpel which may maim or heal.[48] The second frame within which the Piazesner posits the suffering motif is clearly enunciated in early Hasidic thought: "And concerning all that may befall him, let him note that this emanates from God, blessed be He, and if it is proper in His eyes, etc."[49] Yet another Beshtian source directs the sufferer to contemplate the holy spark hidden within suffering. Then will the hidden be revealed and the suffering cease.[50]

> I learned the following significant lesson from my teacher [the Besht]: In all physical and spiritual suffering, if man but consider that within this suffering is God, blessed be He, though in a disguised form. When man becomes aware of this, the disguise is removed, and the suffering and evil decrees are nullified.[51]

Hasidism, along with Rabbi Levi Yitzchak of Berdichev, thus viewed "suffering as having significance only in the temporal,[52] since in the eternal there exists neither suffering nor grief nor sighing."[53] When the component of goodness and kindness *(hesed)* in God's judgment *(Din)* is discovered, the total process of judgment (including suffering) is transformed into *hesed*.[54] When the Piazesner Rebbe defines suffering as *hesed nistar* (hidden kindness), he is consistent with Beshtian thought, which viewed suffering as a hidden manifestation of the divine, purposely hidden in order that it may be sought. Said the Besht: I do not fear the hidden, but rather the hidden which is hidden."[55] Suffering as an opportunity to draw closer to God is enunciated in the Besht's teachings as well.[56] Tribulations serve a divine purpose in creating external fear, in order to stimulate man's inner fear, which, in turn, leads to the acceptance of suffering with love.[57] "Thus, man unites the lower Kingdom of God [this world] with the Kingdom in Heaven, and transforms the *Ani* [I][58] into the *Ayin* [nought],[59] and the evil decree shall be abolished."[60]

Hasidism also perceived suffering as a purposeful contrasting prelude, necessary for the true appreciation of the state of nonsuffering.[61] "The greater the darkness and suffering on the eve of Sabbath, the more brilliant the light of the Sabbath."[62] Rabbi Levi Yitzchak of Berdichev viewed suffering as a tool for salvation: "When one wishes to transform a small vessel into a large vessel, the small vessel must first be broken. So God, blessed be He, in His desire to see man grow, confronts him with suffering or illness, which represents the breaking of the small vessel."[63]

The mutual suffering of God and Israel, highlighted in the Piazesner's *Esh Kodesh*[64] and originating in midrashic literature,[65] is prominently reinforced in Hasidism. "This flows from the simple logic that 'Israel consists of the organs of the Shekhinah.' Thus, if they [Israel] suffer, surely, the Shekhinah feels this, and in order to limit the suffering above, we seek to limit suffering below."[66] Rabbi Levi Yitzchak, in acknowledging this mutual suffering, cautions that man should pray for relief only in order to spare God any suffering.[67] Evident here is the tradition of Dov Ber of Mezritch: "Man should refrain from praying for his own concerns. Rather he should pray always for the redemption of the Shekhinah from exile."[68] The Piazesner Rebbe's comfort in understanding that God shares in the suffering of Israel[69] is anticipated in early Hasidic literature: "And when he [the Jew] realizes that here too [in suffering] God is with him, then the disguise is revealed and removed, and the suffering is abolished."[70]

Because Hasidism recognized the degree to which suffering may disturb the relationship between man and God, it tended to assume a stance of purposeful indifference to suffering.[71] The Piazesner Rebbe's primary concern about radical suffering is precisely that it endangers the relationship of *devekut* between man and God, and disturbs the quality of man's *bitahon* in God.[72] Depression due to existential concerns is a significant deterrent to the service of God.[73]

Depression due to suffering tends to focus man's attention on himself and away from the divine.[74] "If I am not for myself"[75] was altered from its original intent,[76] suggesting that if one is to be fully involved in the service of the Almighty, there is no room for self-concern even when one is tested by suffering. Further, physical suffering may correspondingly affect the holy sparks housed in the body of man, namely, his divine image.[77] The Beshtian tradition indicates that "when the body is sick, the soul too is weakened, and proper prayer is impossible."[78] This is consistent with the Piazesner's observation that suffering prevents *haktanah atzmit* (the diminishing of the ego), the primary condition for proper worship.[79] Finally, the destructive implications of suffering are made clear when Hasidism suggests that the very disappointment triggered by suffering may shut the divine gates of mercy.[80]

Suffering accepted with love was interpreted by the Piazesner as a form of sacrifice, sanctifying God through man.[81] Rabbi Levi Yitzchak formulates this interdependence as follows: "The more one sanctifies oneself, the greater is the strength and sanctity contributed to the realm above."[82] Further, "if we truly conceive the ultimate purpose of all that is, we would most certainly accept all of suffering with longing and love, since it is by means of these beatings that the Name of our Creator will be magnified and sanctified."[83] Man's redemption of God via the process of suffering and sanctification, tied to God's dependence upon man's initiative, is anticipated in Hasidic literature. God's presence within man, represented by the *tzelem* (image [of God]),[84] is redeemed and revealed when Israel cleaves to Him with acts of love and dedication.[85] Man's sacrifice of his own concerns in order to redeem the Shekhinah is summarized in the teaching of Rabbi Dov Ber: "Man should pray, not for his own needs, but for the redemption of the Shekhinah from its exile."[86]

CHAPTER 6

Exile and Redemption

We will now discuss the pattern of Holocaust responses related to the messianic idea and redemption. Once again, we will then demonstrate the relationship between these responses and certain basic concepts in Hasidic thought.

The major source for the pattern of responses related to exile and redemption proved to be Rabbi Yissachar Shlomo Teichthal's *Em Habanim Semehah*. This work by a leading scholarly Hasid of the Rebbe of Munkach itself represents a compendium of Hasidic responses associated with redemption, the messianic period, the land of Israel, and exile, as these were viewed from the standpoint of the Holocaust.

This primary source, other primary sources, and various secondary sources revealed four themes:

1. *Hevle Mashiah:* the attempt to equate Holocaust events with the suffering expected prior to the coming of the Messiah.[1]
2. *Prerequisites for redemption:* Analyses of factors that may hasten or delay redemption; the tension between man's role and initiative, as opposed to "God's hand," in controlling the fate of salvation; imminent, in contrast to gradual, redemption.
3. *The nature of exile and the diaspora:* speculation on the character, purpose, and possible resolution of exile; the Holocaust as a manifestation of Galut.
4. *The Land of Israel:* the relationship of *Eretz Yisrael* to the Holocaust and redemption.

HEVLE MASHIAH

A major section of *Em Habanim Semehah* is devoted to the concept of *Hevle Mashiah* and attempts to draw a connection between contemporary Jewish suffering and the predicted pangs that will precede the coming of the Messiah. "If only the suffering which has come upon us in recent years were indeed the Messiah pains, so that our righteous Messiah could come and redeem us from them."[2] It is, therefore, timely to study the circumstances and conditions by which the obstacles to the coming of Messiah may be removed. One must not prolong the agony of man trapped "in the depths, and one must raise the Shekhinah from this dust."[3] The desire to embrace the redemptive *Hevle Mashiah* was reported by independent eyewitness accounts prior to the death of Rabbi Ben Zion Halberstam, the Bobover Rebbe.[4] When urged to flee in accordance with a contingency plan, the Rebbe responded in the face of certain death: "Why hide? Shall one hide from the *Hevle Mashiah?*"[5] *Hevle Mashiah,* as a forerunner of salvation and as a purifying agent, was noted in a final message of consolation by the Grodzisker Rebbe, Rabbi Yisrael Shapira, in the death camp of Treblinka: "We should not question God's actions. If it is indeed destined that we shall serve as a sacrifice for *Hevle Mashiah* during this period of redemption and thus be consumed in the flames—how fortunate then that we have been privileged for this purpose! . . . we should be happy that our ashes will purify the entire people of Israel."[6] "Is it not worth suffering prior to the coming of the Messiah?" asked Rabbi Yehezkiah Fish, the Matislaker Rebbe, in the Matislaker Ghetto (Hungary, 1944).[7] "When we note a period of great turmoil, we should be aware that the Messiah's coming is imminent. These are all indications of *Hevle Mashiah.* Should he not come, however, we must nevertheless dedicate ourselves to the Almighty."[8] The Spinker Rebbe, Rabbi Yitzhak Eisik Weiss, on a death train from the Selish Ghetto to Auschwitz (1944), responded to a plea from a fellow Jew to intervene with God: "Do not be afraid. We are going to welcome the Messiah. . . . Yes, the Messiah sits in chains in Rome and we must redeem him."[9] Seidman quotes an anonymous Hasid in the Warsaw Ghetto: "Do not worry . . . can't you see that we are going to welcome the Messiah?"[10] The *Hevle Mashiah,* as reflected in Holocaust events, are a prerequisite for redemption. They affect the process of *bitul hayesh* (the dissolving of the ego forces), "since it is impossible for the divine light to penetrate without *bitul hayesh* . . . as the seed rots in the earth [in the process of the creation of plant life]. . . . This is why Israel suffers *hevle leda* (birth pains), and their strength is dissolved. In this process they give birth to the light of the Messiah.[11]

Hasidic responses which identified Holocaust suffering with the birth pangs of the Messiah seemed to go beyond the classic observation in the Talmud: "Rabbi Yohanan said: 'When thou seest a generation overwhelmed by many troubles as by a river, await him [the Messiah].' "[12] The *hakeh lo* ("await him") of the Talmud suggests patience and passive endurance. The *Hevle Mashiah* responses noted in our study imply active anticipation, hope, purpose, and a state of fermentation where the Jew is entreated to "assist" the *Hevle Mashiah* by sharing in the pangs and thus to catalyze redemption. This now leads us to other responses which define the role of man (or God) in hastening redemption.

THE SEARCH AND PREREQUISITES FOR REDEMPTION

Aware of the awesome tragedy which had struck European Jewry and of the threat to the Jews of Budapest, where he had taken refuge, Rabbi Yissachar Teichthal, writing in 1943, vows to take stock of his people's fate and destiny and to seek "to probe and investigate the prolongation of exile and to . . . instruct and advise our people Israel as to what can be done to draw near future redemption, speedily in our day."[13] An investigation in reference to redemption responses reveals two seemingly distinct approaches. One insists on man's active involvement and initiative. The other leads to complete reliance on God. The latter view speaks of imminent *yeshuah* (salvation), the former, of gradual redemption.

The required initiative in shaping human destiny is prominent in *Em Habanim Semehah*. "All that relates to divine matters first requires action by man, only then will assistance follow from heaven."[14] Quoting Rabbi Yaakov Yitzchak (d. 1815), the Seer of Lublin, Rabbi Teichthal acknowledges the nonpermanence of God's unilateral action in Jewish history. "The first periods of salvation were not eternal, since they were not originally initiated by Israel, but came about through God's initiative.[15] . . . Prayer without action, like action without prayer, is not reliable.[16] Passive reliance on the Rebbe, without individual initiative, is ridiculed in a charming anecdote describing the naive faith of the shamash (attendant) in his Rebbe, Rabbi Eliezer of Komarno. Peretz Gabbai (the attendant) was a very simple though pious Jew, a bachelor. When asked why he had not married, he replied: "Why should I marry? With the Rebbe do I lack anything?" "But a man needs offspring!" was the astounded rejoinder.

"Offspring? I will submit a kvittel [petition] to the Rebbe, and I will have children!" Upon hearing this, the Rebbe laughed and responded: "He who completely relies upon a Rebbe has the appearance of a Peretz Gabbai!"[17]

The activist motif in the redemption theme is characterized by the term *tzemah* (growth, flourishing), associated with salvation.[18] In order to reap, one must prepare the ground by plowing and sowing, for the raw seed alone will not suffice to produce growth.[19] Rabbi Teichthal employs numerous sources from the Midrash, Kabbalah and Hasidic literature to develop the principle that the divine "influence does not descend [into the realm of man] until man's response from below is elevated in preparation for divine action."[20] Quoting Rabbi Mordechai Rokeach (the brother of the Belzer Rebbe, and his companion during his escape from Europe, 1943–44, via Budapest), who in turn makes a reference to the Trisker Magid (d. 1887), Rabbi Teichthal summarizes man's role in bringing salvation: "The future redemption shall come about by natural means; therefore, we must do all we can to create these natural elements. Only then will God complete it [redemption] for us, for the good."[21]

While not denying man's role in hastening salvation, the Piazesner Rebbe tempers such activism by stressing "faith and trust in God [which help] bring near our redemption."[22] Concerned with the psychological effect of seeking a rationale for present suffering, which may result in fear and panic, he urges "that we must mainly strengthen our faith and reject probing and conjectures, but rely on God, who will perform good acts on our behalf, and redeem and save us."[23]

The dichotomy between the activism reflected in Rabbi Teichthal's work and the quietism in the Piazesner Rebbe's emerges dramatically in their interpretations of the biblical verse, "Why do you cry out to me? Tell the Israelites to go forward!"[24] Rabbi Teichthal says:

> But faith alone [in redemption] is not sufficient. [It] needs to be supplemented by an act from us, in order to sustain this faith. . . . And it is incumbent upon us to emulate that which was done during the exodus from Egypt, "Tell the Israelites to go forward!" [i.e., they cannot rely on God alone, but must assume some initiative], and then will come the salvation from the Holy One, blessed be He.[25]

In contrast, the Piazesner says:

> At a time when all of Israel is in need of salvation, the major virtue which could bring about such salvation is *emunah* [faith, belief]. Israel would not have been redeemed from Egypt were it not for the merit of *emunah*. "Why do you cry out to me? Tell the Israelites to go forward!" Rashi explains this: "Worthwhile is the virtue of faith."[26]

The utter reliance on divine intervention to bring instant salvation was embodied in the expression *Yeshuat Hashem, keheref ayin* ("Salvation from God [can come] as the blink of an eye"), frequently encountered in Holocaust responses.[27] A Hasid of the Gerer Rebbe in the ghetto of Lodz encourages those about him with the teaching of Rabbi Nahman of Brazlav: " 'There is no such thing as despair in this world,' and, my God, do not despair *(zeit sich nisht meya'esh)* because salvation from God, *keheref ayin* [appears in an instant]."[28]

The *geulah* (redemption) theme in *Em Habanim Semehah* places particular emphasis on the "unexpected" and unorthodox means by which redemption may be realized. Since the return of the Jewish people to its homeland is considered an integral part and requisite of the gradual[29] redemption process,[30] how is it to be explained that the overwhelming number of Zionists,[31] and specifically the pioneers who were settling and developing the land, did not observe the Torah and were often nonbelievers? Rabbi Teichthal proceeds to develop the idea that redemption need not be initiated or stimulated by seemingly holy forces. First, "who is to probe into God's ways . . . and ascertain why He deems it necessary to use this type of creature [the nonreligious Jew] to fulfill His mission?"[32] Suffice it to say that they *are* "God's emissaries,"[33] though we may not be certain why this is so.

In the course of the work, however, Rabbi Teichthal puts forth a number of views which attempt to explain the significance of the redemption process being articulated precisely through irregular and unexpected means. Citing Kabbalah literature, he quotes:

> In an era when God, blessed be He, desires to achieve something of significance in the world, which would bring benefit to cosmic as well as temporal elements, then He disguises it in various cloaks, even in an improper fashion and ugly in dimension, in order that the judges and accusers not be aware of what transpires.[34]

He proceeds to cite a number of Hasidic Rebbes who refused to join in the ultra-Orthodox condemnation of Zionist political activity.

The Komarner Rebbe is said to have stated: "Leave them [the Zionists] alone, since we do not really know how the redemption will unfold. . . . perhaps it is the will of God to build precisely by means of these people."[35] Rabbi Yisrael of Vizhnitz refused to oppose the Zionist movement for a rather paradoxical motive. He believed it proper that God allow the rebuilding of the land and the redemptive process to progress by means of the "uncultured" (*haburyanim*), since it was the boorish element which had destroyed the land and the Temple. "Let them, therefore, rebuild the land and restore what they originally destroyed."[36] This thesis is further strengthened by Rabbi Teichthal's use of the teaching of Rabbi Elimelek of Lizensk (d. 1786). "Thus he wrote in the holy volume *No'am Elimelekh*[37] . . . 'If man ever wishes to break the power of any form, he must do so by employing a similar form.' "[38] Developing the concept of the holy as emerging from the nonholy, Rabbi Teichthal cites the mystical teachings of the Maharal of Prague (d. 1609):

> One should understand that the holy Kingdom of Israel is possessed with an inner divine component which emerged from an unholy kingdom.[39] Thus you will indeed discover that when the fruit is not yet ripe it is encased in a covering until the fruit matures and is on the verge of complete maturation. Then the fruit sheds its covering in the process of growth, since every substance which claims an existence of its own emerges from matter foreign to its existence.[40]

He then invokes talmudic sources as depicting a species of unclean fowl as harbinger of the coming of the Messiah.[41]

> How is it possible that the rebuilding of our Holy Land in our day, which constitutes a sign and omen for the imminent end [of the exile] and the beginning of redemption, should be implemented in the main by desecrators of the Sabbath and violators of the commandments, God forbid? They are practically indistinguishable from other nations, to our great dismay. . . . The *No'am Elimelekh* refers to the sinners of Israel as "unclean fowl." . . . We note how the sages of the Talmud describe the manner in which redemption will be signaled by unclean fowl.[42]

Scholem has described how the mystical consciousness is saturated with paradox.[43] Since redemption is a major concern of Jewish mysticism,[44] Rabbi Teichthal's thesis of a holy–non holy paradox seems not inconsistent with mystical-Hasidic thought.

THE NATURE OF EXILE AND THE DIASPORA

Was the Holocaust perceived as one of the many inevitable consequences of being in exile? What is the nature of exile? How does it affect the personality of the Jew? These were the questions posed by Rabbi Teichthal in *Em Habanim Semehah.*

The Jew is a submissive victim of Galut (exile). At first he welcomes and embraces it. Then he is forced to accept its delimitations. Gradually he is transformed into a Galut Jew (a "Golus Yid" in Yiddish). He then assumes a uniquely characteristic "exile mentality." His Jewish perspective and priorities become blurred and skewed.[45]

> You, the Golus Yid, you, who have become so attached to the clods of earth in the Galut from the moment that you were exiled. If the entire day would echo with the sounds of massive and terrible blows, and then these were to cease but for a moment, you would soon be appeased and reconcile yourself again to this very place. You would never anticipate that the very next day you would again be confronted with more of the same flagellation. . . . You have not as yet learned from the lessons of the past.[46]

Self-deception is a major blunder of the Golus Yid. It is difficult to comprehend why, after generations of persecutions, Jews continue "to contribute their [resources] to the lands of the diaspora, alien countries characterized by an ugly and offensive atmosphere. We expend our resources in vain. Our labor and toil become the focus of extortion."[47] The long Galut has destroyed the Jewish fraternal bond, creating in its wake "controversy, discord, a multiplicity of factions, and hatred without cause."[48]

Rabbi Teichthal reinforces these observations, based on historical considerations, with rabbinic teachings on the nature and consequences of the Galut. He draws upon the literature of the Kabbalah and Hasidism. "The power of the *kelipot*[49] is dependent upon the Galut. With the abolishment of Galut, the *kelipot* will also be abolished."[50] Citing the Hatam Sofer (Rabbi Moshe Sofer of Pressburg, 1763–1839), he makes reference to "Jewish dispersion and exile as the core of our misfortunes."[51]

The Piazesner Rebbe, in *Esh Kodesh,* depicts the Galut as restricting human experience and knowledge. Thus, in essence the experiencing of the divine is limited.[52] Hence, when redemption from Galut is the subject, the prophet employs the dual expression "*Nahamu, nahamu*"

(Comfort ye, comfort ye),[53] since both man *and* God within man, limited heretofore in Galut, will "return"[54] to their original and renewed selves.[55] The mutual interrelationship between God and the Jew, noted above in the discussion of suffering, seems to function as well in the sphere of Galut. If, indeed, the present Galut is not about to terminate and be resolved, "we may be to blame, since we are not sincere in directing our prayers to the redemption of the Holy One, blessed be He, and the Shekhinah from Galut."[56] Following the tragic deaths of his only son, his daughter-in-law, and his sister-in-law in the bombing of Warsaw in September of 1940,[57] the Piazesner Rebbe lamented: "I have lost the battle! May God help the people of Israel to win the war."[58] From that moment on, "nothing else mattered but the existence of the people of Israel. His wounded heart bled for the people of God who were being decimated, for the pure souls of Israel whose blood was being spilled like water, and for the Shekhinah in Galut."[59]

Rabbi Teichthal articulates the abnormality of the Galut for the Jew. "Dispersion is not natural for the Jew and has no basis for existence. . . . Galut is an aberration of, and divergence from, the order which God, blessed be He, designed for every nation."[60] This state of irregularity is the stumbling block for *geulah* (salvation), since it endangers the *ahdut* (unity, solidarity) of a people, which by itself constitutes a "state of normality."[61] The Holocaust represents the nadir of this state of abnormality, which should force the Jew to turn his back, once and for all, on his Galut existence. Breaking through all barriers of restraint, Rabbi Teichthal bitterly explains:

> These countries that have served as the focus for Jewish tragedy in our own day—how can we ever again seek any sort of benefit from them or even travel through them? One would have to pause everywhere along the paths and note how in this place such a person was murdered, burnt, stoned, plundered, and abducted. In another place, another person. . . . How can one imagine ever setting eyes upon them! Anyone with but the slightest sensitivity must surely shudder . . . how can anyone conceive ever rebuilding a home upon this blood?[62]

Bitterness, despair, and procrastination, however, cannot represent the final response to Galut. Neither can one shift the entire burden upon Divine Providence.

> Perhaps, my brethren, you will wish to explain that all this is a decree from heaven, and represents a facet of Galut reality that has been decreed for us by heaven, until the coming of our Messiah; consequently, there remains nothing further for us to do? Then hear this, my brethren, I can never accept this![63]

THE LAND OF ISRAEL

Since 70 C.E., which marked the destruction of the Second Temple in Jerusalem, the Jew has longed to return to Eretz Yisrael. This earnest desire is expressed in the daily, Sabbath, and Festival liturgy, in the traditions and observances, and in the legalistic, popular, and mystical literature.[64] Eretz Yisrael is inseparably tied to the messianic tradition.[65] Understandably, when subjected to persecution, the Jew's negation of exile *(shelilat hagolah)* and love for Zion reached levels of great intensity and fervor.[66]

Rabbi Teichthal's document articulates these sentiments as formulated in the kabbalist and Hasidic tradition and in response to the horror of the unfolding Holocaust. The entire *Em Habanim Semehah,* written in Budapest in 1943, is the fulfillment of a personal *neder* (vow):

> like the vow of Jacob, our Patriarch.[67] [I pledge to] compose this work immediately following God's rescue of me from the enemy—a book devoted to the glorification of Eretz Yisrael; to seek out its merits,[68] to raise its status with honor, to prove to all concerned how vital it is for us to build it and to improve it, to lift it upward and raise it from its dust; [in order to urge] that every Jew share in the upbuilding of our Holy Land, since our redemption is contingent upon it.[69]

Rabbi Teichthal's major thesis suggests that the Jew's neglect of Eretz Yisrael may have contributed to the grave toll taken during the Holocaust.[70] The blame must fall squarely upon the religious leaders who refused to participate with nonobservant Jews in rebuilding the land, and assumed a stance of "sit back and wait."[71]

> Who shall accept the responsibility for the innocent blood shed in our days . . . but the leaders who prevented Jews from participating with the builders [of Eretz Yisrael]. They will not be able to atone [for their mistakes] and claim: "Our hands did not spill this blood."[72]

Had the religious leaders of Eastern European Jewry indeed encouraged active participation in "this holy task, sixty or fifty or forty years ago, this country [the land of Israel] would have been significantly developed. Thousands upon thousands of Jews would have been settled and saved from death."[73] How unfortunate that the enormous resources of Jews throughout the centuries "fell into the hands of Esau . . . [rather than] directed at redeeming and rebuilding our Holy Land."[74] Eretz Yisrael, until now an object of neglect, must be transformed into a source of *tikkun* (reconstruction, restitution).

> Now if we rise and ascend to Zion, we can yet reconstruct[75] the souls of the people of Israel who were murdered while sanctifying the Name [of God],[76] since, due to their sacrifice, we were stimulated to return to our ancestral inheritance . . . thus, we bring about their rebirth.[77]

The *tikkun* potential of rebuilding Eretz Yisrael is such that it has an impact even upon the economic elements.

> It seems to me that should a simple person contribute to building the land, though it may not be for the sake of heaven, but for his own personal interest, he performs a *tikkun*[78] in the upper spheres. [This act] is superior to the *tikkun* of a Zadik, even if he is the greatest of Zadikim, with his *tikkun hazot*[79] accompanied by his crying, bewailing the fate of the Shekhinah in galut. He [the Zadik] may indeed be performing a significant *tikkun*, but it does not compare to the *tikkun* of the simple man, performed by the work of his own hands, actively creating, though not necessarily for the sake of heaven.[80]

In addition to the particular relationship of Eretz Yisrael to the Holocaust and *tikkun*, Rabbi Teichthal describes the permanent contrast between life in the land and Jewish existence in exile. The obvious difference between these two conditions must surely "arouse us to return to our Holy Land."[81] The Holocaust and all that has occurred to the Jew in the exile should be interpreted as a "heavenly call from our King, the Holy One, blessed be He, for us to return to the Holy Land. He brought this all about in order to make it impossible for us to exist any longer among the nations, and thus to undermine any notion of security in exile."[82]

Much emphasis is placed on the interdependence of Eretz Yisrael and *geulah* (redemption). One is the prerequisite for the other. "Since the redemption will develop gradually, not all at once, it is required that [the people of] Israel be gathered into Eretz Yisrael prior to the true *geulah,* in order first to evacuate the very center of evil, namely, dispersion and exile."[82a] Rabbi Teichthal differs sharply with his own Rebbe (the Munkatcher Rebbe) on the issue of whether *geulah* will evolve gradually or erupt cataclysmically.[83]

> The outcry of our master, Rabbi and Holy Gaon, the *Minhat Eliezer* [i.e., the Munkatcher Rebbe, referred to here by the name of his major work], may he rest in peace, [he died in 1937], directed against those involved in the settlement and rebuilding of the land (and I myself was a party to this thinking),[84] was primarily based on [his belief] that everything would occur by means of miracles and wonders, and that all who attempted to intervene [in this process] would be denying redemption, which must be realized through a miracle.[85]

"With all due respect," Rabbi Teichthal dissents on the following counts: (1) Miracles which appear as unnatural events are the select privilege of a world deserving such miracles. "Regrettably, this generation is not deserving. Redemption, therefore, must be garbed in natural form."[86] (2) If the *Minhat Elilzer* were alive to witness "the terrible decrees and murders that have struck us, God forbid, even he would admit that we must evacuate the countries of exile and go to Eretz Yisrael, given to us by the rulers of the world,[87] . . . and not wait for the call of the Messiah."[88]

If Eretz Yisrael is to serve as an effective catalyst for the *geulah shelemah* (the complete and final redemption), the rebuilding of the land must involve all of Israel.

> Our redemption is dependent upon our oneness, all of us united within *Kelal Yisrael* [the totality of Israel], from every corner [of the earth]. This is indeed possible. The common denominator for such solidarity is our total participation in the plan to build the land.[89]

In the background of the Holocaust tragedy unfolding before him, Rabbi Teichthal directs his most bitter comments at the religious elements in Eastern Europe for (1) undermining Jewish solidarity by not participating in the *yishuv* (settlement) and *binyan* (building) of Eretz Yisrael;[90] (2) permitting the secularization of Eretz Yisrael by default;[91] (3) failing to understand the relationship of the settlement and building of Eretz Yisrael to the physical survival of Jews, where all theological, ideological, and legal considerations must be laid aside;[92] (4) placing their own material interests above the interests of all the Jewish people;[93] and (5) failing to strive to bring reality to the longings and yearnings for Zion expressed daily in their own prayers.[94]

Rabbi Teichthal weaves into the contemporary-historical material theological views related to Eretz Yisrael that transcend contemporary history. Citing talmudic sources he equates the inheritance of Eretz Yisrael to the inheritance of the entire Torah.[95] Further, it is only in Eretz Yisrael, due to the merit of the sanctity of the land, that one need not distinguish between the positive and negative characteristics of a human being.[96] Kabbalah teaches that "Eretz Yisrael is located in the highest order of the *sefirot*,[97] in the category of *malkhut*,[98] and *malkhut* is considered to be the mother of Israel. It is she who waits and cries for us, to draw near to her bosom."[99] Eretz Yisrael is the mother of Israel and its heart,[100] whereas exile is the "stepmother."[101]

CHAPTER 7

Hasidic Concepts Related to Exile and Redemption

HEVLE MASHIAH

The talmudic assumptions concerning *Hevle Mashiah* gained new momentum with the kabbalist interpretation of the catastrophic expulsion of the great Jewish community of Spain in 1492. "The birth-pangs of the Messianic era, with which history is to 'end' or (as the apocalyptics would have it) to 'collapse,' were therefore assumed to have set in with the Expulsion."[1] Hasidism similarly chose to weave the periods of intense national suffering into the *Hevle Mashiah* frame. "The concept of *Hevle Geulah* (the pains of redemption), likened to birthpains, is common to all the Hasidic leaders, beginning with the Ba'al Shem Tov, down to our day."[2] "The suffering of the Jewish people" became almost synonymous with *Hevle Mashiah.*[3] It was viewed as "the darkness before the dawn,"[4] and as "the descent for the sake of the ascent."[5] Rabbi Nahman of Brazlav defines this concept as follows: "Descent must precede ascent, since descent makes ascent possible."[6] Rabbi Levi Yitzchak elaborates upon the liturgical hymn "Let Zion and her cities lament like a woman in the pangs of birth":[7]

> The fact is that when a woman prepares for birth she suffers, but following birth she is full of joy. This holds true for all who witness her pains. They too are joyous, since they are confident that she will give birth to a son or a daughter. . . . Thus it is with Zion. Though she is presently in pain following her destruction, she is like a woman in the midst of labor. The Holy One, blessed be He, is happy, since He knows that the suffering is temporary.[8]

The Berdichever explains the rationale for pain prior to redemption:

> That which comes with ease, without suffering, is also devoid of joy. This is the meaning of "God has brought me laughter."[9] God has thus far denied me the fruit of my womb[10] in order that He may bring me laughter and joy.[11] This is the implication of the verse "I will praise You, for You have answered me *(anitani)*, and You have been my salvation."[12] The purpose [of the affliction and oppression] is redemption. This is also the intent of the verse "The stone which was despised by the builders[13] has now become the chief cornerstone," and, therefore, you will say, "This is the Lord's work."[14] In other words, since You first afflicted me, redemption followed. I now realize that all this emanated from God. But this could not have been if God, blessed be He, were to provide man with all the benefits from the time of his youth. He would not discern at all that this is from God. He would be inclined to say: it is coincidental! However, when he at first experiences misfortune, and then God provides him with joy by redeeming him from oppression and distress, he will surely understand that the world is dependent upon Divine Providence. This is from Him and "it is wonderful in our eyes,"[15] and he will exclaim, "The Lord has made this day; let us be glad and rejoice in it."[16]

The Berdichever does not merely view the *Hevle Mashiah* stoically but welcomes them as a necessary antecedent of, and preparation for, redemption.

According to Jewish messianic tradition, Messiah the son of Jospeh must first suffer and be martyred in the cataclysmic wars of Gog and Magog as part of the *Hevle Mashiah* process, prior to the coming of Messiah the son of David, the final redeemer.[17] Hasidic tradition teaches that each generation must produce its own martyred Messiah the son of Joseph in order to hasten the final redemption.[18] Rabbi Shlomo of Karlin would say: "I am ready to be the Messiah the son of Joseph if this would but bring the Messiah the son of David."[19]

Hence, the preparatory stages of suffering prior to the *geulah shelemah* (complete redemption) are integral to the Hasidic messianic tradition.

THE SEARCH AND PREREQUISITES FOR REDEMPTION

Martin Buber has documented the centrality of redemption in Jewish history and thought, and the unique Hasidic variations as expressed in the redemption of the holy sparks, the individual soul, the Jewish nation, and the Shekhinah—and their mutual interrelationship.[20]

Basic to the purpose of Hasidism was the preparation of the Jewish people for *geulah* (redemption). In a rare document from the pen of the Ba'al Shem Tov, the founder of Hasidism confronts the Messiah:

> "When will the master come?" He replied, "You will know it, when your teachings will be disseminated in the world, and your source shall be revealed to the outside . . . then will all the *kelipot* (shells) be destroyed and the time will be ripe for redemption."[21]

The present discussion is limited to the following themes: (1) the extent of man's initiative in the redemption process and the related role of God; (2) the "unholy" or unorthodox forces which may be operating as part of the *geulah* process.

The impact of man's action "below" on the cosmos, already documented in the Midrash and the Kabbalah,[22] is further accented in Hasidism. " 'Thus shall the children of Israel be blessed.'[23] The following is the principle enunciated to the world by the Ba'al Shem Tov in his interpretation of the verse 'God is your shadow;'[24] namely, as the shadow corresponds to the actions of man, so the Creator, blessed be He, relates His actions (so to speak) to those of man."[25] The initiative of man, as an act of preparation for God's ultimate assistance, is viewed as a "planting or sowing" that releases the self-limitations of the divine and allows the unlimited springs of *hesed* (goodness) to well forth.[26] Unlike the redemption in Egypt, which took place in "haste,"[27] the final redemption will evolve gradually, "since it must come through the initiative and action of those below, which will complement the Will of God."[28] The interaction between man and God in bringing redemption is especially evident in the activist thrust of the Hasidic dynasty of Izbitza-Radzin:[29] "*Tikkun* [restoration, completion] must be directed toward the redemption of the Shekhinah [in particular] and redemption [in general]. [These] must be drawn near by action [of man]."[30] The two-directional relationship of the human *I* and the divine *Thou*, clearly enunciated in the Holocaust responses, is summarized by Martin Buber (even as Buber was to incorporate this concept into his own thought system):

> In other teachings, the God-soul, sent or released by heaven to earth, could be called home or freed to return home, by heaven; creation and redemption take place in the same direction, from "above" to "below." But this is not so in a teaching which, like the Jewish, is so wholly based

> upon the double-directional relation of the human *I* and the divine *Thou*, on the reality of reciprocity, on the *meeting*. Here man, this miserable man is, by the very meaning of his creation, the helper of God. For his sake, for the sake of the "chooser," for the sake of him who can choose God, the world is created. Its shells are there in order that he may penetrate through them into the kernel. The spheres have withdrawn from one another in order that he may bring them nearer to one another. The creature waits for him. God waits for him. From him, from "below" the impulse towards redemption must proceed. Grace[31] is God's *answer*. None of the upper, inner worlds, only this lowest and most external world is capable of providing the thrust to transformation in the *Olam Hatikun*, the world of completion in which "the figure of the *Shekhinah* steps out of the hiddenness." For God has contracted Himself to the world. He has set it free; now fate rests on its freedom. That is the mystery of man.[32]

Rabbi Teichthal's documentation for the thesis that redemption will be realized through natural means is independently substantiated in Hasidic literature. Rabbi Shlomo of Luzk (d. 1800), an outstanding disciple of Dov Ber of Mezritch, taught: "Miracles are employed in the event of a contingency. They are, therefore, compared to night.[33] Prior to *geulah* and following *geulah*, one needs neither miracles nor of acts of vengeance."[34]

Rabbi Israel of Rizin (d. 1850) taught that only the type of *geulah* which develops in natural fashion can resist the destructive counteraction of Satanic forces. As evidence he cites the unprovoked attack of Amalek following the redemption from Egypt.[35] Had the *geulah* in Egypt not been made possible by means of the multitude of miracles, the Satanic forces embodied in Amalek would not have asserted themselves.[36]

Rabbi Teichthal's Hasidic documentation, which attests to the realization of *geulah* by means of "unholy" and non-Orthodox elements, may have its basis in Lurianic Kabbalah and the remarkable concepts of *tikkun* (restoration, completion) and *gilgul* (the transmigration of souls). The process of "the return of all things to their original contact with God" rests partly in the hands of man.[37] "Not all the lights which are held in captivity by the powers of darkness are set free by their own efforts; it is man who adds the final touch to the divine countenance . . . ; it is he who perfects the Maker of all things! . . . The 'world of *Tikkun*' is therefore the world of Messianic action."[38]

Tied to the role of man's initiative in the redemption of God, and mankind, is the concept of *gilgul* (transmigration of souls) as a part of the *tikkun* process.[39] "*Gilgul* provides the human soul with an opportunity to redeem itself and atone for not having completed its destined task during a previous stage in its existence. The transmigration represents a second exile in which the soul can find redemption, a mission: its purpose is to uplift the fallen sparks from all their various locations."[40] Zionist activities may have been viewed by the Komarner Rebbe as part of the *gilgul-tikkun* process.[41] At times, in order to uplift the holy sparks, one must descend into the abyss of impurity, for there they may be hidden or imprisoned. Utilizing unholy means in order to attain the holy was most forcefully articulated by the radical Sabbatians, who concluded that "under the law of organic development, which governs every sphere of existence, the process of Salvation is dependent on man's actions being, at least in certain respects and at certain times, dark and as it were rotten."[42] Rabbi Elimelekh of Lizensk (d. 1786) presents the traditional stance of Hasidism regarding the "descent in order to elevate."[43]

> To exploit [his positive role], the Zadik must descend somewhat from his state of *devekut* [clinging to God's Presence] and divert himself [from his normal proper path] in order to view [be sensitive to] the mundane needs of this world. This is the rationale for the statement of our sages, of blessed memory, "A prayer in which there is no sinner of Israel involved is not heeded,"[44] . . . [therefore,] it is necessary to include one sinner in Israel in a quorum of ten [for prayer] so that the influence of the Zadik may be unleashed by his own diversion [from *devekut*].[45]

This concept, namely, that the imperfect, the unholy, the unredeemed, must become an integral part of the *tikkun*-redemptive process, is the basis of the Elimelekh of Lizensk citation employed by Rabbi Teichthal to justify the secular Zionist involvement in Eretz Yisrael: "If ever man wishes to break the power of some substance, he must do so by employing an identical substance."[46] Martin Buber, citing Rabbi Nahman of Brazlav, notes the opportunity for redemption precisely when one is struggling on the brink of the abyss, removed from all contact with holiness: "Because, in truth, sometimes exactly when a person arrives at a very low place far away from holiness, exactly there he may be awakened in a great awakening toward God, blessed be His Name."[47]

THE NATURE OF EXILE AND THE DIASPORA

Though in Hasidism, as noted by Uffenheimer,[48] Galut may also represent personal spiritual limitation, alienation, and estrangement within the human being *(galut haneshamah)* transcending any geographic or national considerations, the physical, material Galut outside the land of Israel was not muted. Hasidism recognized that physical exile may contribute to *galut haneshamah,* even as it is interrelated with *galut hashekhinah* (exile of God's Presence).[49]

In Hasidism, Galut is clearly a tragedy of significant proportions for the individual Jew, the people of Israel, and the God of Israel. It is referred to as the "*galut hamar* [bitter exile] wherein we are hurt, dragged, and pushed in the wake of diminishing [beneficial] influences [emanating from above] to [the people of] Israel."[50] Interpreting the verse "You will surely cry in the night,"[51] Rabbi Yaakov Yosef of Polnoya notes:

> Galut, which is compared to "night,"[52] evokes a twofold cry, since there are two types of Galut: (1) the physical Galut among the nations, (2) the spiritual *yetzer hara* [evil inclination]; [in this instance] the soul is in Galut with the *yetzer hara* . . . and one flows from the other.[53] We are affected by both [types of exile], therefore, the twin cry in the night.[54]

Hasidism perceived Galut as a delimiting experience narrowing the Jew's perspective and depriving him of crucial spiritual and intellectual resources *(histalkut hada'at).*[55] Rabbi Nahman of Brazlav underscores the restricting nature of exile. "All of the centers of exile are referred to as Mitzrayim (Egypt) because they are delimiting to Israel."[56] Galut produces a form of deprivation brought about by "the great forgetfulness *(shikheha)* that is the consequence of this bitter Galut these many days and years."[57] Rabbi Abraham (d. 1776), the son of Rabbi Dov Ber, taught that the "lengthy Galut turns the true Torah into matter."[58]

Such abnormality may lead to the form of self-deceit observed by Rabbi Teichthal,[59] since the Jew does not possess the complete perspective necessary to make decisions in his own best interests. Galut threatens Jewish unity,[60] which in turn prolongs the exile.[61]

Rabbi Teichthal's reference to *kelipot* (shells) in exile[62] is found in kabbalist and Hasidic sources in various forms. Indeed "the main purpose of Galut is only to raise the sparks which fell into the *kelipot*."[63] These holy sparks give sustenance to the Galut. The Jew's purpose in Galut is to rescue the sparks from the prison of exile, thus collapsing Galut entirely.[64]

Though God shares in the suffering of the Jew in Galut, which evidently eases the burden of exile, the abnormality of Galut disturbs the unity of God with His people.

> Presently in this bitter exile, due to our many transgressions, the union and joining [between the Shekhinah and the people of Israel] is not complete, but rather, [it represents a relationship like] *hitun*,[65] until our righteous Messiah will come, quickly, in our day, and then the *zivug* (union) shall be complete.[66]

Galut hashekhinah (the exile of God's Presence), for Rabbi Levi Yitzchak, is God's painful inability to release all the potential sources of benevolence due to Israel's incapability to accept His kindness in Galut.[67] Paradoxically, at this very time, man is urged to redeem the Shekhinah in exile. "Thus, the Shekhinah in this bitter Galut is weary, and only by prayer, the study of Torah, fulfilling the commandments, and benevolent deeds can we sustain the Shekhinah [in Galut]."[68]

Does the Jew play a passive or an active role in responding to the debilitations of Galut? As with redemption, Kabbalah and Hasidism provided an activist option. If indeed the Galut served as a conducive environment for the *kelipot*, sustained only by the imprisoned holy sparks, it is the Jew's responsibility, not the action of the divine, to lower himself into the abyss, rescue the sparks, and thus terminate the exile.[69]

ERETZ YISRAEL

Horodetzky, Buber, Werfel, Dinaburg, Shazar, and Federbush have all documented Hasidism's very special concern for Eretz Yisrael.[70] Buber reflects the general consensus of the authorities: "Hasidism announced with great enthusiasm that Israel, the heart of humanity, and *Eretz Yisrael*, the heart of the world, are required by each other, and without their unity, redemption will not come."[71] The land of Israel was not merely an association of the past, but significant in the present and future. "For mystical Judaism, the bond between the Eretz Yisrael of today in its destruction, and the Eretz Yisrael of the magnificent past was never broken."[72] The modest but continuous waves of aliyah[73] of Hasidim, beginning with Rabbi Avraham Gershon of Kitov, the brother-in-law of the Ba'al Shem Tov attest to the active commitment of representative Hasidim to Israel's geographic centrality.[74] The majority of settlers in nineteenth-century Palestine were Hasidim.[75] Every Hasidic dynasty would eventually be represented in Palestine and Israel.[76]

Among the underlying motives of the Eretz Yisrael responses discussed in *Em Habanim Semehah* one perceives redemption, in general, and Eretz Yisrael in particular, achievable only if coinciding with the *ahdut* (unity) and *shlemut* (completeness) of the people of Israel, in contrast to the fragmentary and debilitating nature of Galut. Interpreting the verses, "And you will return to the Lord your God. . . . He will bring you together again from all peoples where the Lord your God has scattered you. . . . And the Lord your God will bring you to the land,"[77] Beshtian tradition taught: "Everyone in Israel must reconstruct *(letaken)* and prepare the messianic component belonging to his soul . . . then will the total Messiah be composed of all the souls of Israel."[78] Rabbi Levi Yitzhak, paraphrasing Rashi's comment on Leviticus 25:38 ("I the Lord am your God, who brought you out of the land of Egypt, to give you the land of Canaan, to be your God"), perceived Eretz Yisrael as the instrumentality for achieving Israel's completeness: "God took the Israelites out of Egypt in order for you to inherit the land. With your coming to the land, you will have achieved completeness."[79]

In defending the non-Orthodox Zionist elements, Rabbi Teichthal invoked the concept of *Kedushat Eretz Yisrael* (the sanctity of the land of Israel), which obliterates distinctions between good and bad, especially when one is involved in the welfare of the land. Rabbi Nahman relates the impressions of the early Hasidic settlers in Eretz Yisrael in 1763 and 1774. The settlers were so imbued with its sanctity "that they could not conceive of Eretz Yisrael existing in this [mundane] world."[80] Rabbi Nahman of Brazlav[81] viewed Eretz Yisrael as the source of renewal for the world at large.[82] Rabbi Levi Yitzchak associated the eventual ingathering of the exiles to Eretz Yisrael with the *gilgul-tikkun* process, restoring the Jew to his original pure self. "Every Jew will become complete in body and soul on this path to perfection. This [process] prepares one to enter the palace of the King without blemish.[83] Hasidic tradition drew from the writings of the great seventeenth-century mystic Abraham Azulai: "He who enters

Eretz Yisrael receives a newly created soul which joins the old soul. During the first night's sleep in Eretz Yisrael, both souls exit and ascend upwards. Only the new soul returns. He who dwells in Eretz Yisrael is called a Zadik [righteous, saintly], although he may not seem to be a Zadik."[84] Rabbi Pinhas of Koretz, a disciple of the Ba'al Shem Tov taught: "He who has no desire to go up to Eretz Yisrael is poisoned with bitter darkness."[85]

The relationship of the land of Israel to redemption is central to Hasidism and, in particular, to Rabbi Nahman. Eretz Yisrael is conducive to effective prayer[86] and *tikkun,*[87] both essential to individual redemption.[88] Within its environment one may more effectively influence the cosmos and "attract the benefits of the divine" that make the complete and restored individual possible.[89] Charateristically, national and individual redemption merge in the environment of Eretz Yisrael. The evils of the nations, deserving of divine punishment,[90] did not affect Eretz Yisrael.

> It is noted in the Talmud that "the flood inundated the entire world, except for Eretz Yisrael."[91] Now, *mabul* [flood] stems from the term *bilah* [to decay, become worn out], which, in turn, is related to *mebalbel* [to confuse, to mix],[92] since [the world] was mixed [and decayed][93] with good and evil. Except for Eretz Yisrael, since "the environment of Eretz Yisrael makes one wise."[94]

Whereas Rabbi Teichthal accuses the religious leaders of being absorbed with the materialism of the Galut at the expense of Eretz Yisrael and the Jewish people's ultimate national interests, Rabbi Nahman of Brazlav taught: "It is there [in the main, in Eretz Yisrael] that the lust for money is broken."[95] The Komarner Rebbe noted: "In Jerusalem one may guard easily against the evil inclination if one but wishes."[96]

Eretz Yisrael has no national significance or validity unless it is united with the Jewish people.

> On a number of occasions the kingdoms [of the world] desired to establish an effective settlement in Eretz Yisrael to make it like other nations. They did not succeed. Why is this so? Actually God blessed and created the entire earth, and [in the process] designated certain places in the world as [places of] settlement and others as desert. Now, when a settlement is destroyed, it becomes desolate and [reverts to] desert. . . . However, when Israel lives securely in Eretz Yisrael, it is a

> settlement. But when Israel was exiled, though other nations may inhabit it [Eretz Yisrael], it remains a desert.[97]

While Rabbi Teichthal equates Eretz Yisrael with the entire Torah, Hasidism describes Eretz Yisrael "as being the Shekhinah itself."[98] Rabbi Elimelekh of Lizensk equated the unity of the Jewish people and its land with the *shelemut* (completion, perfection) of the Shekhinah. "When Israel dwells in its own land, the Shekhinah is called 'a woman in a state of cohabitation with her husband.' This is not so [when Jews dwell] outside of Eretz Yisrael."[99] The Komarner Rebbe, expounding upon the verse "For the land is mine,"[100] interpreted it to mean, *shaveh beshaveh*—"we are one and the same."[101]

CHAPTER 8

Kiddush Hashem and Kiddush Hahayim

The subject of this chapter is the pattern of Hasidic responses to the Holocaust related to *Kiddush Hashem* (the sanctification of God's Name).

The documentation for the *Kiddush Hashem* pattern of responses was drawn from primary and secondary sources, as well as sources employed in documenting previous responses. In the main, these represent eyewitness accounts in Yiddish and Hebrew periodicals, Holocaust memorial volumes, and the general Holocaust literature. These sources were evaluated in accordance with accepted principles of historical research dealing with problems of authenticity and credibility.[1] Independent corroborating evidence is presented. Wherever possible clusters of similar responses from different sources are grouped in order to depict trends within the *Kiddush Hashem* theme that may possess greater reliability than isolated and solitary instances of response. Data recorded during the Holocaust will be considered more reliable than data recorded in the post-Holocaust period.

The discussion in this chapter, and in the remainder of the study, will be limited to responses that occurred and were witnessed *during* the period of the Holocaust, though the recall (either verbally or in written form) may have been documented in either the Holocaust or the post-Holocaust period. Hasidic responses to the Holocaust subsequent to the liberation of areas conquered by Nazi German (1944–45) will not be considered. The research commences with the German occupation of Poland in September 1939, and the execution of the systematic plan for the displacement and eventual annihilation of European Jewry.

The research will not evaluate responses in terms of their "typical" or "atypical," "positive" or "negative" character.[2] No attempt will be made to compare the pattern of Hasidic responses with other Jewish and non-Jewish data. The only criterion applied to the selection of Hasidic responses, other than their validity and reliability, is whether the data seem related to some aspect of Hasidic thought.

The methodology will not attempt to isolate the Hasidic component or motive of the Holocaust responses. One cannot possibly do so unless employing tools of psychological measurement unrelated to this research. The study will, in the first instance, describe the response of a Hasidic leader or Hasid. The relationship of the response to the Hasidic system of thought and behavior, rather than its motive, will be the focus of the sources.

MANIFESTATIONS OF KIDDUSH HASHEM DURING THE HOLOCAUST

Whenever the subject of *Kiddush Hashem* was under discussion during the Holocaust, Maimonides' classic summary of the various means by which the Jew could fulfill the commandment to sanctify God's Name was often invoked.[3] In the Warsaw Ghetto, Rabbi Shimon Huberband,[4] Rabbi Menahem Zemba,[5] and Hillel Zeitlin[6] all paraphrase Maimonides, applying the term *Kiddush Hashem* to every victim of the Holocaust. "As Maimonides ruled: 'A Jew who is killed, though it may be for reasons other than conversion but simply because he is a Jew, is called *kaddosh* (holy).' "[7] Maimonides, however, clearly reflects the consensus in the Talmud, cautioning against the indiscriminate application of *Kiddush Hashem* by death alone in the event that the Jew has a choice.[8] The Jew is bidden to sanctify God's Name in life,[9] especially when the enemy offers no choice but death.[10] Moshe Prager, a Holocaust researcher especially in the Hasidic area, defines *Kiddush Hashem* in the Holocaust context:

> What is *Kiddush Hashem?* Dr. [Yosef] Burg [Israel's Minister of Welfare] made reference to both passive and active forms of *Kiddush Hashem.* This is not exact. What actually determines *[Kiddush Hashem]* is the very focus of the conflict. If one wishes to really understand the ghetto, one must determine: "What does the enemy want from me?" If the enemy demands my honor, then my honor bids me to sacrifice life for honor. . . . However, the moment the enemy clearly insists: "I demand your life," then a sense of honor compels me to fight for my life.[11]

This contextual and broader concept of *Kiddush Hashem,* tied to the objective of the foe, moved Rabbi Yitzchak Nissenbaum, the president of the Mizrachi movement in Poland prior to and during the early Holocaust period, who died in the Warsaw Ghetto in 1943, to coin the phrase *Kiddush Hahayim* (the Sanctification of Life) as the way to *Kiddush Hashem.*[12]

Though *Kiddush Hashem* was reinterpreted in terms of *Kiddush Hahayim,* the odds during the Holocaust ran high in favor of some form of *Kiddush Hashem* terminating in death rather than life. Here as well, the Holocaust added a new dimension. In the Jewish martyrology of the past, the Jew had the option of choosing life, often by rejecting Judaism.[13] The martyr of the Holocaust, without life options and in full expectations of being murdered, also had a choice: the manner in which he would accept and prepare for death. Freedom to choose between life and religious faith was converted to the option of "going to one's death degraded and dejected as opposed to confronting [death] with an inner peace, nobility, upright stance, without lament and cringing to the enemy. . . . This new option . . . became another attribute of *Kiddush Hashem* during the Holocaust."[14]

Hasidic responses of *Kiddush Hashem* will be interperted against the background of the *Kiddush Hahayim* manifestations, especially as reflected in spiritual-passive resistance and in physical resistance, and then of *Kiddush Hashem* itself, i.e., the manner in which death was faced.

First, one notes the *zekhut* (privilege) motive in anticipation of offering life for *Kiddush Hashem.* The Ostrovzer Rebbe, Rabbi Yehezkel Halevi Halstuk, in garbed talit (prayer shawl) and kittel,[15] confronted the Nazis in Zusmir in the winter of 1943, prior to being shot: "For some time now have I anticipated this *zekhut* [of *Kiddush Hashem*]. I am prepared."[15a] The Koloshitzer Rebbe, Rabbi Hana Halberstam, foreshadowed his own death during the Holocaust in the fall of 1942 as early as 1914. Hasidic tradition relates how, at the age of thirty, he prayed at the grave of Rabbi Elimelekh of Lizensk: "May the Almighty grant that I be privileged to die for *Kiddush Hashem.*[16] Ahron Zeitlin relates the story of an aged Hasidic Rebbe whose only son was murdered during the Holocaust. The night before the planned rescue of the Rebbe, the son appears to his father, in a dream describing the "infinite holiness" of those who die for *Kiddush Hashem.* The following morning the Rebbe refuses to be rescued lest "he be denied the privilege of *Kiddush Hashem.*" The next day the Rebbe joins other Jews being assembled for the journey to their final destination.[17] The Shidlowitzer Rebbe, Rabbi Haim Rabinowitz, comforted those packed in the cattle cars without food and water on a four-day trip to the death camp. "Fellow Jews, do not fear death. To die for *Kiddsuh Hasehm* is a great privilege."[18]

The proper *hakhanah* (preparation) and *kavanah* (concentration on the meaning of a religious act) necessary before the performance of a mitzvah are also essential prior to the act of *Kiddush Hashem.* In discussing the significance of *Kiddush Hashem,* the Koidenover Rebbe, Rabbi Alter Perlow, in the Vilna Ghetto, retold the Hasidic legend of the Zaslover Martyrs, who died for *Kiddush Hashem.* Their souls came to the Ba'al Shem Tov pleading for *tikkun,* since their thoughts during the act of *Kiddush Hashem* had not been pure.[19] The Piazesner Rebbe taught: "Those who fail to praise God in death will not be aware of Him in the world-to-come."[20] Rabbi Mendele Alter, the brother of the Gerer Rebbe, was among a group of Jews in Treblinka during the summer of 1942 who were ordered to undress. Realizing that these were his last moments the Rebbe pleaded desperately for a glass of water. A Jewish guard, usually noted for his cruelty to fellow Jews, was touched by the plea. He provided the water under the impression that the Rebbe wished to quench his thirst before dying. Instead, the Rebbe used the water to cleanse his hands as an act of purification prior to *Kiddush Hashem,* urging: "Fellow Jews, let us say the *Vidui* [the confessional prayer] before dying."[21] The Brezner Rebbe, Zaloshizer Rebbe, Matislaker Rebbe, and Stoliner Rebbe were among a number of Hasidic leaders who led Jews in their final *Vidui* as preparation for *Kiddush Hashem.*[22]

The attitude developed prior to *Kiddush Hashem* determined the manner in which death was actually confronted. The *Kiddush Hashem* reports of the Brezner, Grodzisker, and Zaloshizer Rebbes[23] describe how the Rebbes, by facing death with dignity, had a calming influence on the other victims.[24] In each of these instances the final request included the wearing of a tallit katan or a tallit at the time of death.[25] Other descriptions of *Kiddush Hashem* actually include instances of confronting death with *hitlahavut* (ecstasy), appropriate to the fulfillment of the final and ultimate mitzvah.[26] With a Torah scroll in his hands, Meir Ofen, a kabbalist and a Hasid of the Dzikover Rebbe, led hundreds of Jews during their march to the mass grave reciting Psalm 33:1, "Rejoice in God, righteous ones!"[27] The Grodzisker Rebbe, Rabbi Yisrael Shapira, in an inspiring message prior to entering the gas chamber in Treblinka, urged the Jews to accept *Kiddush Hashem* with joy. He led in the singing of *Ani Ma'amin* ("I Believe").[28] The Dombrover Rebbe, Rabbi Haim Yehiel Rubin, prayed the Sabbath service, his last, with great fervor; sang the Sabbath table songs, and led twenty Jews in a Hasidic dance just before they were all killed and buried in graves dug by themselves.[29] The Spinker Rebbe, Rabbi Yitzchak Isaac Weiss, danced and sang on the death train to Auschwitz, especially the prayer *Vetaher libenu le'avdekha be'emet* ("Purify our hearts so that we may serve You in truth").[30] The Piazesner Rebbe observes that he who is murdered in *Kiddush Hashem* "does not suffer at all . . . since in achieving a high degree of ecstasy, stimulated in anticipation of being killed for the sake of sanctifying His Name, blessed be He, he elevates all his senses to the realm of thought until the entire process is one of thought. He nullifies his senses and feelings, and his sense of the material dissolves on its own. Therefore, he feels nothing but pleasure."[31]

The mutual interrelationship between God and the Jewish people, noted previously in this study, is also evident in connection with the *Kiddush Hashem* motive. The Slonimer Rebbe cites the *Zohar*, observing that God dyes His garments in the blood of the martyrs who die for *Kiddush Hashem*.[32] The Piazesner Rebbe contrasts suffering in punishment for sin with suffering for *Kiddush Hashem*. The latter is not directed only at the individual Jew. The consequences of the suffering affect his faith and way of life. In such instances [as exemplified by the *Kiddush Hashem* during the Holocaust] "it is we [the Jewish people] alone who suffer with Him."[33] Rabbi Yissachar Teichthal discusses a similar interrelationship between *Kiddush Hashem* and Eretz Yisrael. On the one hand, "the current massive *Kiddush Hashem,* sanctified by thousands and tens of thousands [is the cause of the] weakening of the *kelipot* [shells],[34] and enables the gates of Eretz Yisrael to open."[35] In turn, the very realization of Israel's return to Zion will serve to "magnify and sanctify the Name of God."[36]

Kiddush Hashem was also manifested in *Kiddush Hahayim* (sanctifying the Name of God in life). Responses of this kind took the form of modest physical resistance, spiritual and passive resistance, or *mesirat nefesh* (unqualified personal sacrifice, lit., "giving over one's soul") in order to assist others in time of crisis.[37] Rabbi Nehemya Alter, the brother of the Gerer Rebbe, keynoting a meeting of rabbis in Lodz, emphasized that the imperative of *Kiddush Hashem* may assume various forms, but central to the mitzvah is "not to degrade ourselves before the *goyim*."[38] *Kiddush Hahayim* dictates that the Jew face death and live life in dignity, cognizant of the divine component in man. Dignity in response to the enemy's acts of physical and spiritual degradation was dramatically demonstrated in Lublin toward the end of 1939.[39] The German commander had forcibly assembled the Jews in an empty field on the outskirts of the city and ordered them in jest to sing a Hasidic melody. Hesitantly, someone began the traditional melody "Lomir zich iberbeten, Avinu Shebashomayim" (Let us be reconciled, Our Father in Heaven).

> The song, however, did not arouse much enthusiasm among the frightened masses. Immediately, Glovoznik [the commander] ordered his hooligans to attack the Jews because they refused to comply fully with his wishes. When the angry outburst against the Jews continued, an anonymous voice broke through the turmoil with a powerful and piercing cry, "Mir welen sei iberleben, Avinu Shebashomayim" (We will outlive them, O Father in Heaven!). Instantly, the song took hold among the entire people, until it catapulted [them] into a stormy and feverish dance. The assembled were literally swept up by the entrancing melody full of *devekut*, which had now been infused with new content of faith and trust.[40]

The intended derision was turned into a disaster for the bewildered Nazis, forcing the commander, Glovoznik, to order a halt to the paradoxical spectacle.[41] The Zelichover Rebbe, Rabbi Avraham Shalom Goldberg, while hiding in Zelichov in June 1942, responded to the increasingly despondent fellow Jews who shared his hiding place: "We must remain hidden, perhaps it will save the life of but one Jew. Every Jew who remains alive sanctifies the Name of God amongst many. He is indeed a man of courage because he will not submit to the Nazis and will not extinguish his precious life."[42] The Piazesner Rebbe discusses the necessary interrelationship between those who die for *Kiddush Hashem* and the implications of *Kiddush Hahayim* for those who remain alive. Directing his remarks to those in the Warsaw Ghetto whose spirits have fallen, the Rebbe cautions:

> We have always been bidden to control ourselves against temptations and evil inclinations as implied by [the teaching] "Who is strong? He who controls his [evil] inclinations."[43] At present we have been given an additional responsibility: to control ourselves against dejection and

> depression, and to support ourselves in God. True, this is very, very difficult, since the suffering is too much to bear; may God have mercy. However, at a time when many Jews are burned alive sanctifying God, and are murdered and butchered only because they are Jews, then the least we can do is to confront the test and with *mesirat nefesh* control ourselves and support ourselves in God.[44]

Rabbi Menachem Zemba summarized the *Kiddush Hahayim* motif during a zealous plea for resistance prior to the Warsaw Ghetto uprising in April 1943.

> Thus, by the authority of the Torah of Israel, I insist that there is absolutely no purpose nor any value of *Kiddush Hashem* inherent in the death of a Jew. *Kiddush Hashem* in our present situation is embodied in the will of a Jew to live. This struggle for aspiration and longing for life is a mitzvah [religious imperative] [to be realized by means of] *nekamah* [vengeance], *mesirat nefesh* [extreme dedication], and the sanctification of the mind and will.[45]

CHAPTER 9

Hasidic Concepts Related to Kiddush Hashem and Kiddush Hahayim

Hallowing and sanctifying the Name of God is rooted in Hasidism and permeates its teachings and mode of life. In its efforts to achieve *tikkun* in this world as a preparation for *tikkun* in the upper world, Hasidism sought "to overcome the separation between the holy and the profane. . . . Everything wants to be hallowed, to be brought into the holy, everything worldly in its worldliness. . . . Everything wants to come to God through us . . . to let the hidden life of God shine forth."[1] Though Buber viewed Hasidism "as the only mysticism in which time is hallowed,"[2] Hasidism actually elaborated upon Judaism's principle of *Venikdashti betokh benei Yisrael.*"[3]

In Hasidic thought, *Kiddush Hashem* assumes various appearances attainable ultimately in death as well as in life. Interpreting the verse "Because of You, we are killed all the day; we are considered sheep for slaughter,"[4] the second Komarner Rebbe, Rabbi Eliezer Zvi Safrin, echoed the Midrash: "There are not to be found among any other nation those who are ready to sacrifice their souls for *Kiddush Hashem,* blessed be God, as may be found within Israel."[5] According to Hasidic tradition, the Ba'al Shem Tov offered the last two hours of his life as a gift to God, "a true sacrifice of the soul *(mesirat nefesh).*"[6] The traditional view of *Kiddush Hashem* as the supreme test of faith which allows every Jew to reach heights of sanctity was noted by Rabbi Shneur Zalman of Liadi, and incorporated into the Habad school of Hasidic thought. "Even the simplest of Jews, and sinners in Israel, by and large, sacrifice their lives for *Kiddush Hashem* and [in the process] undergo terrible suffering, so as not to deny the One God."[7] The *zekhut* (privilege) motive is also evident in Hasidic thought. Rabbi Levi Yitzchak, discussing "the purpose of all creation," observes: "Thus, every Jew [is prepared to] be killed for *Kiddush Hashem,* happy in the privilege of sanctifying by his own means the Name of Heaven."[8] Rabbi Nahman of Brazlav petitions the "Master of the Universe to grant me the privilege, with your compassion, to be able to sacrifice my life for *Kiddush Hashem,* sincerely, at any time."[9]

Hassidism maintained that all deeds in the service of God should be performed with *mesirat nefesh* (sacrificial devotion). Rabbi Yaakov Yosef of Polnoya draws the following instruction from the saying of the sages: "Who is wise? He who learns from *every* man":[10]

> Even to the extent that he learns from a prohibited act, [for instance] when he sees someone in the act of cohabiting with an animal, [may he apply the following lesson:] if this one endangers his life [since the law of the land prescribes the death penalty for such an act], yet does not hesitate for even one moment, because of the physical pleasure derived—how can he [who observes the act] not fail to sacrifice his life in the service of God, which is an eternal spiritual delight![11]

Rabbi Aaron of Karlin taught: *Es kon nit zein emes afilu ein tnua ketanah, un mesiras nefesh* ("The slightest act cannot be sincerely performed without *mesirat nefesh*").[12] Hasidism often use the terms *Kiddush Hashem* and *mesirat nefesh* interchangeably.[13] In order to dedicate one's soul to God, the soul had to be gradually sensitized and prepared to make the offering. To die for *Kiddush Hashem,* according to Rabbi Nahman Kossover (d. 1775), is the ultimate in altruistic behavior, since "he who is ready to die for God does so because he loves Him, and not as a reward."[14] Rabbi Israel of Rizin interpreted Leviticus 1:2 ("When any man from you shall bring an offering to the Lord") as follows: "Only he who brings himself to the Lord as an offering may be called man."[15] Rabbi Moshe of Kobrin anticipated that man would eventually replace the Temple sacrifices as the ultimate expression of devotion to God. "Lord of the World, we, we shall bring ourselves to You in place of the offering."[16] *Mesirat nefesh* in this context helped prepare the ground for the *Kiddush Hashem* responses noted during the Holocaust.

The related *Kiddush Hashem* motifs of *zekhut* (privilege), *hakhanah* (proper preparation), and *hitlahavut* (ecstatic response to a religious act), as well as the acceptance of death with dignity and honor, were all part of a complex interlocking pattern of consequences, as a result of a special relationship which would be effected and realized between the Jew, the Jewish people, and God via *Kiddush Hashem.* Rabbi

Yechiel Michal of Zlochov (d. 1786), the Magid of Zlochov, applied the kabbalistic formula that man's deeds have an effect upon the cosmos[17] to the concept of *Kiddush Hashem.*[18] The symbiotic relationship between man and the cosmos is dramatized in Hasidic tradition. The Ba'al Shem Tov visited the bereaved mother of a boy who was killed in Polnoya, "a victim of *alilat sheker,*[19] and who very much sanctified the Name. . . . He [the Ba'al Shem Tov] comforted her, saying: 'You should know that all the worlds which were opened for Isaac at the time of his binding,[20] were also opened [for the boy] when he was killed.' "[21] The effect of *Kiddush Hashem* may also reverberate in the region of the *sefirot,* resulting in a repositioning of the various symbolic terms which represent God's mystical qualities.[22] Rabbi Yitzhak Isaac of Komarno, a devout kabbalist, isolated *mesirat nefesh* and *Kiddush Hashem* as the factors enabling the Jew to elevate the divine manifestation of *malkhut* (the "kingdom" of God), the tenth in the series of ten *sefirot,* to the level of *binah* (the "intelligence" of God),[23] The second in the hierarchy of *sefirot.*

Another form of interrelationship between the Jew and the Creator through *Kiddush Hashem* was noted by the Matislaker Rebbe. An identical observation is recorded of the Gerer Rebbe: "Why is man afraid of dying? Does he not then go to his Father!"[24] In a similar vein, Rabbi Moshe Leib Sassov (d. 1807) was seen dancing on a vessel which was threatened with destruction by a terrible storm. When his teacher, Rabbi Schmelke of Nickolsburg inquired as to the reason for his unexpected exuberance, Rabbi Moshe responded: "I am overjoyed at the thought that I shall soon arrive in the mansion of my Father." "I shall join you, then," said Rabbi Schmelke.[25]

Kiddush Hashem and redemption appear as interrelated in Hasidism. In his letter to Rabbi Gershon Kitover, the Ba'al Shem Tov refers to instances of *Kiddush Hashem* in the communities of Zaslov, Sibotke, and Danowitz. "All gave their lives for *Kiddush Hashem* and sanctified the Name of Heaven, thus responding to the test. Due to this virtue, our Messiah will come."[26] The prolonged Galut, and its intensification, can be reversed. Its *tikkun* "consists of self-sacrifice for *Kiddush Hashem,* along with *mesirat nefesh* with all our heart and soul,"[27] taught the Komarner Rebbe.

Despite the evident readiness of Hasidim to die for *Kiddush Hashem* with *mesirat nefesh* when put to the test, "the very purpose of the creation of man is that he observe the Torah and its commandments, 'and live by them'[28] but 'not die by them,'[29] except when the time has come to leave this world."[30] Man's good deeds sanctify the upper and lower worlds. They serve to counter the phenomenon of death, according to Dov Ber of Mezritch.[31] In his prayer requesting the privilege of experiencing *Kiddush Hashem,* Rabbi Nahman of Brazlav straddles the thin line between *Kiddush Hashem* articulated in life and death. On the one hand, Rabbi Nahman pleads: "May I truly be prepared to die any death and to suffer every pain and torment for the sanctification of Your great Name."[32] Yet significantly, in the balance of the prayer Rabbi Nahman clearly makes reference to a vicarious *Kiddush Hashem* death experience, stopping short of death itself. He prays for the ability

> to portray within my mind all of the deaths and torments, in a realistic likeness . . . until I actually sense the pain of death and torment, as if in fact I would be killed or tortured for the sanctification of Your great and holy Name, to the very point when my soul shall practically expire. . . . This would make it necessary to overcome [the final death process] and to diminish these thoughts in order that I not die prematurely, God forbid.[33]

Rabbi Simcha of Parsischa taught that a Jew involved in the process of life, as a partner of God in creation, bears witness to God's greatness. Therefore, "when a Jew dies, a member of God's chosen people, the Lord takes the loss to heart, since this represents one person less to glorify and sanctify His Name."[34]

The Ba'al Shem Tov viewed his own efforts at miracle healing as "only for *Kiddush Hashem.*"[35] The Kotzker Rebbe emphasizes *Kiddush Hashem* as being *Kiddush Hahayim.* Interpreting the verse "You shall be men holy to me,"[36] the Kotzker taught: "Let your holiness be human, and may your human acts be holy. This is the holiness demanded of man. God has no need for angels in heaven."[37] The other world is not to be sought as an escape from the responsibilities of life in this world. Said Rabbi Naftali of Ropshitz: "No Jew can possibly inherit the world-to-come except by means of this world."[38]

CHAPTER 10

Zadik and Hasid

The mutual fraternal bond of the Hasidic fellowship and the unique relationship of the Zadik, or Rebbe, to his Hasidim led, quite naturally, to a very interesting series of responses to the Holocaust. The primary and secondary sources documented in connection with these responses suggested the following themes:

1. *Encouragement and consolation.* Comfort and encouragement from the Rebbe to his Hasidim, with the purpose of strengthening faith and morale.
2. *Refusal to leave community during crisis.* Refusal of Hasidic leaders to abandon their Hasidim despite opportunities for escape.
3. *Assistance and rescue.* Assistance and rescue operations organized through the efforts of the Rebbe.
4. *Devotion of Hasidim to their Rebbe.* Acts of Hasidim aimed at protecting their Rebbe from danger.
5. *Ahavat Yisrael.* Love and compassion for fellow Jews and concern for *kelal Yisrael* (the totality of the Jewish people) under adverse conditions.
6. *The Hasidic meal.* The Hasidic fraternal meal (gefihrt tisch or praven tisch) under adverse circumstances.
7. *The written petition* (kvittel). The Hasid's written petition to the Rebbe under adverse circumstances; this includes occasional challenges to the Rebbe to personally intervene with God.
8. *Neginah* (song). Hasidic melodies under adverse circumstances.

ENCOURAGEMENT AND CONSOLATION

Articulating a special relationship to his Hasidim, the Rebbe played a significant role in raising the morale and spirit of a people caught in an environment of degradation and despair. Providing a framework of hope and a sense of dignity was heretofore documented in responses related to the justifying of God's actions, the purpose of suffering, redemption, and *Kiddush Hashem.* In this chapter, the research will explore general references to acts of encouragement not classified among the responses previously discussed.

Many Rebbes, including the brother of the Gerer Rebbe and the Bukwasser, Brezener, Zichliner, Chenchiner, Komarnor, Kosonier, Radoshitzer, and Piazesner Rebbes, were documented in the process of *hithazkut* (the strengthening of spirit, morale, and will to live).[1] The Ringelblum *Notes* report a Yiddish sign displayed in front of the *shtiebel* (lit. "small room," i.e., the modest quarters associated with Hasidic prayer) of the Brazlaver Hasidim in the Warsaw Ghetto: *Yidden, zeit sich nisht meya'esh!* ("Jews, do not despair!")[2] A special plea for *hithazkut* is contained in a message of the Radziminer Rebbe Rabbi Yaakov Aryeh Morgenstern, to his Hasidim urging them to stand by their faith in order to counter resignation.[3] *Yidden, zeit sich nisht meya'esh!* was also the motto of the Zaviercher Rav Rabbi Shlomo Elimelekh Rabinowitz, in Birkenau camp.[4] An identical plea of the Radziner Rebbe, Rabbi Shmuel Leiner, to his Hasidim (at the time of his arrest in the spring of 1942) was recorded.[5] Despair should be resisted, for

> even though we may be in their [the enemy's] clutches, the Holy One, blessed be He, saves us. "This has always sustained us." With this [thought] we must strengthen our hopes. Though it appears to us that we are already [doomed] in their hands, God forbid, yet He will also save us.[6]

The Rebbe's statements of encouragement asserted the dignity of man, made in the image of God, and urged his Hasidim to resist at all costs being dragged down to the level of their persecutors. "The intent is for man not to conceive himself as void and corrupt, and thus reflect [the persecutor's] actions. Man must feel as a Jew, a Hasid, and a servant of God."[7] The consequences of *hithazkut,* its antithesis—*ye'ush* (despair), are indicated in the responses.

> The severe suffering, aside from its own evil existence, is further compounded by a state of depression, resulting in insensitivity to one's own eminent stature. Thus, we must be strong, even during times of

suffering, as would, indeed, a prince *(ben-melekh)* in captivity. Though he may be beaten, he is, nevertheless, a prince who is thus beaten. So may God be compassionate and save us immediately.[8]

Eyewitness Batya Lieberman reports the following expression of *hithazkut* by the Stoliner Rebbe, Rabbi Moshe Perlow, in the Stoliner Ghetto:

Al ye'ush! [Let there not be despair!] An insolent storm is passing over us all, but it will not attach itself to us. This is not the first time that the community of Stolin has survived a dangerous situation. This time as well God will save us from the murderous enemies. Strengthen yourselves, fellow Jews, and trust in God. "The everlasting glory of Israel [God] does not deal falsely."[9]

The Piazesner Rebbe employs mystical-psychological reasoning in an attempt to demonstrate the positive results of *hithazkut* for both the individual mind and the cosmos.

It is within the power of every Jew to fortify himself in this period of terrible sufferings. Torment [of this dimension, as experienced during the Holocaust] and *Din* [judgment, retribution] are not within the realm of nature [i.e., they are beyond human comprehension]. *Hithazkut,* as well, is an extraordinary phenomenon. Common sense would deny that *hithazkut* [under present conditions] is at all possible. [Precisely] Therefore, *hithazkut* will be successful in transforming *Din* into *Rahamim* [compassion].[10] . . . *Hithazkut,* on its own merit, will convert bad into good and "to bless your people Israel."[11]

Expanding further upon the consequences of *ye'ush,* the Piazesner interprets the biblical commandment to recall the treachery of Amalek,[12] as follows: The enemy can afflict Israel only when there are spiritual stragglers, *die was fallen unter sich* [Yiddish, "those who despair"]. Thus, eyes and hearts should be pointed toward heaven,[13] seeking salvation, though victory may not yet be evident."[14] A further consequence of *ye'ush* is the isolation it brings in its wake. The study of Torah, precisely during time of despair, will permit man to share the burden with God, who suffers with man. Thus, man is strengthened when his sense of isolation is broken.[15]

REFUSAL OF THE REBBE TO ABANDON HIS COMMUNITY

Among the significant patterns of responses emerging from the research is the repeated refusal of numerous Rebbes to abandon their communities during the Holocaust. Extraordinary arrangements for rescue, escape, and concealment, in and outside of Europe, were not exploited.[16] Typical of these responses was the reaction of the Komarner Rebbe, Rabbi Baruch Safrin, when on two occasions he refused to be rescued:[17] *Imam anokhi betzarah* [I am with them in their distress].[18] "*Ich bin nisht besser vun zei.* [I am not better than they are]."[19] A similar statement was made by Rabbi Eliyahu Lifshitz, the Rabbi of Grizah. "I am not permitted to leave my flock in time of crisis."[20] The Trisker's response when rejecting a rare opportunity for escape was: "A captain does not leave a sinking ship until all the passengers have been rescued. . . . I want to be part of the fate of Jews in Poland."[21] The Piazesner Rebbe had long planned to settle in Eretz Yisrael. When an opportunity to escape presented itself in the early days of beleaguered Warsaw, he declined to abandon his Hasidim.[22] Another plan to smuggle the Rebbe into relatively secure Stolin, the seat of his uncle's Hasidic dynasty, at that time under Soviet rule, was also rejected. In a report that reached the *Jewish Daily Forward* in New York, the Rebbe was quoted as having said: "I will not abandon my Hasidim in these difficult times. Wherever my Hasidim are, there I shall be as well. I will not agree to rescue myself and leave my Hasidim in a state of disorder."[23] The Brezener Rebbe, Rabbi Nahum Yehoshua Halevi Pechenik, declined to leave his community in Dombrowitz when the non-Jewish inhabitants of the town offered to help him escape.[24] At great pains, the Hasidim of the Grodzisker Rebbe, Rabbi Yisrael Shapiro, obtained false papers in order to smuggle the Rebbe out of the Warsaw Ghetto. He refused to be removed from the hub of the crisis.[25] The Zvoliner Rebbe, Zabner Rebbe, Lisker Rebbe, Slonimer Rebbe, and Karliner Rebbe all rejected escape plans.[26] Arrangements had been completed to fly the Radomsker Rebbe out of Lodz to Italy, but he declined.[27] Rabbi Avraham Weinberg, a leading Hasidic scholar in Warsaw who was close to the Kotzker and Sochochover schools of Hasidism, was offered a rare work permit in the Warsaw Ghetto; he refused to detach himself from his illegal study group of young Hasidim.[28] Hostages held for the Ostrovzer Rebbe and the Mezibezer Rebbe were in grave danger. The Rebbes rejected all rescue plans and were subsequently murdered when they surrendered together with their families.[29] Refusing to be considered a privileged Jew, the Bianer Rebbe, Avraham Yaakov Friedman, in Belshez, declined to be hidden.[30] The Bukwassker Rebbe, Rabbi Alter Reuven Schapiro in the Samboer Ghetto, did not allow the Judenrat to rescue him during a forced roundup of Jews for the death camps, since someone else would have had to replace him in order to meet the requisite quota.[31] Rabbi Alter Perlow, the Koidenever Rebbe, in the Vilna Ghetto, quoted a Talmudic dictum in his response: " 'Man is directed unto the path of his choice.'[32] I chose to accompany all the Jews, and that is why I am here."[33] The Slonimer Rebbe explained his refusal to leave Barenowich by saying: "Perhaps I erred in remaining here. But what can I do when my little children [his Hasidim] are dependent upon me?"[34]

An unusually conflicted picture emerges of the Alexander Rebbe, Rabbi Yitzchak Menahem Danziger, in the Warsaw Ghetto. Huberband depicts him as constantly discarding Hasidic garb in escape attempts.[35] A different view is provided by eyewitness Yitzchak Farber, a Hasid of the Rebbe. Evidently, the Rebbe had an opportunity to flee to Palestine at the outset of the Holocaust but declined in order to remain with his Hasidim.[36]

ASSISTANCE AND RESCUE

The physical presence of the Rebbe not only enabled him to calm, console, and psychologically support his Hasidim during the Holocaust trauma, but also afforded him the opportunity to utilize his influence and authority to assist in the improvement of the physical plight of the victims, render counsel, and aid in rescue and escape. There is little evidence to suggest that the Hasidic leaders in any way anticipated the ultimate consequences of the Holocaust.[37] When the storm did burst, however, Rebbes utilized every means available in order to blunt the destruction and diminish the losses. They advised and assisted in protection, in the first instance, and, where possible, in escapes.[38] The Belzer Rebbe, who had lost his entire family and was now in Hungary, warned the Hungarian Jews (who considered themselves relatively secure) to seek ways to leave Europe.[39] The Komarner Rebbe urged his Hasidim to escape from the Samborer Ghetto into the forests, where partisan units were active.[40] Appeals for escape and rescue were also transmitted in written messages and by means of Hasidic "torahs."[41] The Trisker Rebbe, employing the latter medium, explained the reason for the "sandwiching" of the biblical ordinance of *eglah arufah*[42] between the verses which deal with war conditions and regulations.[43] The purpose was to dramatize the significance of protecting life at the very time when life could be considered cheap and expendable.[44] Rabbi Yissachar Shlomo Teichthal noted:

> As is well known, at a time when, God forbid, we are aware of brethren in trouble, and, in a position to rescue them, we clearly are bound by the biblical injunction: "You shall not stand upon the blood of your neighbor."[45] However, in our times the suffering exceeds by far that which has befallen us in the past and the punishment for assisting rescue is terribly severe. . . . Should this prevent us from rendering assistance? God forbid, no! God tests our strength in these critical times.[46]

The Rebbes contributed direct assistance as well. The Vishiver Rebbe, Rabbi Baruch Hager, in Vishiv, Hungary, exploited the temporary safety of unoccupied Hungary to direct an operation that forged Hungarian birth certificates for Polish Jews.[47] A Gerer Hasid, Velvel Krutka, exploited connections with the Warsaw Judenrat in order to assist the sick in the ghetto.[48] The Belzer Rebbe, while in the Ghetto of Bochnia, organized an unsuccessful attempt to rescue young Gerer Hasidim who had been discovered in an underground bunker in Cracow in secret and illegal study.[49] In a bizarre episode, the Piazesner Rebbe rescued a Jew from the Gestapo after he was caught attempting to remove jewelry from the bodies of the Rebbe's daughter-in-law and sister-in-law, killed in an air attack.[50]

Numerous reports document the special efforts of the Rebbes on behalf of orphans and refugees. Eliezer Hager, son of the Vishnizer Rebbe, secretly aided Jewish orphans in Nazi-occupied Rumania.[51] The Belzer mobilized assistance efforts in Belz, which was flooded with refugees in the fall of 1940.[52] Meshulam Uri and Alter Yitzhak, the sons of the Stier-Samboer Rebbe, Rabbi Yeshaya Asher Hacohen Yoles, were caught and shot for hiding and supplying food to orphans in the bunkers of the Stier Ghetto. The father continued the work of his martyred sons.[53] The Spinker Rebbe had a bunker built under his home in Selish (Hungary) for the purpose of hiding some of the refugees streaming across the Polish border 50 miles away.[54] The Rebbe of Koznitz, Rabbi Aaron Yehiel Hofstein, risked his life in the

Warsaw Ghetto distributing food to the needy, often amidst gunfire.[55] The Komarner sold all his valuables, including precious ritual articles, in order to assist the poor in his community during the Nazi occupation. He replied to concerned relatives: "If this world remains as it is, then I shall replace them with others just as good. On the other hand, if it is destroyed, of what use will they be?"[56] The homes of the Kosonivr Rebbe in Kosonia and the Razvirter Rebbe in Razeirt, Hungary, served as rescue centers for escapees from forced labor camps.[57] Personal food packages received by the Krimilover Rebbe were redistributed to the poor in the Warsaw Ghetto.[58] The Radziner assisted the refugees in Radzin. Subsequently, he berated the Judenrat in Valodave for aiding the Nazis in their systematic annihilation of Jews, rather than serving as a resource for rescue and escape.[59] The Vorker Rebbe led a 24-hour campaign to raise 6,000 gulden in order to rescue a Jew destined to be burned on Christmas eve, 1939.[60] In rare comic relief, the Komarner Rebbe responded to a Jewish mayor, appointed by the Russians to investigate two hundred Jews jammed about a Passover-night Seder table:[61] "Reb Eliezer, isn't it evident to you that we have no refugees here!"[62]

DEVOTION OF HASIDIM TO THEIR REBBE

The relationship between Rebbe and Hasidim during the Holocaust was reciprocal. At times the zealous devotion of the Hasidim would lead to conflicts, since their attempts to protect the Rebbe would in effect isolate him, thus removing him from a position of influence and leadership. Huberband seemingly disapproved of the manner in which the Alexander Rebbe was secretly moved from place to place, discarding Hasidic garb.[63] The Rebbe was eventually smuggled into the Warsaw Ghetto, where he obtained work in the Schultz shoe factory.[64] The manager of the factory, Avraham Hendel, risked his life in an unsuccessful attempt to bribe officials to remove the Rebbe from a train destined for Treblinka.[65] The rescues of the Gerer Rebbe and the Belzer Rebbe by their Hasidim are well documented.[66] The Bobover Rebbe, Rabbi Shlomo Halberstam, and his son were rescued from certain execution as a result of a daring blackmail effort by a Bobover Hasid in the Ghetto of Bochnia.[67] Hasidim unsuccessfully sought to obtain false foreign passports for the Bianer Rebbe, Rabbi Moshe Friedman, and the Grodzisker Rebbe Rabbi Yisrael Shapira. These efforts were attempted at the risk of life.[68] The Luvitcher Rebbe was "temporarily rescued" through the efforts of Hasidim who raised the required $50,000. The Rebbe and his family were flown out of Livich, but all were killed along the escape route by the Germans.[69] The confidants of the Gerer Rebbe illegally changed his name during the critical registration period in the Warsaw Ghetto.[70] The pages of Holocaust literature are filled with accounts of beatings and murders of Jewish leaders in the first stages of the occupation, basically to create fear and demoralization among the masses. Reb Itche Gabba[71] insisted on accompanying the Zabner Rebbe to forced labor, which resulted in a severe beating for both the Rebbe and himself. "A gabbai cannot live without his Rebbe!"[72] The Belzer Hasidim risked their lives on a number of occasions in order to be close to their Rebbe during his escape from Belz to Hungary.[73] The Kosonier Hasidim refused to be separated from their Rebbe as he was placed aboard the freight car for "relocation." They accompanied him to the Auschwitz death camp.[74] A poignant incident involving the Lisker Rebbe, Rabbi Zvi Hersh Friedlander, symbolized the dedication of Hasid to Rebbe. The gabbai, who refused to be parted from the Rebbe, managed to sneak a bottle of wine aboard the transport to Auschwitz for *kiddush* and *havdalah*.[75] The Rebbe, in turn, requested that the wine be distributed among the children aboard the transport, since "we won't need any wine for *havdalah*."[76]

Extraordinary responses of dedication were recorded of Hasidim who "covered" or substituted for their Rebbe in attempts to protect him against capture, physical violence, or death. Twenty Hasidim of the Ostrowzer Rebbe offered their lives in an attempt to save the Rebbe from execution. They were summarily shot along with their Rebbe.[77] Yeshaya Rawer, a Belzer Hasid who guarded the Rebbe when the Germans entered Parmishlan in 1941, was mistaken for the Rebbe and severely beaten. He responded: "Happy is he who has the privilege to be the scapegoat for the Rebbe."[78] Subsequently, on the escape route to Hungary, a young Hasid masqueraded as the Rebbe while in Bochnia, serving as decoy during the successful escape.[79] The gabbai who impersonated the Radziner Rebbe was shot and killed.[80]

Dedication to the Horondenker Rebbe assumed the form of *hesed shel emet* (a true act of kindness).[81] At great risk, the Hasidim secretly cleansed and buried the body of the Rebbe and covered the grave with a heavy slab to mark the site.[82] Matityahu Gelman, a young Gerer Hasid and the leader of an underground Hasidic cell, endangered his life by returning to Gur to conceal a number of volumes from the valuable personal library of his Rebbe.[83]

AHAVAT YISRAEL

The Hasidic emphasis on *Ahavat Yisrael* (love of, devotion to, and empathy for fellow Jews) found its full expression during the Holocaust.

During the High Holy Day period in the fall of 1940, when news of anti-Jewish atrocities began to reach the Belzer Rebbe, he felt intense emotional pain brought on by his awareness of the plight of the Jewish people. "I can sit no longer. Every limb in my body aches."[84] His empathy with the tragedy of the Jewish people reached such proportions that he did not observe the *yahrzeit* (anniversary of the death of a close relative or a famous personage) of his son, killed the previous year in a synagogue set afire by the Nazis. He refused to demonstrate personal grief because this would have detracted from his grief for *kelal Yisrael* (the totality of the Jewish people).[85] Both the Piazesner Rebbe and Rabbi Teichthal express concern for the centrality of *Ahavat Yisrael* precisely when experiencing personal crisis, since the latter may compromise the former.

> He who demonstrates self-sacrifice for another Jew is on a higher rung than one who does so for God alone. It is comparable to one who sacrifices himself for a prince. He clearly demonstrates supreme love for the king to the extent that he would not limit personal sacrifice to the king, but would apply it to his son as well.[86]

Rabbi Teichthal invokes the example of Moses, who displayed unusual *Ahavat Yisrael* during the critical golden calf episode.[87]

> When Moses realized that Israel was in need of extraordinary *Rahamim* in order for a sin of such magnitude to be forgiven, he was overcome by a tremendous sense of *Ahavat Yisrael*. He was prepared to die for them.[88] [Moses'] readiness [for *Ahavat Yisrael*] was not directed only to the righteous, but also to those who participated in this enormous sin. All this was possible because they [the Jewish people] are the children of God. Because of his sacrificial love for God, Moses was inspired to transfer this love from God to Israel.[89]

The concept of *bittul atzmi* (the dissolution or nullifying of the self) is applied to *Ahavat Yisrael*. The true Zadik is able to achieve total *bittul atzmi*, so that "only *Ahavat Yisrael* and the soul of *kelal Yisrael* [the totality of Israel] were of any consequence to them."[90] The ordinary person, who is usually unable to achieve *bittul atzmi*, is part of *kelal Yisrael* and therefore has the potential to subdue his self-interest. The Jew can become sensitive to the welfare of Israel, "concerned with their concerns and joyous in their joy."[91]

The Piazesner Rebbe's concern for *Ahavat Yisrael* took on special significance in the Holocaust context. The intense suffering engendered by the Holocaust, and the manner in which its victims were degraded, endangered the divine component in man. This godly element provides man with the strength to move beyond himself and to sense the needs of *kelal Yisrael*.[92] One cannot fulfill the will of God unless one fulfills one's obligations in the context of the *kelal* (other-oriented vs. self-oriented) and empathizes with the spiritual and physical suffering of others.[93] The Piazesner Rebbe cites the martyrology of the Talmud to demonstrate the extent to which *Ahavat Yisrael* is to be practiced.[94] During the Roman persecutions (132–135 C.E.) the martyr Rabbi Shimon pleaded: "May I be the first to be killed so that I do not witness the death of my friend."[95] The Piazesner Rebbe adds:

> *Ahavat Yisrael* should reach such proportions that one is prepared to die first rather than witness the death of a friend, though this would in no way benefit the friend. After all, it is the nature of man to prolong his own life, if but for a few hours. Also, according to Jewish law one may desecrate the Sabbath even if one has only a few hours left to live. Furthermore, a miracle may occur during these few remaining hours [of life in order not to witness the friend's death] and his life might be spared. Yet he [Rabbi Shimon ben Gamliel] asked to be killed first. . . . *Ahavat Yisrael* of this kind derives from *Ahavat Hashem* [love of God], an abundance of love combined with *mesirat nefesh* [sacrificial devotion].[96]

Rabbi Teichthal notes the *gematriya* (numerological wordplay) employed by Rabbi Yehoshua Heschel of Apt (d. 1822), whereby *Ohev Yisrael* ("he who loves one of Israel") and *takkanah* (remedial legislation or act) have the same numerical value: 555. "Only it *[Ahavat Yisrael]* can serve as a *takkanah* for Israel, and nothing else. . . . On the other hand, the state of the Jew in the Galut [exile] is the sum product of discord among the Jews split into different parties and [involved in] senseless enmity."[97] In a plea for unity and tolerance, especially between the religious and nonreligious elements in Jewry, Rabbi Teichthal interprets a passage from the Passover Haggadah:

> "Not merely one enemy rose up to destroy us,"[98] that is to say, because of the lack of oneness among ourselves *(shelo ehad),* this alone *(bilvad)* can result in our destruction *(amad alenu lekhalotenu),* God forbid. May God indeed unite our hearts, so that all of Israel will be one.[99]

The mentality of the "Golus Yid" (Galut Jew) is characterized by an insensitivity to the needs of *kelal Yisrael* and an overconcern with the self and one's own limited circle. In sharp criticism of Hasidic groups isolated from the rest of *kelal Yisrael,* Rabbi Teichthal says:

> Let us take as an example this Hasid who cleaves to his Rebbe, and to the Hasidim who circulate in the shadow of their Rebbe. Their entire world consists of this narrow world within which he circulates. This is his *tehum Shabbat.*[100] He neither cares for nor concerns himself with the welfare of Jews spread far and wide in other parts of the world.[101]

Rabbi Teichthal challenges the isolation and divisiveness of contemporary Hasidim by citing a teaching of Rabbi Pinhas of Koretz (d. 1791): "Prior to his death [Rabbi Pinhas] said that all discord among Israel must be laid aside. There must not develop conflict over *any* type of Jew, even the lowest and very worst, since they too are Jews."[102]

During the Holocaust, *Ahavat Yisrael* was well summarized by the *Brezener Rebbe.* Bemoaning the fate of his fellow Jews, he said: "Without the people of Israel, I refuse to and cannot live."[103] Rabbi Nehemya Alter, the brother of the Gerer Rebbe, made the following statement (in the Warsaw Ghetto): "If this does not achieve salvation for the Jews, then what is its purpose?"[104]

"GEFIHRT TISCH": THE HASIDIC MEAL

The significance of "fihren tisch" (lit., "conducting a table"; The term "praven tisch" is also employed), namely, the Hasidic tradition whereby the Rebbe and his Hasidim share a portion or all of the Sabbath and festival meals, will be discussed in greater detail further on in this study. Briefly, the periodic fraternal meal provided Hasid and Rebbe with a unique opportunity for intimacy in an atmosphere of companionship (*hevruta*), song, and dance, and was a setting where the Rebbe could convey important messages to his Hasidim by means of "zogen Torah" (lit., "saying Torah"). This crucial aspect of the tisch consisted of an exposition of biblical and rabbinic thought relevant to the issues of the day, and with a bearing on man's behavior to his fellow man and to God.

Not unexpectedly, the Nazi authorities quickly moved to suppress every expression of communal religious life. Public prayer services,[105] Jewish education,[106] possessing religious articles, [107] wearing traditional Jewish garb, including beard and long side-curls (*pe'ot*),[108] the performance of Jewish ritual, including circumcision (*milah*),[109] ritual slaughter (*shehitah*),[110] ritual immersion (*mikveh*),[111] and the general marking of the Jewish calendar, were all strictly prohibited and often punishable by death. Despite these severe restrictions, Hasidic leaders would attempt to continue with *praven tisch* wherever possible, sometimes under very limited and dangerous circumstances. The Piazesner Rebbe probably gathered his material for the *Esh Kodesh* manuscript from the weekly Sabbath and festival "Torahs" at the *tisch* in the Warsaw Ghetto.[112] The Zabner, Zichliner, Belzer, Karliner, and Dzikover Rebbes illegally conducted fraternal meals in the ghettos of Turna, Zichliv, Bochnia, Sambor, Karlin, and Cracow, respectively.[113] The Belzer *hot gepraved tisch* on Friday night, on a train from occupied Greece to Turkey, during his escape from Holocaust Europe.[114] The brother-in-law of the Radomsker Rebbe, the Rabbi of Zvirtzah, continued to *fihr tisch* in Auschwitz proper.[115] The Rabbi of Bilgure, the brother of the Belzer, conducted a Hasidic meal while in transit in Parmishlan. During the *lehayim* ceremony[116] a young Hasid asked the Rebbe to bestow a blessing on his children, specifically, that they would grow up to be Hasidim and men of good deeds. "All of the participants [in the meal] were amazed that it was possible for this Hasid to be concerned for his children's education during these critical times."[117] The Melitzer Rebbe, Rabbi Elimelech Horowitz, conducted a *tisch* with his Hasidim in an open grave prior to his death.

> When Rabbi Elimelech realized that his end was near, he requested a piece of bread for his final meal. He reclined and ate with his Hasidim in front of the open grave. Following the blessing over the piece of bread, he said "*Torah*" and entered into a state of great *hitalahvut* [ecstasy]. He began to sing a new melody with his Hasidim, *Nishmat Kol Hai* ["The breath of every living creature shall praise Thy name"],[118] and together they danced their final dance. He then approached the German in command and said: "We have done ours, now you may do yours."[119]

A similar episode is related of the Bobover Rebbe. On what was to have been the last Friday evening before their execution, the Rebbe and his son simulated *praven tisch* over a piece of dry bread in a Gestapo jail.[120]

THE KVITTEL

As noted below, the *kvittel* (lit., note) was an accepted tradition among most Hasidim. Written petitions to the Rebbe might concern a great variety of personal or family matters. The Rebbe's role was to assist in elevating the prayer or petition heavenwards.

With the onset of the Holocaust, the Rebbe of Ostrowze, Rabbi Yehezke'el Halstik, went to the graveside of his father, Rabbi Meir Yehiel, and inserted a kvittel into his crypt with the following petition: "Father! Why do you permit the destruction of the holy community of Ostrowze and all the Jews of Poland? Appear before the Almighty and plead for *Rahamim* [compassion] for all Jews, because the danger is great!"[121] The continued acceptance of kvittlech by the Belzer Rebbe in the Ghetto of Bochnia provided comfort and hope to the Hasidim.[122] Reb Berish Ortner, a Hasid of the Belzer who resided in Palestine, presented a kvittel to the Gerer Rebbe (who had previously escaped the Holocaust), on behalf of the Belzer, in which he petitioned for assistance from the Almighty for a safe rescue from Europe.[123] A group of hostages in the Chenstochover Ghetto included a Rebbe who was given kvittlech by some of his fellow hostages.

> He consoled them and asked them to have *bitahon* [trust] in the Master of the Universe, who will and must help them. The religious Jews were encouraged and strengthened by these words of consolation. There was no question but that they [accepted the situation] with greater composure than did the nonbelieving [hostages].[124]

Huberband cites two important letters from the Jewish community in Salomnik, near Cracow, Poland, written to their Rebbe in the spring of 1942 to request his assistance and prayers following one of a series of Nazi "actions." These letters in essence represent a more expanded form of the kvittel. Names of Jews in special need are noted. Significant, however, is the plea for all of Israel: "May *kelal Yisrael* be saved and may it be the end of *Hevle Mashiah* [the pangs preceding the coming of the Messiah], so that our righteous redeemer may come speedily in our own day. Amen."[125]

THE NIGUN

In Hasidism music is both a by-product of joy and a means of enhancing it. Paradoxically, it continued to serve these purposes in several Holocaust responses. As was noted above in chapter 8, Hasidic melodies played a role in a number of *Kiddush Hashem* episodes. The Bobover Rebbe and his son spent a Friday night in a Gestapo jail singing Bobover Hasidic melodies at a symbolic tisch, in the belief that they would be executed the following morning.[126] The Talmatcher Rebbe, Rabbi Yitzchak Hager, on a forced march to the local railroad station, responded to an order to sing with a Hasidic melody the *Shir Hashirim* (Song of Songs).[127] The Belzer Hasidim danced and sang with unusual *hitlahavut* (ardor, ecstasy) on Simhat Torah eve[128] "while outside [the synagogue] fear and confusion reigned."[129] The Slonimer Rebbe quietly hummed Hasidic melodies when he sensed the onset of a state of depression due to the loss of his family in the Holocaust.[130] The Stoliner Rebbe was shot while attempting to protect a pregnant woman in the Warsaw Ghetto. As he lay critically wounded he requested that the *viddui* (final confession) be accompanied by a Stoliner Hasidic melody.[131] A number of eyewitness reports relate the episode of Shlomo Zelichovsky, a Hasid of the Gerer Rebbe, who sang Hasidic melodies on the way to the gallows.[132] Moshe Aaron Wohl, a Hasid fighting in the underground "White Brigade" in Belgium, was caught and tortured. In order to divert his attention from the pain so that he would not give in and reveal secret information, he sang Hasidic *nigunim* (melodies).[133]

The dance, a mode of expressing joy that is central to Hasidic tradition, was the theme of the response of a leading Brazlaver Hasid trapped in the deteriorating ghetto in Lodz. In a letter to his brother Moshe,[134] Simha Bornstein writes:

> While studying the *Zohar* I fell asleep and saw the godly tanna[135] seated and surrounded by great personages, including our Rabbi Nahman [of Brazlav]. I began to cry aloud, "Rebbe! We have been forgotten! Jews are in a state of great plight." I felt the Rebbe taking hold of me, as a master might a novice. He began to dance, and all joined in the dance. Lo and behold, it was a dream! I then opened the Rebbe's book[136] and indeed I discovered that he believes that dancing softens *Din* [retribution]. May God help us.[137]

Eyewitness reports by Leibel Yutzankah and Moshe Brachfeld describe how seventeen young Hasidim from the underground cell in Plashow near Cracow sang and danced in front of the pit which was to become their common grave.[138]

CHAPTER 11

Hasidic Concepts Related to Zadik and Hasid

THE DESCENT OF THE ZADIK

A number of responses in this chapter (encouragement, *Ahavat Yisrael,* the fraternal meal, the kvittel) are variants of a basic Hasidic doctrine: the special relationship of the Zadik to his community. Dresner's study, based on the teachings of Rabbi Yaakov Yosef of Polnoya, deals with the qualities and responsibilities of the leader of a Hasidic community.[1] Of particular interest is the idea of the descent of the Zadik,[2] whereby the leader goes out to meet his people, keeps their welfare constantly in mind, and is willing to suffer for them and with them, in order to join them with God.[3] The Zadik's descent "is the primary expression of his concern for the people."[4] Rabbi Elimelekh of Lizensk defines the descent as the Zadik's temporary disruption of his *devekut* with God, "since it is impossible to exert influence [on behalf of Israel's needs] unless he interrupts and descends somewhat from his *devekut*. . . . In order to accomplish this he must strengthen himself."[5] Rabbi Nahum of Chernibol (d. 1798) compares the descent to "a man who stands on the roof while a precious stone lies on the ground below." It lies out of reach unless he descends to the place where it is situated, takes it, and ascends with it. Thus, the Zadik must at times fall in order to raise the fallen souls.[6] He does not fulfill his role while absorbed in isolated *devekut* from which he alone might benefit. He holds the key for *etaruta delatata* (the impulse from below),[7] the prerequisite for stimulating corresponding impulses from on high. "Thus, the Zadik who wishes to extend divine influence into this world must descend from his rung into the very depths, as it is written:[8] 'Out of the depths I cry unto thee,' "[9] The doctrine of the Zadik's concern for others is the focus of this chapter.

ENCOURAGEMENT

The responses revealed two aspects of encouragement: (1) caution against *ye'ush* (despair), and (2) a plea for *hithazkut* (fortitude and inner strength). Both concepts flow from the doctrine of the Rebbe's concern for his Hasidim.

The attempt to redeem the Jewish masses from *ye'ush* during a period of spiritual disintegration was considered the major achievement of the Ba'al Shem Tov and his school.[10] Hasidism was concerned about *ye'ush* because in effect it questions and challenges God's *Rahamim* (compassion),[11] undermining man's *bitahon* (trust in God) and *emunah* (faith in God).[12] The antidote to *ye'ush* is *hithazkut* in God. "Man is prohibited from despairing, God forbid. Though he may have fallen into the very depths of the abyss, God forbid, nevertheless he should never consider despairing in God. Even there [in the depths], he can come close to God."[13] The Zadik's responsibility is to help strengthen those who have fallen by making them aware that God has not abandoned them. "One is not a true Zadik unless he has the ability to inspire and raise those who have fallen very low. He must strengthen them, and inspire them with an awareness that God is still with them and very near them."[14] Identical with the documented Holocaust responses, the Zadik fulfilled the responsibility of raising the morale of his community by highlighting the Jew's uniqueness and singular stature. The *ben-melekh* (prince) parable of the Piazesner[15] echoes Rabbi Shlomo of Karlin (d. 1792): "The greatest sinner among Jews is he who forgets that he is the son of a King."[16] *Hithazkut* and hope are possible as long as a spark of Jewish consciousness remains. Rabbi Yisrael of Rizin noted: "As long as a Jew has any grasp on Judaism, despair is not possible for him. This may be compared to a pail which has fallen into the depths of a well. Because it is tied to a rope, one can pull it out of the depths."[17] When one comprehends the unique interrelationship between the Jew and God even at the heights of a crisis, one is able to withdraw from a state of *ye'ush*. Said the Komarner:

> Every Jew, according to his level, goes through periods of ascent *(aliyah)* and descent *(yeridah)*. . . . He is cautioned not to enter into a state of despair and has faith and understanding that even in a state of eclipse[18] and darkness, Divine Glory is evident . . . then *he* is saved and he emerges from darkness into light. This is the meaning of the biblical imperative: "I the Lord am your God who brought you out of the land

of Egypt."[19] Note, from the source of impurity [He removed you], there also was the Lord your God.[20]

THE ZADIK'S COMMUNAL INVOLVEMENTS AND RECIPROCAL RELATIONSHIP WITH HIS HASIDIM

The refusal of the Rebbe to abandon his flock is consistent with the expected role of the Zadikim, "who could not be isolated as recluses absorbed in contemplation."[21] The Zadik was intimately involved in the personal, physical, and spiritual affairs of the members of his community in order "to join with them at the very core of their souls."[22]

> He is willing to suffer for them [the people], since they are the "limbs of the Shekhinah"; his life is bound up with theirs, for they are the body of which he is the soul and the matter of which he is the form; a portion of his own self without which he is only half. He strives to save people, for in each of them, no matter how dark the pit into which they have fallen, are sparks of holiness that wait to be redeemed.[23]

The Zadik must be prepared to share in the fate of those whom he wishes to elevate.[24] Rabbi Levi Yitzchak compares the descent to one who wishes to raise his friend from the quagmire and mud. "He must descend close to the mud in order to raise him."[25] Moses is considered the paragon of Zadikim. He gave up his princely comforts in order to join the masses, extending "his hand to Israel so that they would grasp it and be elevated."[26]

The true Zadik cannot fulfill his task when involved solely with his own personal affairs and his own relationship to the divine. In his prayers he must be concerned for *kelal Yisrael* (the totality of Israel), "since [as a result] he brings together all of Israel, which in turn unites the elements in the upper spheres."[27]

The term *Zadik in pelz* (Yiddish, lit. "a Zadik wrapped in furs") was applied by the Kotzker Rebbe to one "who is concerned for his own welfare, supplying heat generated by the fear of heaven, but for himself alone. He may be compared to the miser who refrains from heating the stove in a room which would have provided heat for all. Instead he prefers to be wrapped in furs to warm his own flesh exclusively."[28] Neither can the Zadik achieve his task or "reach any rung [in the hierarchy of holiness] if his soul is not humble, more so than all others in Israel, [and if he does not] attach himself to the people of Israel with love and humility."[29] Moreover, "he shall not isolate himself from the masses, functioning as an individual only, otherwise he cannot serve in the mainstream of *kelal Yisrael*."[30]

The descent of the Zadik was not limited to concern or expressions of solidarity. He was also expected to offer practical assistance and inspire others to emulation. In the tradition of the Ba'al Shem Tov:

> one is required to observe the commandment "Love your neighbor as yourself"[31] with *mesirat nefesh* [great sacrifice and dedication]. The forces of *mesirat nefesh* must be marshaled in order to assist a Jew materially, and most certainly spiritually. At times, a soul descends to this earth and assumes the garb of flesh for seventy or eighty years only for the sake of assisting a Jew.[32]

According to the Brazlaver, the Zadik's assisting of his fellow Jews must reach the point where "he assumes the suffering of Israel . . . [because the true Zadik has great compassion for Israel."[33] Like Rabbi Levi Yitzchak of Berdichev, Rabbi Shlomo of Karlin taught that assistance denotes not merely partial involvement, but radical commitment. "In order to assist a Jew one must be prepared to tread in the mud up to one's neck."[34] Assisting another human being is given such a high priority that Hasidism waived the imperatives of *bitahon* (trust in God) and *emunah* (faith in God), and at times even negated these concepts when in conflict with the immediate welfare of a person. The Yehudi of Pshyscha taught:

> Wherein lies the good spark even in *apikorsut* [denial of divinity and God]? If a poor man approaches you for alms, do not at that moment believe in the Master of the Universe, suggesting: "As He sustains all life, so He will surely in His compassion sustain this poor one. Therefore, I have no obligation to be concerned and involved in his moment of need." But rather this should be your response: "If not I, who else will feed and support him? He will surely die of hunger, God forbid, and even God will not have mercy upon him!"[35]

When we seek concepts that define the reciprocal relationship of the Hasid to the Zadik the pertinent sources appear sparse when compared to those that delineate the Zadik's responsibilities to the Hasid. This difference in emphasis may relate to a number of factors. First, the classic Hasidic literature was written by Zadikim, or by disciples setting down the oral tradition of the Zadikim. A genuine sense of humility characteristic of the Zadik inhibited the formulation of guidelines for the Hasid vis-à-vis the Zadik.[36] Furthermore, the Zadik-Hasid interrelationship was predefined, since a disciple was expected to respond to the master with fervor, fear, love, and dedication. If the Zadik is indeed a Zadik, the result is a Hasid who is indeed a Hasid.[37]

A crisis occurred in the history of Hasidism during the years when the proliferation of Rebbes was unchecked, and "everyone who wanted the name [Rebbe] simply took it."[38] In response, the early literature attempted to define the personality and role of the Zadik, especially in the writings of Rabbis Yaakov Yosef of Polnoya, Shlomo of Luzk, Elimelech of Lizensk, and Nahman of Brazlav. A genuine Zadik may arouse Hasidic fervor to such a degree that a cooling action by the Zadik is necessitated. It was said of Rabbi Simha Bunam of Parsischa: "He would strengthen and assist all who came to him. But basically he wanted everyone to be raised under his own power."[39] Buber summarizes the "helper" role of the Zadik:

> A helper is needed, a helper for both body and soul, for both earthly and heavenly matters. . . . And over and over he takes you by the hand and guides you until you are able to venture on alone. He does not relieve you of doing what you have grown strong enough to do for yourself.[40]

The most authentic of Beshtian traditions depict the zealous dedication of the disciples of the Ba'al Shem Tov, many of whom were originally among his opponents.[41] Rabbi Shlomo of Karlin (d. 1792) describes the Hasid's dedication: "In the upper spheres they measure the fields and forests over which the Hasid travels to his Rebbe."[42] Rabbi Nahman of Brazlav recognizes the efficacy of actually visiting the Rebbe (as opposed to reading an inspiring book) as the opportunity "to purify one's appearance by reflecting his [the Zadik's] face in one's own, as in a mirror."[43] Rabbi Nahman went so far as to say, in his account of the Hasid's relationship to the Zadik, that the Hasid was expected to "pray in order that he may attach himself to the Zadikim of his generation."[44] He was encouraged to confide in and confess to the Zadik, "since when one confesses before the *talmid hakham* [scholar],[45] he [the Zadik] is able to guide him in the proper path in accordance with the source of his own soul."[46] The Komarner reinforces the significance of "clinging to the Zadik of one's own generation. . . . There is nothing superior. . . . One spirit attracts [i.e., raises, inspires] the other."[47]

AHAVAT YISRAEL

The concept of *Ahavat Yisrael* underlies the unique interaction between Zadik and Hasid, in which the latter was provided with moral support that restored his sense of dignity during a period of radical stress.[48] Alfasi has documented the centrality of the *Ahavat Yisrael* motif in the thought and action pattern of Hasidism, especially as articulated by Rabbis Levi Yitzchak of Berdichev, renowned as the "advocate" of the simple Jew before the heavenly tribunal, Zusya of Anipol, and Avraham Yehoshua Heschel of Apt, known as the Ohev Yisrael (Lover of Israel).[49] The selection of *Ahavat Yisrael* motifs in the Hasidic literature for this research was made on the basis of their evident relationship to *Ahavat Yisrael* Holocaust responses. They fall into three categories grouped as follows:

1. *Ahavat Yisrael* as a function of *Ahavat Hashem* (love of God).
2. *Ahavat Yisrael* interrelated with *ahdut ha'am* (national unity) and tolerance for differences among the people.
3. *Ahavat Yisrael* as sensitivity and empathy for the mass of Jews, often subjugating individual to group preferences.

According to early Hasidic tradition, *Ahavat Yisrael* was one of three major objectives of the Ba'al Shem Tov's mission.[50] In response to those who questioned his opposition to the mortification of the body as a means of religious discipline,[51] the Ba'al Shem Tov replied: "I came into this world in order to show another way [to worship God]. It is best for man to adopt the following three principles: *Ahavat Hashem* [love of God], *Ahavat Yisrael* [love of Israel], and *Ahavat Hatorah* [love of Torah]. Therefore, there is no need for self-mortification."[52] The mutually binding interrelationship between the divine and man, evident throughout this study, and noted in the *Ahavat Yisrael* theme by the Piazesner Rebbe, emerges as well in the Beshtian tradition. "He who passes judgment on Israel passes judgment, in essence, on the Holy One, blessed be He, because Israel is part of the total unity of God."[53] This principle is reinforced by Rabbi Yaakov Yosef of Polnoya: "Everyone in Israel is part of the Shekhinah."[54]

Rabbi Nahman of Brazlav notes: "Everyone must make a concerted effort to find merit in every Jew, since every Jew is a diamond in the crown of the Holy One, blessed be He, and one should praise the crown of God."[55] Rabbi Isaac of Komarno articulated the interrelationship of *Ahavat Yisrael* and *Ahavat Hashem* by means of *gematriya*. "Love your neighbor as yourself; I am the Lord"[56] and "You shall love the Lord your God"[57] both have the same numerical values: 907.[58]

Ahavat Yisrael was also related to the ideal of *ahdut* (unity) and the need to be sensitive to different elements within *kelal Yisrael* (the totality of Israel). The Ba'al Shem Tov suggested the following wordplay on *tz(i)bur* (community, congregation): tz*(adik)* [the righteous], be*noni* [the average, common person] ve[59] r*(asha)* [and the wicked person] are all an integral and essential part of community *(tzibur)*. "A *tzibur* without the *rasha* [wicked][60] results in the spelling *tzav* [a species of the lizard family], namely, an animal that is impure [for eating purposes]."[61] *Galut* (exile) and tribulations are a likely result of the negation of *ahdut* (unity) among Israel.[62] Echoing *Em Habanim Semehah*, Yaakov Yosef of Polnoya relates the lack of *Ahavat Yisrael* to the vulnerability of the Jew.[63] Interpreting the verse "You stand this day, all of you,"[64] Rabbi Yaakov Yosef notes: "You will *stand* [upright, firm] when you are all [one, united]."[65] The interrelationship of *Ahavat Yisrael* and *ahdut* with divinity is brilliantly articulated by Rabbi Naftali of Ropshitz (d. 1827) in his exegesis of the verse "Love your neighbor as yourself, I am the Lord."[66]

> The letter *yud*[67] [in the spelling of God's name], if it is equally aligned with its neighboring letter, this is indeed the Name of God.[68] But if it [the *yud*] stands on top of its neighbor,[69] it [the word representing God] is false. This is the meaning of "Love your neighbor as yourself," namely, align your friend alongside of you, then "I am the Lord"—the merging of you both becomes My Name.[70]

For Rabbi Yitzchak Isaac of Komarno, *Ahavat Yisrael* and *ahdut* asume significance when the cumulative effect of merging oneself with the good in another person builds a totality of good, which in turn unites man with the ultimate Good and the ultimate Unity.[71]

The Belzer's empathy with the pain of *kelal Yisrael* is reflected in Rabbi Israel of Rizin's teaching:

> When, God forbid, Israel is in trouble, then I am sick and saddened. When compassion [toward Israel] is displayed, I am well and happy,

> because a Zadik can feel in his body all the vacillations in this world—from *Din* [stern judgment] to *Rahamim* [compassion], and, God forbid, from *Rahamim* to *Din*.[72]

Rabbi Abraham Yehoshua Heschel of Apt wished at times that he did not possess such extreme sensitivity for *kelal Yisrael*. The cumulative sympathetic pain was too much for one person to bear.[73] On the other hand, to exist outside and beyond the concerns of Israel is absurd and meaningless. The "world iteslf is meaningless without Israel."[74] To share the fate of Israel and to contribute to *Ahavat Yisrael* is to enhance total existence. The specific is a prelude to the universal. Said the Kotzker: "By means of true *Ahavat Yisrael* one can achieve *Ahavat Ha'olam* [love for mankind, the universe]."[75]

THE FRATERNAL MEAL AND THE ZADIK'S "TORAH"

The fraternal meal has a special place in many religious movements. Josephus describes the rituals of the fraternal meal of the Essenes, a Jewish sect in Palestine during the Second Commonwealth.[76] Talmudic tradition identifies the table as more than a mere platform upon which food and drink is to be consumed.[77] Hasidism merged the centrality of the Zadik with the sanctity of the table, "elevating the fraternal meal in which the Zadik participated to new and unimagined heights."[78] Hasidim would periodically leave their families and travel great distances in order to share the Sabbath and festival meals with their Rebbe.[79] Praven tisch could extend many hours beyond normally designated mealtimes. Secondary to the actual consumption of food was the interspersion of the Rebbe's "Torot," Hasidic melodies, reciprocal exchanges of *leha'im*,[80] and Hasidic dances.[81] At many Hasidic "tables" *(tischen)* the custom of *shirayim* (remnants) was prevalent.[82] Hasidim would zealously attempt to partake of the remnants of food left for them by the Rebbe. Various mystical traditions have sanctified and blessed these *shirayim* as "beneficial to those who consume them."[83] Among all of the fraternal meals, the *se'udah shelishit* (the third [Sabbath] meal),[84] the *melaveh Malkah* (the farewell [meal] for the Sabbath Queen),[85] and the *hilule* festivities commemorating the *Yahrzeit* (memorial anniversary) of a noted personage[86] were the most prominent.

THE KVITTEL

The Hasid would turn to the Zadik for advice concerning every aspect of personal life, especially in the areas of health, economy, and matrimony, or any crisis of the moment.[87] Rabbi Nahman of Brazlav encouraged Hasidim to seek advice from the Zadik as a means to attain truth: "It is impossible to attain truth except by drawing near to the Zadik and following their advice. By following their advice, the truth shall be engraved [into one's consciousness]".[88] Visits to the Zadik were usually accompanied by a monetary contribution, the *pidyon nefesh* (lit., "redemption of the soul"). The Hasid indeed believed that by means of such visits he could redeem his own life and that of his loved ones. The *pidyon* was therefore not a gift, but a form of ransom payment.[89] The unique Hasidic invention was the kvittel (lit., "note"), employed by the Hasid to forward a request directly, or by means of a messenger, to the Rebbe. The Rebbe, in turn, would either respond orally during a personal interview or transmit his reply in writing.[90] The origin of the kvittel is nebulous. Wertheim attempts to trace it to Kabbalah and specifically to Nahmanides (Rabbi Moses ben Nahman, 1194–1270).[91] The Ba'al Shem Tov was evidently aware of the tradition and personally utilized the kvittel.[92] Following the death of the Rebbe, the kvittel could still be employed by placing it upon his grave.[93]

THE NIGGUN

Gershuri's study of the central position of music in Hasidism documents the manner in which the Hasidic melody "was transformed into a vital means for the contemplation of the divine *(hitbonenut Elohit)*, the stripping of the material *(hipashtut hagashmiyut)*, and its most significant objective—to remove depression and dejection from the Jewish home, and teach the worship of the Creator with joy and gladness."[94] When the Temple in Jerusalem was destroyed, in the year 70 C.E., the highly developed system of religious music that had accompanied the Temple service came to an end. In the centuries that followed, Rabbinic Judasim sought to mute efforts to reconstruct Jewish music in the diaspora.[95]

The Hasidic revival of Jewish music, especially at the Sabbath and festival table and in the house of prayer, represented more than an antidote to depression. Hasidic melody served as a path to God, since the source of musical creativity "is drawn from holiness."[96] Hasidic melodies were also drawn from shepherd's tunes, regional folk melodies, and songs heard in the inns, since this was a form of *ha'alat hanitzotzot* (the rasing of the holy sparks) hidden in the *kelipot* (shells) of the melodies awaiting *tikkun* (restoration).[97] Hasidic muscial tradition originated in melodies said to have been composed by the Ba'al Shem Tov and by Rabbis Dov Ber, Shneur Zalman of Liadi, Levi Yitzchak of Berdichev, and Nahman of Brazlav, among the fathers of Hasidism. Characteristic of the manner in which Hasidism sought to address itself to the needs of the simple and ignorant, Hasidic music involved all of the participants in the prayer and festivity experiences. Song and dance provided each individual with an opportunity to discover and simultaneously dissolve his individual ego *(bittul atzmi)* in the process of uniting with the divine in musical *devekut*.[98]

> Know that every area of knowledge has its particular melody, each according to its own level and degree. . . . Faith as well has its own song, particularly that melody corresponding to the ultimate faith, higher than all wisdom and faith in this world, namely, the faith in the *En Sof* [Infinite Being]. This [melody] is higher than all the melodies and songs in this world. All other melodies . . . derive from this superior melody. . . . It is natural that the soul which is tuned in to this melody and follows its movements will become dissolved within it [the melody] and practically vanish.[99]

Rabbi Naftali of Ropshitz synthesized the negative and positive elements in the search for the path to true melody and to heaven: "By way of the *niggun* one can indeed open all the gates of heaven. Sadness shuts them. All melodies have their source in holiness. Impurity cannot create melodies, since it is the source of sadness."[100]

CHAPTER 12

Resistance

The area of resistance, both physical and passive, by Hasidic leaders and Hasidim encompasses a wide range of Holocaust responses. Before we proceed, an observation is in order regarding the use of the terms "physical" resistance and "passive" or "spiritual" resistance. As Jacob Robinson has noted, in the Holocaust context passive resistance cannot be distinguished from active or physical resistance.[1] In contrast to the "noncooperation" policy of the Indian bureaucrats and Gandhi's nonviolent resistance in pre-1947 India, which were recognized as passive resistance by the British colonial government against which the passive struggle was directed, the German regime during the Holocaust made virtually no distinction between the smuggling of food and the smuggling of arms, between failure to report to work on Yom Kippur and striking an SS officer, between illegally studying Torah and planning to sabotage a munitions train. The manner in which the Germans defined these crimes and responded to them blurred any distinctions between the various forms of resistance, differing perhaps in degree but not in essence.[2]

Why, then discriminate between "physical" and "passive" resistance? The distinction between the two is made because the research attempts to correlate responses with select aspects of Hasidic doctrine, and this study notes the manner in which Hasidic thought offers a spiritual interpretation of the subject of war and violence (evidently alien to Hasidism).

PHYSICAL RESISTANCE

Among the few responses of physical resistance were instances of cooperation with partisan resistance units operating in neighboring forests. The Brezener Rebbe urged collaboration with partisan units in the Dombrowitz Ghetto.[3] The Slonimer's basement served as a storage area for arms for partisan groups operating in the vicinity of the Baranowich Ghetto.[4] The Radziner was one of the most militant Hasidic leaders, calling upon Jews in Vlodove to join the partisans in armed resistance. Subsequently he urged a full-scale revolt, including the burning of the ghetto. He was publicly hung for his illegal activities.[5] Rabbis Zemelman and Zemba, both close to the Hasidic movement, were among the minority of Jewish leaders in the Warsaw Ghetto who called for armed resistance.[6] The son of the Radoshitzer Rebbe led a partisan unit in the Lazisker forests.[7] The Rovner Rebbe joined a partisan group.[8] Moshe Aaron Wohl, a Hasid, fought in the "White Brigade" resistance units in occupied Belgium.[9] Yehiel Ashkenazi Badi, grandson of the Sereter Rebbe, served as a captain in the French underground resistance movement.[10]

Individual as well as group patterns of physical resistance were noted. The Stoliner Rebbe personally emerged from his hiding place to attack a Ukrainian guard in the process of killing a pregnant Jewish woman.[11] Rabbi Yitzchak Mordechai Rabinowitz, the grandson of the founder of the Radomsker Hasidic dynasty, was shot to death in Plavneh for rescuing a Jewish woman who was being harassed by a German soldier.[12] The Slominer was frequently beaten for physically intervening when another Jew was attacked.[13] The Chenchiner was shot for refusing to be touched by a German soldier.[14] Leib Schzeransky, in Hasidic garb, was a member of Mordecai Anilewitz's inner headquarters command during the Warsaw Ghetto revolt.[15] Remnants of Rabbi Avraham Weinberg's illegal study group also fought in the uprising.[16] The Hasid Simha Holzberg fought with the militant Revisionist group in the Warsaw Ghetto revolt.[17] Yisrael Holzkenner, a Gerer Hasid, served as leader of a Revisionist armed resistance group in the Warsaw Ghetto.[18]

Rare and atypical are the responses that call for *nekamah* (revenge).[19] The Matislaker Rebbe called for revenge while undergoing the ordeal of being transported to Auschwitz.[20] The Konstantinover Rebbe was quoted as saying: "If any Jew, in any generation, ever forgets what Hitler has done to the Jewish people and does not thirst for revenge, may his name be wiped off the face of the earth."[21]

PASSIVE RESISTANCE

In contrast to the meager evidence of resistance by physical or violent means, the research noted a very significant pattern of responses related to passive resistance. Passive or spiritual resistance in this research refers to noncompliance with the various regulations and prohibitions aimed at destroying the religious and spiritual life of the Jew, including edicts forbidding specific Hasidic practices.[22] It is not possible to determine clearly whether such noncompliance was motivated by conscious efforts to frustrate Nazi plans, as the term "resistance" would normally suggest.[23] Incidents of spiritual resistance by Hasidim may primarily have been efforts to preserve their basic way of life.

The refusal to remove Hasidic garb, beard, and *pe'ot* (side-curls), despite stringent prohibitions, constituted a form of passive resistance.[24] The Grodzisker, Zabner, Zichliner, Tomashover, and Strikover Rebbes and Reb Feivel Zusman, a prominent Lubavicher Hasid, refused to cut off their beards.[25] The Chentchiner Rebbe resisted a German officer who was about to shear his beard, and was shot to death.[26] Huberband described groups of young Gerer Hasidim in the Warsaw Ghetto who continued to wear the traditional Hasidic dress.[27] Eliezer Unger and Moshe Prager provide supporting evidence for the Warsaw Ghetto underground group of young Gerer Hasidim who refused to change into conventional garb.[28] Yad Vashem documentation cites an illegal Hasidic group in the Ghetto of Cracow who wore kerchiefs covering their faces in order to hide beard and *pe'ot*.[29] Yosef Friedenson, who had personal contact with the underground cells of young Gerer Hasidim and their legendary leader Mattityahu Gelman in the Ghetto of Shidlowitz, noted that Hasidic dress was even worn by those who were assigned to the dangerous task of maintaining liaison between the various ghetto cells.[30] Young Hasidim in the Lodzer Ghetto went underground and continued to wear Hasidic dress.[31] In addition, Hasidic dress was the norm for illegal cells operating in Michov, Pinz'ev, Williz'kah, Wloshozwah, Stofnitz, Diyaloshitz, Slomnik, Zavirzah, and Bochnia.[32] The elder Bobover Rebbe, Rabbi Ben Zion Halberstam, confronted a Ukrainian and German contingent dressed in Hasidic Sabbath garb, including the *shtreimel*,[33] prior to being murdered.[34] Belzer Hasidim continued to wear *shtreimlech* in the Ghetto of Bochnia.[35] Rabbi Eliezer Horowitz, the Grodsisk-Tarna Rebbe, continued in Hasidic dress despite the local edicts.[36] The Zabner Rebbe proceeded to march to the train station with both hands covering his head in defiance of the Germans who had forcibly removed his hat during a beating.[37] The Piltzer

Rebbe, Rabbi Hanoch Gad Yustman, in the Chenstochover Ghetto, refused to remove his *tallit katan*[38] despite a beating.[39]

Documentation is available on the continued use of the mikveh (ritual bath), vital in Hasidic tradition, despite stringent prohibitions.[40] The Tomashover Rebbe illegally continued to utilize the mikveh in occupied Lodz during the winter of 1939–40.[41] When the brother of the Gerer Rebbe pleaded for a glass of water prior to his death, he may have been following the contingency guidelines of the great kabbalist Rabbi Isaac Luria (1534–1572) in the event that a mikveh was not available for the purification ritual.[42] Young Gerer Hasidim, operating as an illegal underground group in the Ghetto of Cracow, improvised a miniature mikveh with a cleaning pail.[43] Eyewitness Mendel Brachtfeld describes how a group of young Hasidim, captured in an underground cell in Cracow, used the pipes in the jail's plumbing system as a mikveh.[44] The Ostrowzer Rebbe entered the mikveh prior to his execution.[45] The martyred shamash of the Radziner Rebbe used the mikveh prior to his death, after posing as the Rebbe in Waldowa.[46] Huberband provides a detailed account of an unnamed Rebbe who risked death in the Warsaw Ghetto in order to observe the laws of mikveh on the day prior to Yom Kippur, the holiest day on the Jewish calendar.[47]

A form of passive resistance was the manner in which Hasidim countered German strategy measures to deprive them of their leaders. Unger cites two instances of the sons of a Rebbe being "crowned" (appointed as successors) amidst Holocaust events following the deaths of their fathers.[48]

Prayer and Jewish rituals related to prayer were often prohibited. Nonetheless, the Horodenker Rebbe continued to use the tefillin (phylacteries) during impromptu prayer services conducted on the death march from Chernowitz to Yampola.[49] The Novominsker Rebbe prayed daily with tefillin in Block 22 of the Birkenau concentration camp.[50] Dr. Levinbach relates how the Slonimer Rebbe ignored danger and prayed daily with tallit (prayer shawl) and tefillin in the Ghetto of Baranowich.[51] Eyewitness Avraham Handel reports on the many illegal prayer services in the Warsaw Ghetto. In particular he singles out the groups meeting secretly in the houses at 3 and 5 Malavska Street, in the apartments of Rabbi Avraham Haim Danziger (the brother of the Alexander Rebbe), David Gelbart (a Hasid of the Sochochover Rebbe), and Yankel Bash (a Hasid of the Mezeretcher Rebbe).[52] The Kosonier Rebbe endured a beating by SS personnel for attempting to retain his watch so that he could determine the proper times for prayer services to take place.[53] In a rare description of the activities of Hasidic women, Joseph Fuchsman cites the illegal organization of women's prayer and study sessions in the Vilna Ghetto by Perele Perlow, the wife of the Koidenever Rebbe.[54] The Zarwicher Rebbe illegally organized High Holy Day services in the Birkenau camp.[55] A prominent Sochochover Hasid, Rabbi Eliyahu Laskowsky, conducted daily services in the Dvart Ghetto under the threat of death.[56] The day following the public hanging of Shlomo Zelichovsky, a secret prayer service was held in the Zadunska-Vellya Ghetto.[57] The Hasid Mendel Yokowitz utilized tefillin at an impromptu prayer service held during a marathon three-day "roll call" at the cemetery of the ghetto.[58] Eyewitness Yisrael Tabaksblatt reports on the Hasidic environment created in one of the Auschwitz barracks by means of prayer, snatches of study, even song and dance.[59] Avraham Weissbrod documents how young Hasidim conducted secret prayer services in the Skalat camp.[60]

Efforts to maintain the Jewish festival and Sabbath routines are noted. Rabbi Yehoshua Hager, the son of the Vishnitzer Rebbe, sold his furs in order to buy wheat for matzah (unleavened bread) in the Verchovke Ghetto, for the Passover festival.[61] The Strikover-Kinnover Rebbe restricted his diet to ground sugar during the 1943 Passover holiday in the Warsaw Ghetto rather than partake of leavened food.[62] The Piazesner Rebbe set up a special religious court in the Warsaw Ghetto, in April 1943 (immediately before the outbreak of the armed uprising), in order to determine which of the foods still available could be eaten during Passover.[63] Avraham Hendel describes the meticulous preparations for the baking of matzah and the "selling" of the *hamez* (leavened food articles) in the Warsaw Ghetto in March–April 1943.[64] The procedures for the Passover arrangements, all involving significant risk, were supervised by the Krimilover Rebbe, the Piazesner Rebbe, and the Sokolover Rebbe.[65] The Zarchiver Rebbe, at great risk to his life, baked matzah in the Birkenau camp prior to Passover of 1944.[66] A young Polish Hasid, Itche Motel, led a symbolic Passover Seder in Block 14 of the Auschwitz death camp.[67] Avraham Weissbrod cites a similar observance of the Passover Seder tradition by a group of young Hasidim in the Skalat work camp in 1943.[68] Shlomo Glazer, a member of the underground Hasidic group in the Warsaw Ghetto, describes a secret Seder in the apartment of an Ostrovzer Hasid, Rabbi Silberberg.[69] Hasidim in the Warsaw

Ghetto openly celebrated Simhat Torah, the concluding day of the Sukkot festival, in the face of strict prohibitions. When fellow Jews cautiously warned against doing so, they responded: "We are not afraid of the murderer! The devil with him!"[70] Young Gerer Hasidim in the Plashow camp near Cracow smuggled a Torah scroll from an SS warehouse on Simhat Torah and danced with it in the tradition of the festival.[71] Eyewitness Leibel Yud tells how the young Gerer Hasidim courageously emerged from their bunkers in the Warsaw Ghetto on the festival of Purim in 1943 and danced in the spirit of this joyous festival. When they were cautioned on the danger of the act, they responded: *"Arur Haman!"* (Curse Haman!)[72] Young Gerer Hasidim lit the Hannukah candles over a period of ten days in the forced-labor camp of Ovornik, since they were not certain as to the exact dates of this eight-day featival.[73] Eyewitness Yaakov Frankel relates how a group of Hasidim in the Buchenwald concentration camp conspired to piece together a Megillah (Scroll of Esther) in time for its traditional reading on Purim.[74]

Rabbi Nehemya Alter, the brother of the Gerer Rebbe, utilized an onion for a symbolic *shalosh sudos* (third Sabbath meal) in the Lodz and, subsequently, the Warsaw Ghetto.[75] A young Hasidic group in Warsaw took the time to conduct a *shalosh sudos* "meal" at the Umschlag Platz[76] during the deportation procedures.[77]

Jewish ritual slaughter *(shehitah)* was included among the numerous prohibitions in the ghettos.[78] Kaplan's diary cites the death of a Hasidic *shohet* (ritual slaughterer) who was murdered with his own *halaf* (ritual slaughtering knife).[79] Moshe Rabinowitz, the son of a prominent Gerer Hasid, was shot to death in the Ghetto of Lodz when he refused to eat *taref* (nonkosher food).[80] The Hasid Yaakov Pik in Gerlitz not only refused to eat the meager portions of nonkosher soup but declined to "trade" the soup for bread, since this would have implied that he was deriving personal benefit from the nonkosher food.[81]

The rituals related to birth, marriage, and death were observed and encouraged in the face of severe prohibitions. The Piazesner Rebbe secretly performed the *brit milah* (circumcision) ceremony of a newborn child in the Warsaw Ghetto during the winter of 1943 amidst the singing of Hasidic melodies.[82] The Hasidic leaders in the Warsaw Ghetto encouraged marriages. The brother of the Gerer Rebbe, Rabbi Moshe Bezalel, indicated that marriage in time of grave crisis represents an extraordinary degre of *emunah* (faith).[83] Among the mitzvot (commandments) most actively encouraged by Matityahu Gelman, the leader of the underground Hasidic cells, was *hakhnasat kalah* (providing the bride with a dowry).[84] Eliezer Unger describes the sacrificial devotion of an elderly Hasid, Reb Yehiel Meir, who time and again risked his life to provide proper burial *(kever Yisrael)* for those who died in the ghetto and was eventually killed while doing so.[85] Eyewitness Leibel Pinkoswitz describes the unusual devotion of his father, who arranged for the proper ritual burial of many Hasidim in the Warsaw Ghetto.[86]

Illegal study was one of the most common patterns of spiritual resistance. Activities of this kind took various forms; they frequently involved individuals and groups who refused to register with the German authorities and operated underground study cells. Yaakov Sternberg describes one such group:

> I also recall the passive type of rebels in the ghetto of Cracow. These were young people who fought with spiritual weapons; namely, they sat day and night in a cellar without ever seeing the light of day, absorbed in study. This group consisted of an amalgamation of various Hasidic streams (Belz, Gur, Bobob, Radomsk, etc.). This youth was fortified with sacrificial dedication *(mesirat nefesh)* to the service of the Creator. Following the liquidation of the ghetto, these young "Zadikim" were forced out of the cellar by the impure Gestapo, and all were killed with the Name of God on their lips.[87]

Two eyewitness reports in a Yad Vashem document depict an illegal Hasidic study group operating in and near Cracow.[88] Prager and Eliezer Unger document the underground Gerer Hasidic study cells operating in the Cracow, Lodz, and Warsaw ghettos among others.[89] Rabbi Shimon Engel, a Koznitzer Hasid, is cited as the leader of another illegal study group in the Cracow Ghetto.[90] Huberband documents a variety of Hasidic study cells in Warsaw.[91] Rabbi Avraham Weinberg, a Kotzker and Sochochover Hasid, led an underground Hasidic group in the Warsaw Ghetto.[92] Seidman devotes three citations in his *Warsaw Ghetto Diary* to a young Hasidic group studying in a secret bunker.[93] In the Ghetto of Lodz a substantial study group of Gerer Hasidim and a more modest-sized group of Alexander Hasidim operated illegally.[94] Rabbi Efraim Fishel Rabinowitz, a prominent Gerer Hasid, was constantly absorbed in study in the Ghetto of Lodz.[95] A number of Hasidim somehow found the inner strength to convene a regular study circle under extreme conditions in the Sakazisk and Buchenwald death camps.[96] Prager devotes a considerable portion of *Eleh Shelo Nikhne'u* to the "Mati" episodes. Under the leadership of the charismatic young Gerer Hasid Matityahu Gelman, a number of underground Hasidic cells operating in various ghettos were coordinated in illegal study, rescue, and assistance activities.[97] Nathan Pik documents the activities of Hasidim who studied Talmud on their daily six-kilometer march from the Garlitz death camp to forced labor.[98] Rabbi Moshe Bezalel Alter, brother of the Gerer Rebbe, and other Rebbes studied Mishnah, the Zohar, and Psalms in the Schultz factory in the Warsaw Ghetto, disguised as shoemakers.[99] The Piazesner Rebbe, who was among those "working" in the Schultz factory, urged Jews who were now unemployed to exploit the time for "study and Psalms."[100] Rabbi Mendel Alter, the other brother of the Gerer Rebbe, sent an *igeres* (public letter) to all the ghettos in the winter of 1941, urging concerted study of Torah, based on a dream in which his father, the previous Gerer Rebbe, known as the Sefat Emet, had pleaded with him: "This is a time of tribulation for Jacob. Days of darkness lie ahead for the Jew. Only the study of Torah will strengthen the Jew."[101] The call led to the formation of numerous study cells in the ghettos.[102]

A contrasting and unusually militant group of young Gerer Hasidim, bordering on the nihilistic, operated in the Warsaw Ghetto, according to a detailed documentation by Huberband.[103] Some fifty young men banded together under a code of cooperative discipline. They severed all their family and community ties and displayed utter disdain for the feelings and emotions of their neighbors, claiming loyalty only to the Gerer Rebbe.[104] Their bizarre behavior and obsession with Hasidic song, dance, and alcoholic drink, and their eventual involvement in petty theft and extortion in order to support their "orgies," aroused the contempt and opposition of the Gerer elders and the neighbors at 9 Mila Street.[105] A formal protest was lodged with Rabbi Moshe Bezalel, the brother of the Gerer Rebbe. Rabbi Moshe responded with a brisk letter to the group, reprimanding it for its excesses, especially in the background of the Holocaust tragedy. "The main objective at this particular time [should be] to strengthen the zealous and regular study of Torah; at least eight hours each day without employing any pretexts."[106] He berated them for violating the honor due to parents and the Rebbe, as well as for dishonoring Torah and Hasidism.[107]

Forms of resistance included various modes of refusal to obey orders and general noncooperation. The Radomsker refused to participate in "transportation arrangements" as part of the liquidation of the Warsaw Ghetto.[108] The Germans found little when they searched the Radomsker shtiebel because it had been emptied earlier in order to prevent them from obtaining valuable objects.[109] The Koznitzer refused to perform on the violin as ordered since he did not wish to submit to obvious ridicule.[110] Rabbi Eliyahu Laskowsky, a Sochochover Hasid, refused to cooperate with the Judenrat in the Dvart Ghetto.[111] Two unnamed young Hasidim refused to provide a list of ten Jews for execution. They were consequently included in the public massacre.[112] The brother of the Belzer Rebbe (Rabbi Mordechai Rokeach) reported the heroism of a young Hasid in the Ghetto of Bochnia who was shot in the Jewish cemetery for refusing to reveal a particular hiding place. Prior to his death the Hasid noted with satisfaction that God had rewarded him with burial among Jews *(Kever Yisrael)*, frustrating Nazi intentions.[113] Rabbi Menahem Zemba, despite a severe beating, refused to provide the Gestapo in Warsaw with the names of thirty wealthy Jews.[114]

CHAPTER 13

Hasidic Concepts Related to Resistance

The subject of physical resistance during the Holocaust has been the focus of heated controversy and polemics. The thesis of Hannah Arendt, which emphasizes "the contrast between Israeli heroism . . . [and] the submissive meekness with which Jews went to their death,"[1] and Jewish cooperation in their own destruction, is refuted by Jacob Robinson.[2] He counters with elaborate documentation of Jewish resistance and noncooperation. Moreover, he focuses upon the characteristic Nazi strategy of the combined use of sudden terror, brutality, and deception, which made any form of resistance extremely difficult. Meticulous research he says, reveals a pattern of Jewish heroism in the struggle for "survival with dignity." According to Robinson, Arendt inaccurately evaluated the Jewish response because her expectations and preconceptions were inconsistent with and unrelated to Holocaust conditions.[3] Pertinent to the present research is Robinson's insight into the historical and ideational context of the Jewish response to violence and terror:

1. In responding to adverse circumstances, the Jew *least* applied the option of violence and war (in the diaspora).
2. The emphasis throughout Jewish history was on continuity and survival.
3. Judaism stressed the value of time as *the* precious commodity in the existence of the individual and community.[4]

Raul Hilberg, leaning toward Arendt's views, characterizes the Jewish reaction/response to force and adversity throughout Jewish history as reflected in various forms of "alleviaton," "anticipatory compliance," and "recurring readjustments," playing "along with an attacker . . . in the knowledge that their policy would result in least damage and least injury."[5] This cautious and defensive character, according to Hilberg, was indigenous to Jewish life under alien diaspora conditions. "It should be emphasized again that the term 'Jewish reactions' refers only to ghetto Jews. This reaction pattern was born in the ghetto and it will die there. It is part and parcel of ghetto life."[6]

Neither Arendt nor Hilberg, nor to some degree Robinson, seems to take cognizance of Jewish tactics that may indeed have been submissive, passive, or delaying in nature, but aimed not at mere physical survival but at the type of continuity that would preserve and sustain Jewish identify and character.[7] This type of resistance, though distinct from the physical kind, demanded an equal degree of dedication, raw defiance, and fortitude. If historical precedent was indeed the determinant of the Jew's behavior during the Holocaust, as Hilberg suggests,[8] then resistance that sought to preserve spiritual authenticity, thus countering the objectives of that which was resisted, cannot be isolated from the heroic response pattern of the Jew during the Holocaust. In such a framework, the research cited Hasidic resistance responses and presently seeks to indicate related concepts in Hasidic thought.

PHYSICAL STRUGGLE AND VIOLENCE

As one might assume from a system of religious experience based upon the three principles of *Ahavat Hashem* (love of God), *Ahavat Yisrael* (love of Israel) and *Ahavat Hatorah* (love of Torah), the motif of violence is absent from Hasidic thought. Furthermore, scriptural references to physical resistance are spiritualized. for example, "Israel's warfare with Amalek[9] is [in essence] a battle with the *yetzer hara* [man's evil inclination]. [It represents] the prince of Amalek. [The staging of this war] is our responsibility and not in the hands of God," according to Yaakov Yosef of Polnoya.[10] Similarly, the violent action of Simeon and Levi against the male population of the city of Shechem actually symbolizes man's life-and-death struggle with the *yetzer hara,* notes Rabbi Elimelech of Lizensk.[11]

> "For when angry they slay men,"[12] . . . at first the *yetzer hara* is called "guest" [i.e., an occasional visitor]; then someone who "comes" [regularly]; and finally a "man" [referring to the term *ish* (man) in Genesis 49:5] who has made himself at home [i.e., a *ba'al habayit;* the term is

> appropriate because Shechem and its people, who symbolize the *yetzer hara,* were the natives of the land in which Jacob dwelled]. Thus one must employ great force in order to break and destroy him. . . . And this is the meaning of *be'apam* ["for when angry" or "with their anger"], namely, they provoked the *yetzer hatov* [man's good inclination] against the *yetzer hara,*[13] and they killed him even though he was in the form of a man.[14]

In fact, man's purpose in life and ultimate reward focus upon the extent of his warfare against the *yetzer hara.* Expounding upon the biblical phrase *Vayehi Ya'akov* ("and Jacob lived"),[15] Rabbi Elimelech notes:

> The major reason for achieving our reward is that our Creator, blessed be His Name, placed within us the *yetzer hara,* who provokes us at every moment and tempts us with evil thoughts so that we transgress, God forbid. . . . Man, however, is to resist [the *yetzer hara*] . . . and conceive tactics to wage war. . . . One must respond with warfare and great effort in order to break the power of the temptations of the *yetzer hara.* It is a tortuous process.[16]

The term *milhamah* (war) is also associated with the process of prayer.[17] In this vein, Rabbi Nahman of Brazlav spiritualizes the verse "When you go out to war against your enemies . . . and you take some of them captive":[18]

> For he [the enemy] is the *yetzer hara.* . . . Therefore, the Torah provides the [following] exhortation: "And you take them captive,"[19] that is to say, with the very thing that he wishes to overpower you, namely, with pride, proceed to overpower him. Say to him, how can I be in control when I am conceited and the Holy One, blessed be He, is not with me?'[20]

The Kotzker Rebbe elaborates on the manner in which violence and warfare were spiritualized in Hasidism. In comparing Numbers 10:9 ("When you are at war in your own land against an aggressor who attacks you, you shall sound short blasts on the trumpets, so that you may be remembered before the Lord your God and be delivered from your enemies") with Deuteronomy 21:10 ("When you take the field against your enemies and the Lord your God delivers them into your power and you take some of them captive"), the Kotzker taught:

> [In neither instance] does one note the action of man. But the difference [between the verses] is clear. When man assumes the offensive against the *yetzer* [the (evil) inclination], he is confident that he will be victorious and take captives from him. If he is worthy he will bring him [the *yetzer*] into the realm of *Kedushah* [sanctity][21] and will convert her to good. . . . But if man waits until the *yetzer* approaches him and only then engages in war with him, then he will not easily vanquish the enemy unless he blasts the trumpets and cries unto God and pours out his heart and soul before God. Then salvation will come.[22]

The idea of vengeance is not encountered in the Hasidic literature. References to *nekamah* when they do occur are associated with God. Even so, according to Rabbi Levi Yitzhak of Berdichev, God's vengeance is only directed against the nations of the world who are the source of injustice against the people of Israel. *Nekamah* is an extension of God's special affection for His people.[23] Rabbi Yehiel Mechel Lipshitz, (d. 1888), the Rabbi of Gastinin, interpreted "Let men be chosen from among you . . . to wreak the Lord's vengeance on Midian[24] as follows:

> This is what Moses our teacher counseled the Israelites. When they wreak vengeance on Midian let them disregard their own emotions. This means that although they are certainly pent up with anger and zealously intent on vengeance for all the evil perpetrated against them, nevertheless, they should remove these inclinations and be motivated exclusively by the imperative of God's commandments.[25]

The spiritualization and allegorization of warfare is consistent with Uffenheimer's documentation of the Hasidic tendency to spiritualize the material and physical aspects of everyday life, requests in prayer, and national and messianic concepts.[26] The objective was to strip away the material *(hitpashtut hagashmiyut)* and obliterate the ego forces in man *(bittul atzmi)* so as to clear the path for a union of man with the divine.

SPIRITUAL AND PASSIVE RESISTANCE

Violence and physical resistance evidently were not within the ideational and experiential framework of the Hasid, as previously noted. This research has indicated the manner in which Hasidism educated its adherents to assume various postures in response to all aspects of life, especially when its religious integrity was threatened.[27]

Two patterns of Hasidic teachings could conceivably have directed the Hasid to the response of spiritual resistance. All of the concepts that comprise these patterns were introduced earlier in this research in the context of other responses. At present the study seeks to integrate them into a unified whole suggesting the cumulative relationship of a number of pertinent Hasidic concepts to the response of spiritual resistance. The first pattern relates to the absolute primacy of the Divine Will (*Hashgahah Elyonah*) and is interrelated with faith (*emunah*) and trust (*bitahon*) in His ways.[28] This foundation of faith enabled the evolvement of the concepts of *Ahavat Hashem* (love of God), *Ahavat Hatorah* (love of God's teachings and law), and *Ahavat Yisrael* (love of the Jewish people). Further, life, representing the unique manifestation of divine creativity, was to be invested with sanctity *(Kiddush Hahayim),* and in the process, one paid tribute to the Creator of all by sanctifying God *(Kiddush Hashem). Kiddush Hahayim* was to be attained by simply making the most of this precious commodity within the comprehensive frame of the mitzvot (God's commandments), which were to be fulfilled with joy (*simhah*) and ecstasy (*hitlahavut*). Suffering and concern for the mundane are to be seen in the total context of God's interaction with man and to be accepted with love (*kabalah be'ahavah*). One must be prepared to demonstrate love and devotion for the Creator by responding to every challenge with sacrificial dedication (*mesirat nefesh*) and fortitude (*hithazkut*).

The second pattern focuses upon the limitation of the human being, the futility of the search for material achievement, and the absurdity of existence in a world insensitive to the reality of the divine. The Hasid could readily disengage from the swirling events of life, as in the case of the underground groups. Moreover, the Hasid could ignore and resist decrees intended to limit or destroy his spiritual way of life, since he was the product of a behavioral system which placed a premium on the dissolution of the ego and the self (*bittul atzmi, hitbatlut*), and of material reality (*bittul hayesh, hitpashtut hagashmiut*); and by doing so he would assume a stance of indifference (*hishtavut*) to the intentions of others who sought to exert their will in contradiction to his value system.[29] The net effect of these patterns—one focusing on the primacy of the spiritual, the other on the limitations of the physical—could have produced forms of spiritual resistance to the events of the Holocaust like the ones documented in this study.

The mikveh (ritual pool for immersion) is an example of a concept given new weight in Hasidic tradition and particularly articulated under radical stress in the framework of the two patterns formulated above. The Ba'al Shem Tov taught: "One is to be especially careful to observe immersion (tevilah) at all times and to concentrate when in the mikveh upon the kavvanot [intentions] related to the mikveh."[30] What indeed was the purpose of mikveh, and upon what "intentions" should the Hasid focus? For the Hasid, immersion in the mikveh was an opportunity to reject "the impurity of the body [or the physical] and to elevate in the mikveh all that is holy."[31] The mikveh also symbolized *hitpashtut hagashmiut* (the stripping away of the material)[32] and *bittul atzmi* (dissolution of the self or the ego).[33] In the event that a ritually designated mikveh was not available, one simply washed one's hands and recited a brief prayer formulated by Rabbi Isaac Luria. The prayer beseeches God to convert *Din* (judgment) into *Rahamim* (mercy) on the basis of fulfilling the mitzvah of mikveh.[34] The experience of mikveh is associated with *mesirat nefesh* (sacrificial devotion).[35] Hasidic tradition describes the use of the mikveh "during the severest frost of winter [when] they broke the ice in the stream in order to immerse themselves in the flowing water."[36]

Sociological as well as ideological elements may have stimulated resistance responses. Prager indicates that the following elements helped to galvanize the Gerer underground cells:

1. The social cohesion among the various Hasidic *shtiblech* (centers of Hasidic study, prayer, and social life) in most Eastern European communities prior to the Holocaust and the periodic visits to the Gerer Rebbe.
2. The Rebbe's plan to organize the young Hasidim into self-contained study, prayer, and social units (also prior to the Holocaust), each with a local leader and coordinated by regional leaders ("Commandanten").
3. The Rebbe's inclination to be involved in the political affairs of the Jewish community in Poland for the purpose of protecting and safeguarding religious observance and tradition.[37]

Buber summarizes the cumulative effect of the Hasidic teachings that may have accounted for the conviction and fortitude reflected in the patterns of resistance cited in this research:

> If you direct the unlimited power of your fervor to God's world destiny, if you do what you must do at this moment—no matter what it may be!—with your whole strength and with *kavanah* [utter and undivided concentration] with holy intent, you will bring about the union between God and Shekhina, eternity and time. You need not be a scholar or a sage to accomplish this. All that is necessary is to have a soul united within itself and indivisibly directed to its divine goal.[38]

Buber's use of the terms "undiminished power," "fervor," "strength," "intent," and "soul united" suggests the kind of spiritual arsenal employed in confronting the "no matter what it may be"—in this instance, the supreme test of the Holocaust.

CHAPTER 14

Summary and Conclusions

Having examined the available documentation, we sought to correlate Hasidic responses to the Holocaust with certain basic concepts in Hasidic thought. In doing so we assumed that Hasidism sought to apply its doctrines and teachings to the behavior of its adherents. We were correct to do so, for our study indicates that the documented Holocaust responses of Hasidic leaders and Hasidim clearly derived from fundamental Hasidic tenets. Our findings are summarized below in more specific terms.

GOD'S RELATIONSHIP TO MAN AND THE JEWISH PEOPLE

One response pattern comprised efforts to justify God's role during the Holocaust. Man's limited perspective does not permit a full grasp of the interrelationship of divine *Din* (justice) and *Rahamim* (compassion), unless it is viewed in the context of God as the source of the ultimate good. Hence, a Jew must accept everything with love *(kabalah be'ahavah)*, inspired by *bitahon* (trust) and *emunah* (faith) in God's benevolent relationship to man. Within this framework, man responds to God by cleaving to Him in mystical union *(devekut)* and joy *(simhah)*. This process leads to the dissolution of the forces of ego *(bittul hayesh)* and a stance of indifference to material and physical adversity *(hishtavut)*. Despite (or because of) this special relationship, some responses questioned God's role in the Holocaust, maintaining that it was incompatible with God's purpose in the universe. The research documented rationales for suffering and seeming evil. "Positive" and "negative" consequences of suffering were noted. Some significant responses held that the bond between God and His people is forged by mutual suffering. Man's love for God is simultaneously tested and articulated by means of sacrificial devotion *(mesirat nefesh)* in suffering. Noteworthy was the relative absence of responses that saw the Holocaust as retribution for the sins of the Jewish people.

The teachings of Rabbi Israel Ba'al Shem Tov and his disciples focus upon man's duty to accept personal adversity and suffering within a framework of *bitahon* (trust) in God's ways and in His Will. Man is to discover the inherent goodness in misfortune and to accept it with love *(kabalah be'ahavah)*. Other Hasidic interpretations of suffering are offered, including the mutual suffering of God and man as part of the general interaction and interdependence of God and man. Man is to convert *(hithapkhut)* his concern for himself *(ani)* to a concern for the *tikkun* (restoration) of the Shekhinah (God's presence).

Hasidism's predominantly quietistic stance, documented in Uffenheimer's work, is contrasted with the activist tradition of Rabbis Levi Yitzchak of Berdichev and Mordechai of Tchernibol, who challenged God to assume his role as *Shofet kol Ha'aretz* (Judge of All the Earth).[1]

REDEMPTION AND THE MESSIANIC ERA

Some Hasidic thinkers related the Holocaust to the *Hevle Mashiah* (the suffering prior to the coming of the Messiah). Generally, the "birth pangs of the Messiah" are to be welcomed. A variant response prefers to delay the coming of the Messiah so that Israel may be spared the suffering. Both activist and quietist notions emphasized the role of the individual in hastening redemption. The activist notion relies on man's initiative to stimulate redemption. The quietist notion views redemption as a supernatural phenomenon outside man's sphere of action. In either case, the responses acknowledged the "unexpected" sources from which redemption may spring—unexpected as to the time as well as the source of the redemption. Attention was focused on the nature of Galut (exile), its negative impact on the personality of the Jew, and its role as breeding ground for tragedies like the Holocaust. Dominant is the bias of Rabbi Teichthal in *Em Habanim Semehah*, supported in Kabbalah and Hasidism, that man must assume the initiative in countering Galut "realities." Eretz Yisrael alone can provide the Jew with a national-religious framework of normalcy. Rabbi Teichthal accuses religious and Hasidic leaders of making exile seem normal by establishing the idea of its permanency and by undermining the Zionist initiative in Palestine. The responses invoke classic Hasidic sources to support the centrality of Eretz Yisrael in the essential *tikkun* (restoration) process of the Shekhinah (God's presence) and *kelal Yisrael* (the totality of Israel), and as a precursor of the *geulah shelemah* (final redemption).

These responses were positively correlated with aspects of Hasidic thought. The classic Hasidic teachers also welcomed the *Hevle Mashiah* as the necessary forerunner of redemption, the "darkness before the dawn." Consistent with Kabbalah, Hasidism urged man to initiate action "below" in order to arouse a response "above." As applied to redemption, this suggested that man's initiative in utilizing material and natural resources would trigger a similar response from the cosmic elements. The "double directional relationship" (Buber's term) thus operates not only in the sphere of man's misfortunes but in the quest for ultimate *tikkun* (restoration). All elements in *kelal Yisrael* must play a role in the redemption process. While Eretz Yisrael is central to ultimate redemption, exile inhibits and obstructs the Jewish soul struggling to return to its holy origin.

KIDDUSH HASHEM AND KIDDUSH HAHAYIM

Responses related to *Kiddush Hashem* (the sanctification of God's name) assumed the classic form of Jewish martyrdom as well as forms related to *Kiddush Hahayim* (the sanctification of God in life) in defiance of the enemy's objective to degrade and terminate life. The study noted the concern for the proper stance and attitude a Jew should assume in preparation for *Kiddush Hashem*. The privilege of *Kiddush Hashem* enabled the Hasid to anticipate his tragic fate with some comfort and dignity. *Kiddush Hashem* also strengthened the bond between God and His people and between the people and its land. It was the opportunity to counter the satanic and the impure with the elements that were the most difficult to destroy—the spiritual and divine in human existence. *Kiddush Hashem* allowed the Jew to transcend the uneven battle of material forces.

Mesirat nefesh (sacrificial devotion to religious imperatives) is central to Hasidism and related to *Kiddush Hashem*. The Jew should indeed seek the privilege of experiencing *Kiddush Hashem*, which in essence is the ultimate form of *Ahavat Hashem* (love of God). *Kiddush Hashem* is facilitated by achieving the desired state of *devekut* (cleaving to God in search of a mystical union with the divine). Though *Kiddush Hashem* in martyrdom is unquestionably a religious imperative, the Hasidic teachers, especially Rabbi Nahman of Brazlav, seem to prefer *Kiddush Hashem* as articulated in *Kiddush Hahayim*. This tendency is consistent with the Hasidic concept of *avodah begashmiut* (worshiping God through the mundane and material).

ZADIK AND HASID, HASIDIC TRADITIONS, THE HASIDIC FRATERNAL BOND

The Hasidic elements are most conspicuous in responses related to the unique mutual attachment of Hasid and Rebbe. We noted the consistent refusal of Rebbes to abandon their communities despite offers of protection and rescue. By sharing the Holocaust plight with them and seeking to counter the tendencies toward *ye'ush* (despair), the Rebbes were a source of comfort for their Hasidim. If God is indeed "with them in their distress," the Zadik could do no less. The investigation documented the assistance and rescue efforts of the Rebbe implemented by the Hasidic fraternal structure. The Rebbe as a source of comfort and assistance was a natural extension of the ideal of *Ahavat Yisrael* (love for fellow Jews). Hasidim attempted to continue to observe Hasidic traditions despite the severe restrictions of Holocaust life. These included the fraternal meal (praven tish), the petition to the Rebbe (the kvittel), and the Hasidic melody (niggun). (In a subsequent section the continued use of the immersion pool [mikveh] is cited.)

The Zadik and his concern for his Hasidim are fundamental to Hasidic doctrine, especially as developed by Rabbis Yaakov Yosef of Polnoya, Elimelech of Lizensk, and Nahman of Brazlav. The role of the Zadik as one of concern for his people is related to the doctrine of the descent of the Zadik, and the Hasidic emphasis on *Ahavat Yisrael* (love for fellow Jews). The Zadik played a major role in reversing the mood of *ye'ush* (despair) which was a cardinal sin in the Hasidic system of behavior. The Zadik helped the Hasid focus on aspects of daily existence that reflect the divine spirit and thus were to be experienced with *simhah* (joy). Hasidic traditions flowing from this mutual relationship—the fraternal meal (praven tisch), the kvittel (petition), and the *niggun* (song) and dance—are all documented in primary and secondary Hasidic sources.

PHYSICAL AND PASSIVE RESISTANCE

While any distinction between physical and spiritual resistance in the Holocaust context is superficial, we nevertheless separated resistance into these two categories because of the spiritualization of physical violence and warfare in classical Hasidic thought. Evidence of physical resistance during the Holocaust is sparse and correlates with the Hasidic spiritualization of violence and warfare.

Passive and spiritual resistance was evident, however, especially in response to edicts restricting or prohibiting religious and specifically Hasidic traditions. Prominent were the underground cells of young Hasidim operating in the various ghettos. They pursued a policy of complete disengagement from the occupation authorities. Evidence was cited of noncompliance with prohibitions against the wearing of Hasidic dress, the use of the mikveh, the observance of Jewish rituals related to birth, marriage, death, prayer, study, ritual slaughter, dietary laws, the Sabbath, and the festivals.

The absolute primacy of the Divine Will, the limitations of the material sphere, and the Hasidic declensions of these concepts may have enabled the Hasid to assume a posture of spiritual resistance.

COMMON MOTIFS

In addition to the five categories of responses summarized in the preceding sections, the study accumulated evidence of two other apparent motifs.

The first of these was the mutual relationship between God and man in which both share in, as well as seek to shape, the ultimate destiny of salvation. Holocaust events were interpreted within this God-man partnership context.

The second motif focused on man's initiative *(etaruta deletata)* in the process of *tikkun* as the essential prerequisite for the ultimately successful struggle against the negative-satanic forces (the *kelipot*) that prevent salvation.

These motifs may have provided the Hasid with an additional frame of reference within which the Holocaust assumed meaning. In the first instance the terror of facing Holocaust events in isolation was either removed or reduced. Second, the Hasid could function as part of a larger, meaningful struggle transcending Holocaust events. This too may have provided a degree of comfort, fortitude, and stability during extreme crisis.

PSYCHOLOGICAL IMPLICATIONS

In addition to providing the Hasid with a general frame of faith and some guidelines for response to radical crisis, the research suggested that traditional Hasidic thought offered various "pegs" upon which the Hasid might hang interpretations of the unfolding horror. These were ideational as well as structural in character.

Hasidism offered a system of concepts that could be used to interpret the Holocaust. Further, Hasidism provided both a social framework and a leadership[2] to articulate these concepts. The general frame of faith, the specific concepts, and the social units may have served as the type of shock absorbers and defenses reported by Bruno Bettelheim in his psychoanalytic studies of concentration camp inmates.[3] He noted that the more substantial and sustained the realm of "private behavior,"[4] the more bearable and, possibly, meaningful was the trauma of Holocaust events. Private behavior evidently provided the victim with the resources to maintain the self-respect essential to resist the disintegration of personality. Bettelheim depicts the exaggerated states of depression and agitation of

> non-political middle-class [gentile] prisoners [who] were those least able to withstand the initial shock [of extreme situations]. They were utterly unable to understand what had happened to them and why. . . . They had little or no resources to fall back on when subject to the shock of imprisonment.[5]

In contrast, he notes the following responses of prisoners who were Jehovah's Witnesses:

> They were even less affected by imprisonment and kept their integrity thanks to rigid religious beliefs. . . . Such integrity was evident to some extent in their relationship to other prisoners even when they were selected as foremen of work groups in the camps. . . . they were the only group of prisoners who never abused or mistreated other prisoners.[6]

This research did not reveal any instances of cruel or abusive behavior by Hasidim during extreme situations. Seidman in his *Warsaw Ghetto Diary* verifies the consistency of religious integrity during radical crisis.

> People in the ghetto whose normal moral resistance had been low descended to an even lower level [in the ghetto]. The corrupt [prior to the Holocaust] became yet more corrupt, while those of high moral integrity rose to even greater heights. [This is] the interpretation of the

> *Sefat Emet* [i.e., Rabbi Yehuda Aryeh Leib Alter, the elder Gerer Rebbe and author of the *Sefat Emet* commentary on the Pentateuch] of the verse, "The Egyptians dealt harshly with us."[7] The verse should have read *lanu* and not *otanu*.[8] However, the intent of the verse [was to demonstrate] that they [the Egyptians] transformed *otanu* [us] into worse beings.[9]

This interpretation was borne out in the ghetto.

> The Germans exploited every means, organized every Satanic device in order to break the moral defenses of the Jew and to stimulate his most primitive senses. They initiated a difficult and inhuman war of survival so that a Jew could only continue to exist at the expense of another [Jew]. Yet the elements in the [ghetto] police,[10] with exceptions, were not of the highest caliber.[11] At the time of the deportations it [the Jewish police force] was composed of converts, assimilated Jews, radicals, dishonest individuals, those without moral scruples, the "golden youth,"[12] and many from the underworld. It can be ascertained that the entire police force did not include even one observant Jew. . . . (This was also true in the camps. Among all the various overseers . . . there were no religious Jews. This is confirmed by all who were in the camps.)[13]

Bettelheim's psychological observations on "private behavior" may well have applications in understanding Hasidic responses during the Holocaust. Baruch Kurzweil's distinction between mysticism and tragedy may also be pertinent to this research. "The tragic personality is an entity sealed up within itself, whereas emphasis of the self within an entity higher than itself characterizes the mystic personality."[14] Tragedy and true mysticism are thus incompatible. Steinman notes Hasidism's search for the "entity higher than itself" documented in this study.

> Central to Hasidism are spiritual values endowing man with dignity. They provide him with a sense of trust emanating from a soul which originates in the Holy Source. They [the spiritual values of Hasidism] enhance the image of man and arouse within him courage inspired by a Holy Spark *(azut dekedushah)*.[15]

Bibliography

GENERAL WORKS ON HASIDISM

Primary Sources

Aaron of Apt and Yaakov Yosef of Polnoya. *Likute Keter Shem Tov.* Israel: Hotza'at Talpiot, 1965.

Aaron of Karlin. *Bet Ahron.* Brody, 1873.

Barukh of Mezbiz. *Buzina Denehorah* [The shining light]. Lvov: Ksieg. Margulies, 1879–80 (Film Production, New York Public Library, Jewish Division).

Dov Ber of Mezritch. *Magid Debarav Leya'akov.* Korzec, 1781.

———. *Torat Hamagid.* Edited by Yisrael Klapholz. 2 vols. Tel Aviv: Pe'er Hasefer, 1969.

Elimelech of Linzensk. *No'am Elimelekh.* Lemberg, 1874.

Israel Ba'al Shem Tov. *Igeret Hakodesh* [The holy letter]. In *Shivhe Habesht.* Israel: Hotza'at Talpiot, 1965.

———. *Kuntrus Meirat Enayim.* Israel: Hotza'at Talpiot, 1965.

———. *Zava'at Haribash.* Israel: Hotza'at Talpiot, 1965.

Levi Yitzchak of Berdichev. *Kedushat Levi.* Munkatch, 1939.

Menahem Mendel of Kotzk. *Emet Ve'emunah* [Truth and belief]. Brooklyn, N.Y.: Ahavat Hakadmonim, 1971.

Menahem Mendel of Vitebsk. *Likute Amarim.* Lemberg, 1911.

———. *Pri Ha'aretz im Etz Pri.* Jerusalem: Sifre Musar Vehasidut, 1953.

Menahem Mendel Schneerson of Lubavich. *Likute Sihot* [Collection of talks]. Brooklyn, N.Y.: Otzar Hahasidim, 1971.

Nahman of Brazlav, *Likute Ezot.* Jerusalem: Haside Brazlav, 1956.

———. *Likute Mohran.* Bnei Brak: Yeshiva-Brazlav, 1965.

———. *Me'olamo Shel Rabbi Nahman Mebrazlav* [From the world of Rabbi Nahman of Brazlav]. Edited by David Hardan. Jerusalem: World Zionist Organization, 1971.

———. *Zimrat Ha'aretz* [The choice products of the land]. Lemberg, 1876.

Pinhas of Koretz. *Nofet Tzufim* [Flowing honey]. Warsaw, 1929.

Shivhe Habesht. Israel: Hotza'at Talpiot, 1965.

Shne'ur Zalman of Liadi. *Likute Amarim (Tanya)*. Slobuta, 1795.

Ya'akov Yosef of Polnoya. *Toldot Ya'akov Yosef*. Brooklyn, N.Y.: Yosef Weiss Publishers, n.d.

Yechiel Meir Lifshitz of Gastinin. *Sefer Me Hayam* [The waters of the sea]. Edited by Menachem Berber. Brooklyn, N.Y., 1964.

Yitzchak Isaac of Komarno. *Hekhal Habrakhah*. Lemberg, 1858.

———. *Netiv Mitzvotekha*. Jerusalem, 1947.

———. *Notzar Hesed*. Lvov, 1856.

Secondary Sources

Alfasi, Yitzchak. *Hahasidut* [Hasidism]. Tel Aviv: Hotza'at Zion, 1969.

———. *Sefer Ha'admorim* [The book of Hasidic rabbis]. Tel Aviv: Ariel, 1961.

Barzowski, M. "Gedole Hahasidut Haslonima'it Umanhigeha Bebaranowich" [Slonimer Hasidism and its leadership in Baranowich]. In *Baranowich*. Tel Aviv: Irgun Yoz. Baranowich, 1953.

Berl, Hayim Y. *Reb Yitzhak Isaac Mekomarno* [Rabbi Yitzchak Isaac of Komarno]. Jerusalem: Mosad Harav Kook, 1965.

Buber, Martin. *The Origin and Meaning of Hasidism*. New York: Harper & Row, 1960.

———. *Tales of the Hasidim: Early Masters*, New York: Schocken, 1961.

———. *Tales of the Hasidim: Later Masters*. New York: Schocken, 1961.

Dresner, Samuel H. *The Zaddick*. New York: Abelard-Schuman, 1960.

Dubnow, Simon. *Toldot Hahasidut* [The history of Hasidism]. 3 vols. Tel Aviv: Dvir, 1930–32.

Ehrenberg, Elimelech E. *Arze Lebanon* [Cedars of Lebanon]. Jerusalem: Ehrenberg, 1967.

Federbush, Simon. *Hahasidut Vezion* [Hasidism and Zion]. New York: Moriah, 1963.

Fox, Joseph. *Rabbi Menahem Mendel Mekotzk: Toldot Hayav Vedarkho Behasidut* [Rabbi Menahem Mendel of Kotzk: His life and approach to Hasidism]. Jerusalem: Mosad Harav Kook, 1967.

Frankel, Issar. *Rabbi Meir Yehiel Meostrovzeh: Hayav, Shitato Vetorato* [Rabbi Meir Yehiel, the Ostrowzer rebbe: His life, method, and teaching]. Tel Aviv: Netzah, 1953.

Gershuri, Meir Simon. *Haniggun Veharikud Behasidut* [Song and dance in Hasidism]. 3 vols. Tel Aviv: Netzah, 1954–59.

Gutman, Ezekiel M. *Migdole Hahasidut: Rabbi Shalom Mebelz* [Great Hasidic personalities: Rabbi Shalom of Belz]. Bilgoraj: N. Kronenberg, 1935.

Halachmi, David Weisbrod. *Arze Halevanon* [Cedars of Lebanon]. Tel Aviv: Alter-Bergman, 1956.

Horodetzky, Samuel. *Hahasidut Vehahasidim* [Hasidism and the Hasidim]. 4 vols. Tel Aviv: Dvir, 1953.

———. *Hahasidut Vetoratah* [Hasidism and its teachings]. Tel Aviv: Dvir, 1944.

Landau, Bezalel, and Natan Ortner. *Harab Hakadosh Mebelz* [The holy Belzer rebbe]. Jersualem: Or Hassidim, 1967.

Maimon, Cohen. L. Y., ed. *Sefer Habesht* [The Ba'al Shem Tov volume]. Jerusalem: Mosad Harav Kook, 1960.

Malach, Avraham. *Hesed Le'abraham* [Kindness to Abraham]. Jerusalem: Lewin-Epstein, 1954.

Minz, Benjamin. *Rabenu Sa'zal Megur* [Our Gerer Rebbe of blessed memory]. Tel Aviv: Shearim, 1949.

Newman, Louis. *Hassidic Anthology*. New York: Schocken Books, 1963.

Rabinowich, Ze'ev. *Hahasidut Halita'it* [Lithuanian Hasidism]. Jerusalem: Mosad Bialik, 1961.

Rotenberg, Yehezeke'el, and Moshe Sheinfeld, eds. *Harebi Mekozk Veshishim Giborim Saviv Lo* [The Kotzker Rebbe and the sixty mighty men around him]. 2 vols. Tel Aviv: Nezah, 1959.

Rudavsky, David. *Emancipation and Adjustment: Contemporary Jewish Religious Movements, Their History and Thought*. New York: Diplomatic Press, 1967.

Scholem, Gershom G. *Major Trends in Jewish Mysticism*. New York: Schocken Books, 1954.

Steinman, Eliezer. *Sha'ar Hahasidut* [The Gate of Hasidism]. Tel Aviv: Hotza'at Sefarim Neuman, 1957.

Uffenheimer, Rivka Schatz. *Hahasidut Kemistika* [Hasidism as mysticism]: *Quietistic Elements in 18th Century Hasidic Thought*. Jerusalem: Magnes Press, 1968.

Werfel, Isaac. *Hahasidut Ve'eretz Yisrael* [Hasidism and the Jewish homeland]. Jerusalem: Hotza'at Sefarim Ha'eretz Yisraelit, 1940.

———. *Mema'ayanot Ha'folklor Hahasidi* [From the fountain of Hasidic folklore]. Jerusalem: Ahiasaf, 1945–46.

Wertheim, Aaron. *Halakhot Vehalikhot Behasidut* [Laws and traditions in Hasidism]. Jerusalem: Mosad Harav Kook, 1960.

Yashar, Baruch. *Bet Komarno* [The house (dynasty) of Komarno]. Jerusalem: Baruch Yashar, 1965.

Zevin, Shlomo Yosef. *Sipure Hasidim* [Hasidic legends]. Tel Aviv: Avraham Zioni, 1963.

Secondary Sources: Articles

Alfasi, Yitzhak. "Ahavat Yisrael Behasidut" [The love of Israel in Hasidism]. In *Hahasidut* [Hasidism], pp. 177–183. Tel Aviv: Hotza'at Zion, 1969.

Brayer, Menahem. "The Hasidic Rebbes of Romania, Hungary, and [their relationship to] *Eretz Yisrael.*" In *Hasidut Vezion* [Hasidism and Zion], edited by Simon Federbush, pp. 190–245. New York: Moriah, 1963.

Dinaburg, Ben Zion. "Reshitah Shel Hahasidut Visodotekha Hasozialiyim, Vehameshihiyim" [The beginnings of Hasidism and its social and messianic foundations]. *Zion* 7, no. 2 (January 1943): 107–115; 8, no. 3 (April 1943): 117–134; 8, no. 4 (July 1943); 179–200; 9, no. 1 (October 1943): 39–45; 9, nos. 2–3 (January–April 1944): 89–108; 9, no. 4 (July 1944): 186–197; 10, nos. 1–2 (November 1944–February 1945): 67–77; 10, nos. 3–4 (April–July 1945): 149–186.

Gershuri, M. S. "Letoldot Hahasidut Vehanegina Hahasidit Bekrako" [The history of Hasidism and Hasidic music in Cracow]. In *Sefer Krako* [The book of Cracow], edited by Aryeh Bauminger et al., Jerusalem: Hotza'at Mosad Harav Kook, 1959.

———. "Letorat Hanigun Behasidut [Concerning the doctrine of the *niggun* in Hasidism]. In *Sefer Habesht,* edited by L. Y. Cohen Maimon, pp. 70–83. Jerusalem: Mosad Harav Kook, 1960.

Heschel, Abraham Joshua. "Umbekante Dokumenten zu der Geshichte fun Chassidus" [Unknown documents in the history of Hasidism]. *Yivo Bletter* 36 (1952): 113–135.

———. "R'Gershon Kitover, Parshat Hayav Ve'aliyato Le'eretz Yisrael" [Rabbi Gershon Kitover, his life and settlement in Eretz Yisrael]. *Hebrew Union College Annual* 23, pt. II (1950–1951): 17–71.

Ibn Shmuel, Yehudah. "Memishnato shel Rabi Yisrael Ba'al Shem Tov" [From the teachings of Rabbi Israel Ba'al Shem Tov. In *Sefer Habesht* [The Ba'al Shem Tov volume], edited by Y. L. Maimon, pp. 84–90. Jerusalem: Mosad Harav Kook, 1960.

Kahane, S. Z. "The Foundation of Redemption in Hasidic Thought."

In *Hasidut Vezion* [Hasidism and Zion], edited by Simon Federbush, pp. 289–398. New York: Moriah, 1963.

Pechenik, Aaron. "Zadike Rizin Vechernibol Veyahasam Le'eretz Yisrael," (The Zadikim of Rizin and Chernibol and their attitude to Eretz Yisrael). In *Hasidut Vezion* [Hassidism and Zion], edited by Simon Federbush. New York: Moriah, 1963.

Schatz, Rivka. "Hayesod Hameshihi Bemahshevet Hahasidut [Messianic foundations of Hasidic thought]. *Molad* 211, (May–June 1967): 105–111.

———. "Lemahuto Shel Zadik Behasidut" (The essence of the Zadik in Hasidism]. *Molad* 18:144–145 (1960): 365–378.

Shazar, Zalman. "Kisufe Hage'ulah Vera'ayon Ha'aliyah Behasidut" [Longing for redemption and aliyah in Hasidism]. In *Sefer Habesht* [The Ba'al Shem Tov volume], edited by Y. L. Maimon, pp. 93–106. Jerusalem: Mosad Harav Kook, 1960.

Schechter, Solomon. "The Chassidim." In *Studies in Judaism,* First Series, pp. 150–189. New York: Atheneum Press, 1970.

Scholem, Gershom. "Demuto Hahistorit Shel Habesht" [The historical image of the Ba'al Shem Tov]. *Molad* 18:144–145 (1960): 335–356.

Tishby, Isaiah. "Ben Hasidut Leshabta'ut" [Between Hasidism and Sabbatianism]. *Knesset* 9 (1945): 238–268.

———. "Hasidut" [Hassidism]. *Ha'enziklopedia Ha'ibrit* [Hebrew Encyclopedia], vol. 17, pp. 769–822. Jerusalem: Massada Press, 1965.

Zeitlin, Hillel. "Hahavaya Hahasidit" [(essays on) the Hasidic experience]. In *Gevul Shne Olamot* [Between two worlds], pp. 225–374. Tel Aviv: Yavneh, 1965.

Zevin, Shlomo Yosef. "HABAD" [The Lubavitcher system of Hasidism]. In *Sofrim U'sefarim* [Authors and texts], pp. 239–281. Tel Aviv: Avraham Zioni, 1959.

GENERAL WORKS ON THE HOLOCAUST

Arendt, Hannah. *Eichmann in Jerusalem: A Report on the Banality of Evil.* New York: Viking Press, 1963.

Avtichi, Aryeh, and Ben Zakai Avtichi, eds. *Stolin; Sefer Zikaron* [Stolin: a memorial volume]. Israel: Irgun Yoze Stolin Vehasevivah Beyisrael, 1952.

Bauminger, Aryeh, Meir Bosk, and Natan Michael Gelber, eds. *Sefer Kraka; Ir We'em Beyisrael* [The book of Cracow: mother-city in Israel]. Jerusalem: Mosad Harav Kook, 1959.

Bettleheim, Bruno. *The Informed Heart.* New York: Free Press of Glencoe, 1960.

Blumenthal, Nachman, and Meyer Kozin, eds. *Lublin.* Vol. 5 of *Enziklopedia Shel Galuyot* [Memorial volumes of the diaspora countries and their communities]. 7 vols. Jerusalem and Tel Aviv: Enziklopedia Shel Galuyot Co., 1956.

Braham, Randolph L. *The Hungarian Jewish Catastrophe: A Selected and Annotated Bibliography.* Joint Documentary Projects, no. 4. New York: Yad Vashem and Yivo, 1962.

Brand, Joel, and Hansi Brand. *Hasatan Vehanefesh* [The Satan and the soul]. Israel: Ledori, 1960.

Buber, Martin. "Das Echte Gesprach und die Moglichkeiten des Friedens" [True dialogue and the possibilities of peace]. In *Address on the Occasion of the Award of the Peace Prize of the German Book Trade.* Frankfurt a.M., 1953.

Davidovitz, David. *Bate Kneset Bepolin Vehurbanam* [The destruction of the synagogues in Poland]. Jerusalem: Mosad Harav Kook, 1960.

Eck, Nathan. *Hatoim Bedarkhe Hamavet* [Wandering on the roads of death]. Jerusalem: Yad Vashem, 1960.

Feikatch, Mendel. *Bibliography of Hebrew Periodicals and Newspapers on the Catastrophe and Heroism.* 4 vols. Joint Documentary Projects, nos. 5–8. Jersualem: Yad Vashem and Yivo, 1966.

Fisher-Schein, Zeev. *Besod Yesharim Ve'edah: Mazevat Zikharon Likhilat Levov,* [In the council of the just and [their] community: a memorial to the community of Lvov]. Bnei Brak: Netzah, 1969.

Flinker, Moshe. *Hana'ar Moshe: Yomano Shel Moshe Flinker* [The lad Moses: the diary of Moses Flinker]. Jerusalem: Yad Vashem, 1961.

Frankel, Issar. *Yehide Segulah* [Extraordinary personalities]. Tel Aviv: Alif, 1955.

Friedman, Philip, ed. *Bibliografia Shel Hasefarim Ha'ivri'im al Hashoah Ve'al Hagevurah* [Bibliography of Hebrew books on destruction and heroism]. Joint Documentary Projects, no. 2. Jerusalem: Yad Vashem and Yivo, 1960.

Gar, Joseph. *Bibliography of Articles on the Catastrophe and Heroism in Yiddish Periodicals.* Joint Documentary Projects, no. 9. New York: Yad Vashem and Yivo, 1966.

———. *Bibliography of Articles on the Catastrophe and Heroism in North American Yiddish Periodicals.* Joint Documentary Projects, no. 10. New York: Yad Vashem and Yivo, 1969.

———, and Philip Friedman, eds. *Bibliografia Fun Yidishe Bicher Vegen*

Churban un Gevura [Bibliography of Yiddish books on destruction and heroism]. Joint Documentary Projects, no. 3, New York: Yad Vashem and Yivo, 1962.

Gelber, N. M., ed. *Lvov.* Vol. 4, pt. 1 of *Enziklopedia Shel Galuyot,* [Memorial volumes of the diaspora countries and their communities]. 7 vols. Jerusalem and Tel Aviv: Enziklopedia Shel Galuyot Co., 1956.

Glatstein, Jacob, Israel Knox, and Samuel Margoshes, eds. *Anthology of Holocaust Literature.* Philadelphia: Jewish Publication Society, 1969.

Greenbaum, Yitzchak, ed. *Warsaw.* Vol. 1, pt. 1 of *Enziklopedia Shel Galuyot* [Memorial volumes of the diaspora countries and their communities]. 7 vols. Jerusalem and Tel Aviv: Enziklopedia Shel Galuyot Co., 1953.

Gutman, Israel. *Anashim Va'efer: Sefer Auschwitz-Birkenau* [People and Dust: The Auschwitz-Birkenau Volume]. Merchavyah: Sifriat Hapoalim, 1957.

Hakibbutz Hame'uhad. *Dafim Leheker Hashoah Vehamered* [Tracts for research on the Holocaust and the revolt]. Tel Aviv: Hotza'at Hakibbutz Hame'uhad, 1951.

Hilberg, Raul. *The Destruction of the European Jews.* Chicago: Quadrangle, 1967.

Huberband, Shimon. *Kiddush Hashem* [Writings on the Holocaust from the hidden Ringelblum archives in the Warsaw Ghetto]. Tel Aviv: Zachor, 1969.

Kaplan, Hayyim Aaron. *Megilat Yisurin: Yoman Ghetto Warsha 1 BeSeptember, 1939–4 BeAugust, 1942* [The Stroll of agony: The Warsaw Ghetto diary, September 1, 1939–August 4, 1942]. Tel Aviv: Am Oved, 1966.

———. Scroll of Agony: *The Warsaw Diary of Chaim A. Kaplan.* Translated and edited by Abraham I. Katsh. New York: Macmillan, 1965.

Katzenelson, Yizhak. *Ketavim Aharonim: T'SH-TSH'D* (His Last Works: 1940–1944). Tel Aviv: Hotza'at Hakibbutz Hame'uhad Ubet Lohame Hageta'ot, 1951.

Korngreen, Philip, ed. *Tarnopol.* Vol. 3 of *Enziklopedia Shel Galuyot,* [Memorial volumes of the diaspora countries and their communities]. 7 vols. Jerusalem and Tel Aviv: Enziklopedia Shel Galuyot Co., 1955.

Landau, Yaakov. *Orot Meofel* [Light from darkness]. Bibliography of

Religious Works Published from 1933 to 1945. New York: Research Institute of Religious Jewry, 1957.

Lansky, Mordechai. *Meme Hayehudim Begetto Warsha* [The life of the Jews in the Warsaw ghetto]. Jerusalem: Yad Vashem, 1961.

Levin, Nora. *The Holocaust.* New York: Cromwell, 1968.

Mark, B., ed. *The Report of Jurgen Stroop.* Warsaw: Zydowski Instytut Historycny, 1958.

Margolit, Aryeh, ed. *Sefer Hazikharon Likhilat Ostrow* [Memorial volume of the Ostrow-Mezuveyzk community]. Tel Aviv: Irgun Ole Ostrow-Mezuveyzk B'Yisrael, 1960.

Mered Ghetto Warsha Be'ene Ha'oyev: Haduhot Shel Hageneral Yargen Stroop [The Warsaw Ghetto revolt from the perspective of the enemy: the reports of General Jurgen Stroop]. Jersualem: Yad Vashem, 1959.

Niger, Sh., ed. *Kiddush Hashem.* New York: Cyco Bicher Ferlag, 1948.

Oshry, Efraim. *Mimaamakim* [From out of the depths]. 2 vols. New York: Efraim Oshry, 1959–63.

Ringelblum, Emanuel. *Notizen Fun Warshaver Ghetto* [Notes from the Warsaw Ghetto]. Warsaw: Verlag Yiddish Buch, 1952.

Robinson, Jacob. *The Crooked Shall Be Made Straight: The Eichmann Trial, the Jewish Catastrophe and Hannah Arendt's Narrative.* Philadelphia: Jewish Publication Society, 1965.

———, and Philip Friedman. *Guide to Jewish History Under Nazi Impact.* Joint Documentary Projects, Bibliographical Series no. 1, New York: Yad Vashem and Yivo, 1960.

Seidman, Hillel. *Yoman Getto Warsha* [Warsaw Ghetto diary]. New York: Hotza'at Hashevuon die Yiddishe Woch, 1957.

Steinman, Eliezer, ed. *Brisk Delita* [Brisk in Latvia]. Vol. 2 of *Enziklopedia Shel Galuyot* [Memorial volumes of the diaspora countries and their communites]. 7 vols. Jerusalem and Tel Aviv: Enziklopedia Shel Galuyot Co., 1954.

Tabaksblat, Yisrael. *Hurban Lodz* [The destruction of Lodz]. Buenos Aires: Central Farband Fun Poilisha Yidden in Argentina, 1946.

Trunk, Isaiah. *Lodz-Ghetto: A Socio-Historical Study of the Second Largest Jewish Community in Poland Under the Nazi Rule.* New York: Yad Vashem and Yivo, 1962 [in Yiddish].

Unger, Eliezer. *Zekhor: Mime Kronot Hamavet* [Remember: From the days of the transports of death]. Tel Aviv: Hotza'at Massada, 1945.

Waga, Shlomo. *Hurben Chenstochow* [The destruction of Chenstochow]. Buenos Aires: Central Verband fun Poilishe Yidden in Argentina, 1949.

Weissbrod, Avraham. *Es Shtarbt a Shtetel: Megilas Skalat* [A town is dying: the scroll of Skalat]. Munich: Central Comitet fun die Bafreite Yiden, 1948.

Yad Vashem. *Jewish Resistance During the Holocaust: Proceedings of the Conference on Manifestations of Jewish Resistance. Jerusalem, April 7–11, 1968.* Jerusalem: Yad Vashem, 1970.

Articles

Agus, Jacob B. "God and the Catastrophe." *Conservative Judaism* 18, no. 4 (Summer 1964): 13–21.

Bettelheim, Bruno. "Individual and Mass Behavior in Extreme Situations." *Journal of Abnormal and Social Psychology* 38 (1943): 417–452.

Blumenthal, Nahman. "Mekorot Lamehkar Ha'amidah Hayehudit" [Sources for research on Jewish resistance]. In *Proceedings of the Conference on Manifestations of Jewish Resistance, Jerusalem, April 7–11, 1968*, pp. 34–36, Jerusalem: Yad Vashem, 1970.

Esh, Shaul. "Kiddush Hahayim Betokh Hahurban" [The sanctification of life during the destruction]. *Molad*, nos. 153–154 (1961), pp. 106–199.

Dvorzeski, Meir. "Ha'amidah Behaye Yom Yom Begeta'ot U'vemahanaot" [Resistance during daily routines in the ghettos and camps]. In *Jewish Resistance During the Holocaust: Proceedings of the Conference on Manifestations of Jewish Resistance, Jerusalem, April 7–11, 1968.* Jerusalem: Yad Vashem, 1970.

Kersh, Y. M. "Brief fun Churef-Gevorene Yiddishe Shtet un Shtetlech" [Letters from destroyed cities and towns]. *Forvertz,* July 11, 1946, p. 8.

Kurzweil, Baruch. "Job and the Possibility of Biblical Tragedy." In *Arguments and Doctrines: A Reader of Jewish Thinking in the Aftermath of the Holocaust,* edited by Arthur A. Cohen, pp. 325–344. New York: Harper & Row, 1970.

Poliakov. L. "Jewish Resistance in France." *Yivo Annual of Jewish Social Science* 8 (1953): 252–263.

Simon, Ernest, and Alexander, Donat. "Revisionist History of the Jewish Catastrophe." *Judaism* 12, no. 4 (Fall, 1963): 387–435.

Wiesel, Elie. "Jewish Values in the Post-Holocaust Future: A Symposium." *Judaism* 16, no. 3 (Summer 1967): 281–282.

Yahil, Leni. "Ha'amidah Hayehudit-Aspaklarya Lekiyum Hayehudi

Lezuroteha Hape'ilot Vehasebilot Bitkufat Hasho'ah" [Jewish resistance in its active and passive forms as a reflection of Jewish existence during the Holocaust]. In *Jewish Resistance During the Holocaust: Proceedings of the Conference on Manifestations of Jewish Resistance, Jerusalem, April 7–11, 1968*. Jerusalem: Yad Vashem, 1970.

HASIDISM, HASIDIM, AND THE HOLOCAUST

Eliav, Mordechai, ed. *Ani Ma'amin: Eduyot al Hayehem Umotam shel Anshe Emunah Bime Hashoah* [I believe: documentation on the life and death of believing Jews during the Holocaust]. Jerusalem: Mosad Harav Kook, 1969.

Levin, Isaac, ed. *Eleh Ezkerah: Osef Toldot Kedoshe, T'a's'h-Tash'Heh* [These will I remember: biographies of leaders of religious Jewry in Europe who perished during 1939–45]. 6 vols. New York: Research Institute of Religious Jewry, 1956–65.

Prager, Moshe. *Eleh Shelo Nikhne'u: Korot Tnuat Meri Hasidit Begeta'ot* [Those who did not succumb: the Hasidic resistance movement in the ghettos]. 2 vols. Bnei Brak: Nezah, 1963.

———. *Nitzotze Gevurah: Alilot Kiddush Hashem Beyamenu* [Sparks of heroism: incidents of martyrdom in our times]. Tel Aviv: Nezah, 1952.

Rothstein, Shmuel. *Rabbi Menahem Zemba: Hayav Upe'ulotav* [His life and achievements]. Tel Aviv: Nezah, 1948.

Spiro, Kalmish Kalonymus. *Esh Kodesh* [Holy fire]. Jerusalem: Va'ad Haside Piazesne, 1960.

Teichthal, Yissachar Shlomo. *Em Habanim Semeha* [The mother of children is happy]. Budapest: Zalman Katz Katzburg, 1943.

Unger, Menashe. *Sefer Kedoshim: Rebeim of Kiddush Hashem* [The book of martyrs: Hasidic rabbis as martyrs during the Holocaust]. New York: Shulsinger, 1967.

Yehezke'eli, Moshe. *Hatzalat Harebe Mebelz Megay Haharegah Bepolin: Mesupar Mipi Ed Re'iyah* [The rescue of the Belzer Rebbe from the valley of death in Poland: an eyewitness report]. Jerusalem: Yeshurun, 1962.

———. *Nes Hahatzalah Shel Harebe Megur: Sipuro Shel Ed Re'iyah* [The miraculous rescue of the Gerer Rebbe: an eyewitness report]. Jerusalem: Yeshurun, 1959.

Yeshivat Bet Abraham. *Zikhron Kadosh* [A holy remembrance]. Jerusalem: Yeshivat Bet Abraham, 1967.

Articles, Interviews, Letters

Bar Sarharitz, Beila. "Yamav Ha'aharonim Shel Habunker Hahasidi Begeto Warsha" [The last days of the Hasidic bunker in the Warsaw Ghetto]. *Bet Ya'akob* 25 (Sivan 5721–June 1961): 17, 19.

Bein, L. "Belzer Rebbe." *Unzer Weg* (Paris), August 20, 1948, p. 3.

———. "Wishnitzer Rebbe." *Unzer Weg* (Paris), September 11, 1947, p. 5.

Bobover Rebbe (Rabbi Shlomo Halberstam). Personal interview held in Brooklyn, New York, July 30, 1969.

Cahane, Lazer. "Der Piazesner Rebbe hot Verloiren Finf fun zein Familia in der Milchume" [The Piazesner Rebbe lost five members of his family in the war]. *Forward,* March 30, 1940, p. 8.

"Delegat Shildert Letzte Minuten fun Ostrovzer Rebbe," [Delegate describes last moments of Ostrovzer Rebbe]. *Morgen Jornal* (Jewish Morning Journal), June 3, 1946, p. 3.

Frankenthal, Yoel. "Nerot Hanukah Shehe'iru et Ofel Ha'abdut" [The Hanukah candles which brightened the atmosphere of slavery]. *Bet Ya'akob* 43 (December 1962): 9–10.

Friedensohn, Moshe. "Harab Reb Yehezkel Halevi Halstuk, Ha'admor Me'ostrowze" [Rabbi Yehezkel Halevi Halstuk, the Ostrowzer Rebbe. In *Eleh Ezkerah* [These I shall remember], vol. 4, edited by Isaac Levin. New York: Institute for Research of Orthodox Jewry, 1961.

Friedenthal, Aharon. "Der Ostrowzer Rebbe, H'Y'Di." *Unzer Weg* (Paris), November 18, 1949, p. 3; November 25, 1949, p. 3.

Ger, M. A. "Der Dombrover Rebbe Tanzt mit Zeine Hassidim" [The Dombrover Rebbe dances with his Hasidim]. *Der Tag* (The Day), March 3, 1946, p. 2 (sec. 2).

Gordon, Nisan. "Der Neder fun a Ruv a Kodosh Sich Unzunemen far Eretz Yisrael" [The vow of a martyred rabbi to devote himself to Eretz Yisrael]. *Tug–Morgen Jornal,* May 22, 1969, pp. 5, 14.

———. "Wurnung fun a Ruv Eyder Er iz Umgekummen in Nazi Eirope," [A warning of a rabbi prior to his death in Nazi Europe]. *Tug–Morgen Jornal,* May 15, 1969. pp. 5, 10.

Granatstein, Yehiel. "Protim Wegen Umkum fun Slonimer Rebbin" [Details concering the death of the Slonimer Rebbe]. *Poalei Emunei Yisrael, Bulletin* (Lodz), February 1947, pp. 57–58.

Kehilat Haharedim Collection. 344 files on the activities of the Habad movement (Lubavitcher Hasidim) during the Nazi occupation of France. In Yivo Archives (New York).

Kolitz, Zvi. "Yossel Rokover's Appeal to God." In *Out of the Whirlwind*, edited by Albert H. Friedlander, pp. 390–399. New York: Union of American Hebrew Congregations, 1968.

Meislitch, Zvi H. "Ma'asim Nifla'im Bemahaneh Oschwitz" [Remarkable happenings in Auschwitz]. *Bet Ya'akob* 4 (Elul 5719—August 1959): 74.

Nelkenbaum. Eliezer. "Der Sokolower Rebbe S'Z'L'." *Poale Emune Yisrael Bulletin* (Lodz), December, 1946, pp. 10, 18.

Oshry, Efraim. "Wie Azoi a Teil Litvishe Rabonim Zenen Umgekumen Al Kiddush Hashem" [How a number of Latvian rabbis went to their martyrdom]. *Poale Emune Yisrael Bulletin* (Lodz), February 1947, pp. 19–23.

Pardes, Y. "R'Aharon Eliyahu Gad S'Z'L." *Bet Ya'akob* 12 (Iyar, 5720—May 1960): 12.

"Die Petiere Fun Tchortkover Rebin S'Z'L." [The death of the Chortkover Rebbe of blessed memory]. *Wochenzeitung* (London), March 29, 1946, p. 1.

Prager, Moshe. "A Chassidic Underground in the Polish Ghettos." *Yad Vashem Bulletin*, nos. 6–7 (June 1960), pp. 10–12.

———. "Agadah Sheterem Nikhtebah al Mekadshe Hashem Bedorenu" [Unwritten legends concerning the sanctification of God's Name in our generation]. *Bet Ya'akob* 4 (Elul 5719—August 1959): 6–7.

———. "Krakow—Yerushalayim D'Polin" [Cracow—The Jerusalem of Poland]. *Bet Ya'akob* 10 Adar 5720—March 1960): 16–17.

———. "Lapid Hai Shel Kiddush Hashem" [A flaming torch of *Kiddush Hashem*. *Bet Ya'akob* 12 (Iyar 5720—May 1960): 12.

———. "Reb Mendel M'Pavianich Holekh Letreblinka" [Rabbi Mendel from Pavianich goes to Treblinka]. In *Sefer Milkhamot Hageta'ot* [The Book of the Ghetto Wars], edited by Yitzchak Zuckerman and Moshe Bsok, pp. 517–519. Tel Aviv: Hakkibutz Hame'uhad, 1956.

———. "Tnu'at Hahasidut Bitkufat Hashoah" [The Hasidic movement during the Holocaust period]. In *Sefer Habesht* [The Ba'al Shem Tov volume], edited by Y. L. Maimon, pp. 265–273. Jerusalem: Mosad Harav Kook, 1960.

Rochman, Leib. "Yumim Noroim Bei Die Zwei Greste Rebeyim" (Belzer un Gerer) [High holy days with the two greatest Hasidic Rebbes]. *Unzer Weg* (Paris), October 6, 1950, p. 3.

Schwartz, Elimelech Hacohen. "Agudisten in Lodzer Ghetto" [Members of the Agudah movement in the ghetto of Lodz]. *Dos Yidishe Wort* 82 (November 1963): 108–109.

———. "Der Zadik fun Ostrowze" [The Zadik from Ostrowze]. *Unzer Leben* (Berlin), December 27, 1946, p. 30.

Segalawitch, Z. "Der Yid in Der Lange Kapote" [The Jew in the long caftan]. *Unzer Weg* (Paris), April 13, 1949, pp. 3–4.

Seidman, Hillel. "Gadlus in Kedush-Gettlecher Ploim" [Greatness within holiness—godly wonders]. *Beshaar* (Paris), July 1948, pp. 2, 4.

"Hillel Zeitlin." *Morgen Jornal*, January 26, 1947, p. 7.

"Letzter Brief vun Hillel Zeitlin" [The last letter of Hillel Zeitlin]. *Unzer Weg* (Paris), Pentecost Eve, 1946, p. 3.

Stein, David. "Hasidishen Yid Hot Ungefihrt mit Untergrunt in Belgia" [Hasidic Jew led underground in Belgium]. *Morgen Jornal*, July 26, 1945. p. 5.

Sternberg, Ya'akov. "Hahavai Hayehudi Bime Hashoah" [The Jewish essence during the Holocaust]. In *Sefer Kraka* [The book of Cracow], edited by Aryeh Bauminger et al. Jerusalem: Mosad Harav Kook, 1959.

Weiss, Yosef. "Oshviz Ha'aheret: Seder Hashai in Zemer *Had Gadya*" [The other Auschwitz: a secret Seder with the *Had Gadya* melody]. *Bet Ya'akob* 59 (March 1964): 6–7.

Zeitlin, Ahron. "A Maise mit a Rebben un Zein Zuhn" [An occurrence of a Rebbe and his son]. *Morgen Jornal*, July 12, 1946. p. 5.

GENERAL WORKS

The Bible

Mikra'ot Gedolot [The Complete Scriptures]. 10 vols. New York: Pardes Publishing House, 1951. (Including commentaries of Rashi and Nahmanides.)

Pentateuch and Haftorahs. Edited by J. H. Hertz. London: Soncino Press, 1952.

The Torah: The Five Books of Moses. Philadelphia: Jewish Publication Society, 1962.

The Talmud and Rabbinic Literature

Ayin Ya'akob. 6 vols. Vilna: Hotza'at Rom, 1936.

Kaddushin, Max. *The Rabbinic Mind*. New York: Jewish Theological Seminary, 1952.

Maimonides, Moses. *Igarot Harambam* [The letters of Maimonides]. Jerusalem: Mosad Harav Kook, 1960.

———. *Mishneh Torah.* 5 vols. New York: Hotza'at Feldheim, 1953.

Midrash Rabbah. 2 vols. New York: Hotza'at Hil, 1953.

Talmud Babli (The Babylonian Talmud). 16 vols. New York: Pardes Publishing Co., n.d.

Yalkut Shimoni. 2 vols. Jerusalem, 1960.

Liturgy

Daily Prayer Book. Translated by Philip Birnbaum. New York: Hebrew Publishing Co., 1949.

Daily Prayer Book. Edited by Joseph H. Hertz. New York: Bloch Publishing Co., 1957.

Kinoth for the Ninth of Av. Translated by Abraham Rosenfeld. London: I. Labworth, 1965.

The Passover Haggadah. Translated by Philip Birnbaum. New York: Hebrew Publishing Co., 1953.

The Prayer Book. Edited by Ben Zion Bokser. New York: Hebrew Publishing Co., 1961.

The Standard Prayer Book. New York: Bloch Publishing Co., 1957.

Kabbalah: Primary Sources

Sefer Hazohar [The Book of the Zohar] Edited by Yehudah Rosenberg. 3 vols. New York: Chorev Printing, 1924.

Kabbalah: Secondary Sources

Ginzberg, Louis. "The Cabalah." In *On Jewish Law and Lore.* New York: Atheneum Press, 1970.

Scholem, Gershom G. "Isaac Luria and His School." In *Major Trends in Jewish Mysticism*, pp. 243–286. New York: Schocken Books, 1954.

Jewish History and Thought

Baron, Salo. "The Emergence of Israel." In *Great Ages and Ideas of the Jewish People*, edited by Leo W. Schwartz, pp. 420–448. New York: Modern Library, 1956.

Buber, Martin. *Israel and Palestine: The History of an Idea.* New York: Farrar, Straus & Young, 1953.

Dubnow, Shimon. *Divre Yeme Olam* [World Jewish history]. Tel Aviv: Dvir, 1954.

Klausner, Yosef. *Historiya shel Habayit Hasheni* [History of the Second Temple]. 5 vols. Jerusalem: Achiasaf, 1958.
Rabinowich, Israel. *Of Jewish Music.* Montreal: Book Center, 1952.
Selzer, Michael, ed. *Zionism Reconsidered.* New York: Macmillan Co., 1970.
Speigel, Shalom. *The Last Sacrifice.* New York: Schocken Books, 1969.
Zoref, Efraim. *Haye Harab Kook* [The life of Rabbi Kook]. Jerusalem: Hotza'at Hasefarim Ha'aretz Yisraelit, 1947.

Historical Research

Gottschalk, Louis. *Understanding History: A Primer of Historical Method.* New York: Alfred A. Knopf, 1950.

Notes

NOTES TO INTRODUCTION

1. For the purposes of this study, a response to the Holocaust is defined as any properly documented and confirmed activity, demonstration, written or oral communication, or instruction by a Rebbe (Hasidic leader), ordinary Hasid, or group of Hasidim that pertains to Holocaust events, took place during the Holocaust, and is documented in accordance with standard historical methods.

NOTES TO CHAPTER 1

1. Deuteronomy 25:19, Exodus 17:14.
2. Genesis 18:26, Psalms 13:22:2, Job 9:21.
3. For examples of talmudic exposition of the theodicy theme, see Talmud Berakhot 7a, Genesis Rabbah 49.
4. "What constituted the uniqueness and the greatness of Hasidism is not a teaching, but a mode of life . . . that shapes a community." Martin Buber, *The Origin and Meaning of Hasidism*, p. 24.
5. Gershom Scholem, *Major Trends in Jewish Mysticism*, pp. 324–350.
6. The two terms are not interchangeable. Zadik is a generic, used in the impersonal sense. When referring to his own master, the Hasid refers to the *Zadik* as *Rebbe*, which is derived from the term *Rav*, indicating "teacher" or "master." Aaron Wertheim, *Halakhot Vehalikhot Behasidut*, pp. 231–234.
7. Nora Levin, *The Holocaust;* Joseph Guri, "The Jewish Holocaust in Soviet Writings," pp. 4–5; Andrew Sharf, "The British Press and the Holocaust," pp. 169–191.
8. Max Kadushin, *The Rabbinic Mind*, p. 44. See also Talmud Sanhedrin 74b.
9. Kadushin, p. 214.
10. Martin Buber, "Das Echte Gespraech und die Moeglichkeiten des Friedens, p. 5; Jacob Robinson and Philip Friedman, *Guide to Jewish History Under Nazi Impact*, pp. xxi, xxvii.
11. Elie Wiesel, "Jewish Values in the Post-Holocaust Future," pp. 281–282.

12. As noted in the indices of the ten volumes of Holocaust bibliography prepared by Yad Vashem–Yivo. See Bibliography for full citation.

13. Samuel Abba Horodetzky, *Hahasidut Vetoratah*, p. 100. See also Buber, *Origin and Meaning of Hasidism*, pp. 24–25. "[Hasidism] remolds the basic motif of mystical speculation into life motifs, not merely in the presentations of the teaching, but above all in life itself." Ibid., p. 63.

14. Scholem, *Major Trends*, p. 347.

NOTES TO CHAPTER 2

1. Robinson and Friedman, *Guide to Jewish History Under Nazi Impact*, pp. 115, 119.

2. Zeev Fischer-Schein, *Besod Yesharim Ve'edah*, p. 9.

3. Ibid. "As a native of Lvov I was invited to participate in the writing of the Book of Lvov prepared as one of a series." N. M. Gelber, *Lvov*, vol. IV, pt. 1. "[At] A meeting of the writers' panel for this volume, I met some thirty people: doctors, lawyers, poets, writers and journalists and among these were to be found only two observant Jews. . . . During the discussions and arguments that followed, the nature and contents [of the proposed volume] became evident. I realized that they would falsify completely the traditional Jewish image of Lvov and would describe it as a secular-nationalist, proletarian, and socialist city devoid of its most important source—that of authentic traditional Judaism. I have seen this time and again in the hundreds of memorial volumes which ignore the truth, that the great majority of Jews in the destroyed communities were believing Jews." Since 1971, when this study was completed, the "religious gap" in the literature on the Holocaust has been filled to a great extent, and consequently an updated bibliographic survey would be a desideratum. The author is grateful to be included among the pioneers in this specialized field, which deserves continued critical attention.

4. Joseph Gar, pp. 165–185.

5. Ibid. The secularist Jewish political movements were highly vocal. Of the 258 Yiddish periodicals published during and immediately following the Holocaust, only fourteen were sponsored by Orthodox religious groups. Ibid., pp. 193–200.

6. Seidman, *Yoman Getto Warsha;* Huberband, *Kiddush Hashem.*

7. *Hana'ar Moshe: Yomano Shel Moshe Flinker.*

8. Ringelblum, *Notizen Fun Warshaver Ghetto.* In English: Chaim Aaron Kaplan, *Scroll of Agony: The Warsaw Diary of Chaim A. Kaplan.*

9. These are referred to as "Torahs," an abbreviation of *divre Torah* ("words of Torah"). See Wertheim, *Laws and Traditions in Hasidism*, p. 165. It is not certain under what conditions the Torahs of the Piazesne Rebbe were delivered. Following each Sabbath day, they were recorded in his own handwriting (letter from Mr. Joseph Shapiro, October 13, 1970, p. 2).

10. *Esh Kodesh* will hereafter be cited as *EK*. The biographical material given here was drawn from "The History of the Piazesner Rebbe," edited by Aaron Soresky, in the appendix of *EK*. Information was also obtained by personal

correspondence with the Rebbe's nephew, Mr. Joseph Shapiro of Tel Aviv, October 13, 1970.

11. Herafter cited as *EHS*.

12. *EHS*, introduction (pagination by researcher, p. 21). See also the biographical introduction to vol. 1 of Rabbi Teichthal's responsa, *Mishne Sachir*.

13. *EHS*, pp. 14–17.

14. Prager, "The Hasidic Movement During the Holocaust Period," p. 270.

15. Prager, *Eleh Shelo Nikhne'u*.

16. Yehezke'eli, *Nes Hahatzalah Shel Harebe Megur* and *Hatzalat Harebe Mebelz Mege Haharegah*.

17. Yehezke'eli, *Nes Hahatzalah*, p. 118.

18. Menashe Unger, *Sefer Kedoshim*.

19. Isaac Levin, *Eleh Ezkerah*. Mordechai Eliav, ed., *Ani Ma'amin*. Yaffa Eliach, *Hasidic Tales of the Holocaust*.

NOTES TO CHAPTER 3

1. The interrelationship between Sabbatianism and Hasidism, reflected in a number of points of contact during the critical transitional period at the onset of the eighteenth century, is discussed by Scholem, *Major Trends*, pp. 330–334. See also I. Tishby, "Ben Shabtaut Vehasidut," pp. 238–268.

2. Scholem, *Major Trends*, pp. 233–234, 341–342.

3. Buber, *Origin and Meaning of Hasidism*, p. 24. See also Scholem, *Major Trends*, p. 338.

4. Ibid., p. 344.

5. Rivka Schatz Uffenheimer, *Quietistic Elements in 18th Century Hassidic Thought*, p. 16.

6. Yaakov Yosef of Polnoya, *Toldot Ya'akov Yosef*, p. 96d, 165d (hereafter cited as *Toldot*). See also Buber, *Origin and Meaning of Hasidism*, p. 208.

7. *Tolodot*, p. 49b.

8. *Zava'at Harivash*, in *Shivhe Habesht*, p. 21.

9. Buber, *Origin and Meaning of Hasidism*, p. 75.

10. "He should strive to petition the Almighty only for that which God conceives as good for him [man], and not what appears so to man's understanding, since what seems in his [man's] opinion as good may not be so in reality. He should simply thrust all his concerns and necessities upon Him, blessed be He." *Zava'at Harivash*, p. 3. See also *Toldot*, p. 97b.

11. Buber, *Origin and Meaning of Hasidism*, p. 137, 180–181.

12. Scholem, *Major Trends*, p. 335.

13. Dov Ber of Mezritch, *Magid Debarav Leya'akov*, p. 5a.

14. *Toldot*, pp. 86b, 86c.

15. Shneur Zalman of Liadi, *Likute Amarim Tanya*, p. 18b. See also Scholem, *Major Trends*, p. 262, elaborating on the concept of man as a "micro-cosmos" and God as a "macro-Anthropos."

16. Uffenheimer, *Quietistic Elements*, pp. 22–31.

17. Ibid., p. 13.

18. Buber, *Origin and Meaning of Hasidism,* p. 206; Nahman of Brazlav, *Zimrat Ha'aretz,* p. 2b.

19. Menahem Mendel of Vitebsk, *Pri Ha'aretz,* p. 5.

20. *Toldot,* p. 195b.

21. *Zohar,* Ahare Mot, pp. 62, 75.

22. Uffenheimer, *Quietistic Elements,* pp. 41–53.

23. Shneur Zalman of Liadi, *Likute Amarim,* pp. 30b–33a.

24. "I have placed the Lord always before me" (Psalms 16:8). *Shiviti* [I have placed] is also related to *hishtavut* [from *s-w-h,* meaning equal], implying that all events were received with equanimity, irrespective of whether people will praise or insult him"; *Zava'at Haribash,* p. 14.

25. Also referred to as *bittul atzmi.* Uffenheimer, *Quietistic Elements,* pp. 16, 30. See also Menahem Mendel of Vitebsk, *Pri Ha'aretz Im Etz Pri,* p. 76.

26. In Hebrew, the term *Ayin* is obtained by juxtaposing the three letters in *Ani.* See Uffenheimber, *Quietistic Elements,* p. 24.

27. Uffenheimer, *Quietistic Elements,* pp. 155–167, see esp. fn. 29, p. 164.

28. Nahman of Brazlav, *Likute Mohran,* p. 244. Manahem Mendel of Vitebsk, *Likute Amarim,* p. 55.

29. Scholem, *Major Trends,* p. 343. See also Buber, *Origin and Meaning of Hasidism,* p. 41.

30. Wertheim, *Laws and Traditions in Hasidism,* p. 158.

31. *Toldot,* p. 151.

32. Wertheim, *Laws and Traditions in Hasidism,* p. 156; Scholem, *Major Trends,* p. 347.

NOTES TO CHAPTER 4

1. *Shalosh Seudot,* the third of the four traditional Sabbath meals, held to be of mystical significance. The "meals" were likely performed symbolically or under severely limited circumstances.

2. "Until I entered into the sanctuary of God, and considered their end." When the Messiah reestablishes the sanctuary of God, only then will man understand the "end" (goals, objectives) of God's ways.

3. Already established in biblical tradition. See Isaiah 55:8, "For My thoughts are not your thoughts, neither are your ways My ways."

4. Unger, *Sefer Kedoshim,* p. 151.

5. Yehezke'eli, *Hatzalat Harebbe,* p. 51. See ibid., p. 27, for a similar response.

6. In a letter to his brother in Palestine (Rabbi Yeshiah Shapiro), in the winter of 1943; *EK,* p. 8 (introductory pagination by the researcher).

7. *EK,* p. 97., with reference to Genesis 27:22. In rabbinic tradition the "hands of Esau" symbolize warfare, while the "voice of Jacob" refers to study of Torah.

8. Bereshit Rabbah, p. 12; *Yalkut Shimoni,* Genesis 1:13, 2:19.

9. *EK,* pp. 75–76.

10. A basic, complex theosophic doctrine of Rabbi Isaac Luria, the leader of the sixteenth-century Palestinian kabbalistic school. Lit., "the breaking of

the vessels," in which the divine lights flowing from primordial space had to be "caught and preserved" in special vessels—the transfer from infinite to the finite realms. The lower six of the ten *sefirot* could not contain the powerful lights and were shattered. For full treatment of the implications of *Shevirah* see Scholem, *Major Trends*, pp. 265–268, or the chapter dealing with Lurian Kabbalah, pp. 244–286.

11. *EK*, p. 124.

12. Lit., the "hidden countenance" (of God). Based on Deuteronomy 31:18, "Yet I will keep My countenance hidden on that day, because of all the evil they have done," the absence of revelation or God's apparent presence has signified the severe, unrelenting, and punishing deity in biblical and rabbinic tradition.

13. *EK*, pp. 40–41, 130–131.

14. Yehezke'eli, *Hatzalat Harebbe*, pp.120–121.

15. *EK*, pp. 15–16. Actually, the midrashic literature speaks of God's dilemma of a world without either *Din* or *Rahamim*. See Midrash Rabbah, Genesis 12:15, and *Yalkut Shimoni*, Genesis 2:19.

16. *EK*, p. 42. Employing kabbalistic letter-word manipulation, *EK* notes the presence of the Divine Name of *Shadai*, which symbolizes God's attribute of protection, in the pronounced Hebrew letters of *y*=*tz*=*r* (the root of *yetzer*): *yud-tzadi-resh*.

17. Ibid., pp. 68–69.

18. Ibid., p. 163.

19. Baruch Yashar, *Bet Komarno*, p. 130.

20. Unger, *Sefer Kedoshim*, pp. 237, 239.

21. "From the beginning, Thou hast distinguished man by endowing him with reason and filled him with the desire to seek Thy presence." Morris Silverman, High Holiday Prayer Book, p. 456.

22. Close to a literal reading of the Hebrew *Atah hivdalta enosh merosh* ("Yet from the first you singled out mortal man"), the second half of the exegesis reverts to its original context, *Vatakirehu laamod lefanekha* ("and you consider him worthy to stand in Thy presence").

23. Yashar, *Bet Komarno*, p. 130. Yashar's version differs from that of Unger, *Sefer Kedoshim*, p. 352, with the Komarnor's application of the following talmudic dictum: "When a king stands before you, do not dare raise an eyebrow, though a scorpion may sting you or a serpent is wrapped about your ankle." Talmud Berakhot 30b, and related dicussion, p. 33a.

24. "Therefore, the limbs which Thou hast spread forth upon us . . . all my bones shall exclaim, 'Lord, who is like unto Thee!' " *Standard Prayer Book*, p. 183.

25. *EK*, p. 36.

26. Amalek (Exodus 17:8–16, Deuteronomy 25:17–19) was the archadversary of the Israelites in the biblical period and later represented the eternal foe of the Jewish people.

27. *EK*, p. 169. Among the "acceptance with love" motifs, see Unger, *Sefer Kedoshim*, p. 151 (the Zaloshizer Rebbe); *EK*, pp. 74, 169.

28. *EK*, p. 55.

29. Ibid., p. 26

30. In an earlier passage (p. 172) *EK* points to the total immersion in the mikveh (ritual pool, central to Hasidic doctrine and observance) as the symbol of *bittul hayesh* and complete subjugation to God's will.
31. Ibid., p. 179.
32. Unger, *Sefer Kedoshim*, p. 419.
33. Talmud Sotah 14a.
34. The functioning of finite creatures within the universe was made possible by the withdrawal of God, as it were, into a *concentrated* and *self-limited (tzimtzum)* space. Some kabbalists interpret this act as the divine's self-imposed exile from his own infinite existence. See Scholem, *Major Trends*, pp. 260–264.
35. *EK*, pp. 168–169.
36. Ibid., p. 177, quoting Talmud Berakhot 63a.
37. The thief has complete faith in God (that he will not be caught). The talmudic text makes no such reference. But see *Ayin Ya'akov*, Berakhot, p. 112.
38. Unger, *Sefer Kedoshim*, p. 419.
39. *EK*, p. 175.
40. Ibid., p. 97.
41. Ibid., p. 44
42. Probably during the Bar Kokhba revolt, 132–135 C.E. A synthesis of a number of talmudic sources, the Yom Kippur litany *Eleh Ezkerah* records the angels' challenge and God's angry response thus: "The angels of heaven called out in bitterness, 'Is this the Torah and this its reward? Behold, the foe blasphemes Thy great and revered name and vilifies and scorns Thy Torah!' Whereupon a voice from heaven replied, 'If I hear another sound uttered I will turn the world to water, I will devastate both heaven and earth.' " Philip Birnbaum, *High Holy Day Prayer Book*, pp. 841–842.
43. *EK*, p. 187.
44. Moshe Friedensohn, "Harab Reb Yehezkel Halevi Halstik, Ha'admor Meostrowze," p. 55.
45.For a full discussion of Hasidic allegorization of mitzvot, see Wertheim, *Laws and Traditions in Hasidism*, pp. 52–56.
46. *EK*, p. 11, with reference to Deuteronomy 22:1–4 and Exodus 23:4.
47. *EK*, pp. 126–27.
48. No specific passage is cited, but *EK* does cite Rashi's commentary to Numbers 20:15 (the patriarchs are filled with anguish when suffering befalls the Jew).
49. *EK*, p. 38.
50. Talmud Ta'anit 11a. For the Hasidic teaching that temporary suffering in this world makes it possible to enjoy the full benefits of the world-to-come, see *Likute Shem Tov*, p. 35.
51. Leviticus 10:3. Moses quotes God's response following the sudden death of the two sons of Aaron. The Rebbe employs the root *k-b-d* = "heavy" "burden," rather than *k-b-d* = "honor" "glory."
52. Unger, *Sefer Kedoshim*, p. 353, interpreting "It will be difficult for the simple people to comprehend, etc., "fails to note that God and not the people is the subject of *ekaved*. Yashar's more accurate version includes the

Rebbe's pleas for Jews to be among "those near to God" and sanctify and honor His Name in unquestioning martydom. Baruch Yashar, *Bet Komarno*, p. 130. This does not detract from the critical thrust of this interpretation.

53. Deuteronomy 33:1.

54. Deuteronomy 34:12.

55. Genesis 1:1. Seeking to establish a frame of unity and continuity between Deuteronomy and Genesis is acceptable in Hasidic and mystical exegesis and consistent with Jewish tradition. At the festival reading of Simhat Torah, when Deuteronomy is completed, it is customary to renew the reading cycle immediately with Genesis. This is to indicate that a Torah study never ends.

56. Implied in the term *bereshit*, Genesis 1:1.

57. Implied in the combined phrases "This is the blessing" and "*before* the very eyes of all Israel" from the closing readings in Deuteronomy.

58. *EK*, p. 134.

59. Ibid., p. 139.

60. Ibid., p. 69.

61. *Gevurah*, the divine attribute of might or power, is utilized when God overcomes His enemies or dispenses judgment and punishment. Also referred to as *Din*. One of the "ten spheres or *sefirot* of Divine manifestation in which God emerges from His hidden abode." Scholem, *Major Trends*, pp. 212–213. The attributes of *Hesed* (kindness or love) and *Rahamim* (compassion) referred to throughout his study are also among the ten *sefirot*.

62. *EK*, p. 165. The *Zohar* makes reference to indiscriminate destruction. "For when the angel of destruction obtains authorisation to destroy, he does not discriminate between innocent and guilty." The *Zohar*, vol. I, p. 113.

63. *EK*, p. 10, referring to Sarah's sudden death when she learned of the binding of her son Isaac (Kohelet Rabati 9:2). *EK* cites the teaching of Rabbi Menahem Mendel of Rimanov (d. 1815), who sees in this Midrash a veiled protest to God, alerting Him (!) to the consequences of excess suffering.

64. Though *EK*, p. 108, offers the traditional response of *tehiat hametim* (the resurrection of the dead during the messianic period), Hasidism placed a great premium on living life in the here and now. The challenge, therefore, stands. "The Kotzker Rebbe said that he could likely bring life to the dead, but would prefer to inject life into the living." *Emet Ve'emunah*, p. 135.

65. *EK*, p. 49.

66. Ibid., p. 114. "*Wehakadosh barukh hu lo abid dina, beli dina.*" The benevolent and virtuous nature of God is firmly established in Rabbinic literature, *Talmud Berakhot*, p. 60b, "*Kol de'abid rahmana, letab abid.*" (All that which is done by God is for the good.)

67. *EK*, p. 115.

68. Ibid., pp. 157–158.

69. Ibid., pp. 56–58, 100.

70. *EK*, p. 137.

71. Ibid., pp. 5, 9, 81.

72. Ibid., p. 9.

73. Ibid., p. 147, referring to the intense Jewish life which existed in Eastern Europe prior to the Holocaust.

74. *EHS*, pp. 78–79.

75. *EK*, pp. 21–22, 114. *EK* utilizes the Midrash which describes the giving of the Torah in the desert under adverse conditions.

76. Shemini Atzeret, the eighth and concluding day of the festival of Booths (Sukkot) is portrayed in rabbinic literature (*Tanhuma Hakadum*, Pinhas) as the time of year when God and His people are alone to themselves following the first seven days of the festival, in which the "seventy nations of the world" were honored with pomp and circumstance. *EK* interprets the contrasting conclusion of the festival (see Numbers 29:36 vs. Numbers 29:32, 29:29, etc.) as a symbol of God's *tzimtzum* (self-limitation) and a state of the suffering of God with His beloved people. *EK*, p. 76.

77. Ibid., pp. 81–82.

78. Ibid., p. 83. Since God is without limits, his suffering, unlike man's is limitless. Ibid., p. 159.

79. Ibid., p. 191.

80. Ibid., p. 9.

81. Ibid., pp. 27–28. Thus even the psychological relief valve of someone else's empathy for another's suffering is not evident.

82. Ibid., p. 11.

83. Ibid., pp. 16–17.

84. Ibid., pp. 190–191.

85. Ibid., p. 100. The example of the Nazarite (Numbers 6:1–21) is invoked, pointing to the biblical negation of needlessly bringing suffering and self-denial upon oneself. At the conclusion of the Nazarite's period of self-imposed abstinence, he is required to bring a number of sacrifices, including the sin offering (Numbers 6:14).

86. *EK*, p. 27.

87. Ibid., pp. 70–71. By implication, man contributes to God's sanctity—*Kiddush Hashem*. Further, since God suffers together with man, the opportunity presents itself to sympathize with God in His suffering.

88. Genesis 22:1–19; *EK*, pp. 72–73.

89. *EK*, p. 129.

90. Exodus 13:21.

91. *EK*, p. 20.

92. Yehezke'eli, *Hatzalat Harebe Mebelz*, pp. 8, 27. Bezalel Landau and Nathan Ortner, *Harav Hakadosh Mebelz*, p. 95.

NOTES TO CHAPTER 5

1. Dov Ber of Mezritch, *Magid Debarav Leya'akov*, p. 14.

2. *Likute Keter Shem Tov*, p. 11 (hereafter cited as *LKST*). The *mahshavot zarot* (alien thoughts) distort God's true presence in the world. It is man's duty to "rescue" the alien sparks and hasten the process of *tikkun* (rehabilitation) which, in turn, will stimulate the coming of the Messiah and salvation.

3. Uffenheimer, *Quietistic Elements*, p. 21.

4. "As a result of this outlook (namely, man is not in a position to judge that which is beneficial to him), Hasidic circles did not hesitate to determine

that there is little purpose in praying for the abolition of suffering. It is best to pray for man's benefit in accordance with God's will." Ibid., p. 35.

5. *Zava'at Harivash*, in *Shivhe Habesht*, p. 3.

6. "For the believing Hasid the attributes of *Din* and *Rahamim* were blurred and it did not matter which attributes God applied to him." Uffenheimer, *Quietistic Elements*, p. 34.

7. *Mah shepagam beolamot haelyonim* ("that which He made defective in the cosmic realm"). A veiled reference to *shevirat hakelim*. *Or Hameier*, p. 27.

8. Uffenheimer, *Quietistic Elements*, p. 33. An extreme example of a positive Hasidic interpretation of the catastrophic *shevirat hakelim* is to be found in the work of Rabbi Haim Haika of Admor. He views the Shekhinah as part of the *tikkun* process; thus the shattering of the vessels is no longer a catastrophe, since their *tikkun* involves the divine. Ibid., pp. 125–126.

9. *LKST*, p. 8.

10. *Zava'at Harivash*, in *Shivhe Habesht*, p. 15.

11. "There is the principle that God, blessed be He, projects goodness and mercy upon His people Israel. And when at times, God forbid, an evil occurrence strikes Israel, it is only because the final product will prove to be beneficial to Israel. However, if God forbid, the net result will not prove to be beneficial, then God [to begin with] will refrain from bringing evil upon Israel." Levi Yitzchak of Berdichev, *Kedushat Levi Hashalem*, pp. 32, 59.

12. *Zava'at Harivash*, p. 21; identical with the Response of *EK*, p. 57.

13. The Hasidic emphasis on *kabalah be'ahavah* has its roots in the Midrash: "Rabbi Yitzchak taught: 'They justify and accept with love all the decrees that You may bring upon Your creations' " (*Yalkut Shimoni* 1:3). Bereshit 1:10 has the variant reading, "They accept it with faith."

14. The following was the reply to the Besht: "Will you then pray that God, blessed be He, will give me strength to enable me to accept all with love?" To which the Besht responded: "You speak the truth. One must pray for this." *Heikhal Haberakhah*, p. 258.

15. Uffenheimer, *Quietistic Elements*, pp. 35–38.

16. *LKST*, p. 37.

17. *EK*, p. 55.

18. Shlomo of Luzk, *Divre Shlomo*, vol. II, p. 57b.

19. *EK*, p. 26.

20. "Self," in Hasidic terminology *ani* or *yesh*, refers to the inhibiting ego forces that make it impossible to achieve *devekut* and *bitahon*.

21. *LKST*, p. 29. A person embued with complete *bitahon* does not seek the material.

22. Referring to the talmudic caution against theodic and theosophic speculation (Mishnah Hagigah 2:2). Only Rabbi Akiba, of the four scholars who entered the "garden" of speculation (*pardes*), "left in peace" (Talmud Hagigah 14b).

23. Rabbi Yitzchak Isaac of Komarno, *Netiv Mitzvotekha*.

24. Rabbi Yitzchak Isaac of Komarno, *Heikal Haberakhah*, p. 95.

25. *Quietistic Elements*, p. 37.

26. *Kedushat Levi*, p. 40. The Nahshon reference is from a midrashic source, Talmud Sotah 37a.

27. "For he who believes in *Hashgahah Pratit* . . . and is aware that all that occurs to man emanates from Him, etc." *LKST*, p. 11. "All that occurs in this world is surely *hashgahah pratit*." Menahem Mendel Shneersohn of Lubavich, *Likute Sihot*, p. 10.

28. *Zava'at Harivash*, p. 9.

29. Uffenheimer, *Quietistic Elements*, pp. 46–47.

30. Ibid., p. 22.

31. *Netiv Mitzvoteka*, Shvil Emunah 1:7.

32. *Zava'at Harivash*, pp. 4, 9.

33. Uffenheimer, *Quietistic Elements*, pp. 26–27.

34. *Netiv Mitzvoteka*, Shvil Emunah 3:15. "*Simhah* [joy] is the expansion of the holy," says the Kotzker Rebbe. *Emet Ve'emunah*, p. 34. God reaches out where there is joy.

35. Uffenheimer, *Quietistic Elements*, p. 18.

35a. Meister Eckhart, German mystical theologian (c. 1210–c. 1328). Miguel de Molinos, Spanish mystic (1640–1697).

36. Ibid., p. iii.

37. David Rudavsky, *Emancipation and Adjustment*, pp. 61, 109, 256.

38. Uffenheimer, *Quietistic Elements*, p. 18.

39. Scholem, *Major Trends*, pp. 315–319.

40. *Kedushat Levi*, p. 40. "For all depends upon the acts of those below, etc." Ibid., p. 27.

41. Ibid., p. 153. The allusion is to a selection from the liturgy repeated thrice daily, "Sound the great *shofar* for our freedom." Philip Birnbaum, *Daily Prayer Book*, pp. 87–88. Zvi Kolitz's "Yossel Rakover's Appeal to God" is a work of fiction which attempts to recreate a Rabbi Levi Yitzchak figure in the ruins of the Warsaw Ghetto, taking God to task, yet believing in Him, despite all.

42. *Sefer Habesht*, pp. 317–318.

43. Uffenheimer, *Quietistic Elements*, pp. 17, 35, 39. The general absence of activism, especially in the secular realm, may account for the virtual nonexistence of Hasidic underground press activities noted above. Certainly, except for sacred writings or material related to Hasidism, including letters of the Rebbe to his Hasidim, neither Hasidim nor their Rebbes contributed anything of significance to the field of journalism or secular literature. Hasidic activism assumed different forms, as will be noted below.

44. Buber, *Origin and Meaning of Hasidism*, pp. 36–37.

45. Yehudah Ibn Shmuel, "Memishnato shel Rabbi Yisrael Ba'al Shem Tov," pp. 85–87.

46. Ibid., p. 86.

47. Ibid., pp. 86–87. "It is easier for the body to tolerate every kind of physical torture than to endure the yoke of the Kingdom of Heaven." *Emet Ve'emunah*, p. 34. The Kotzker Rebbe underscores the Besht's teachings on the relativitism of suffering.

48. *EK*, p. 76.

49. Ibid., p. 81–82. *Zava'at Harivash*, p. 3.

50. *LKST*, p. 18. Earlier it was indicated that the revealing of *hester panim*

(God's hidden countenance) occurs precisely when God's role in suffering is acknowledged.

51. *Toldot Ya'akov Yosef*, pp. 38, 74.

52. When God's eternal component in suffering is not acknowledged.

53. *Kedushat Levi*, p. 29. By definition, when the divine, or eternal, component in suffering is acknowledged, suffering cannot exist. When the divine in suffering is not recognized, suffering operates in the temporal sense.

54. *LKST*, p. 8.

55. Ibn Shmuel, "Memishnato shel Rabbi Yisrael Ba'al Shem Tov," p. 87. The ultimate fear results from man's inability to recognize that God is the source of all that is.

56. *LKST*, p. 5, based on the Besht's exegesis of Exodus 14:10 and Psalms 4:2.

57. Ibid., p. 30.

58. The egoistic forces in man, the mundane and temporal.

59. The pinnacle of human humility, when cognizant of God's greatness. *Ani* and *Ayin* are easily transformed in Hebrew wordplay by transposing the letters of their roots.

60. *LKST*, p. 30. Identical with the *EK* source cited above, p. 26.

61. Rabbi Aaron of Karlin carefully develops his thesis of *berurim* (selection) around the concept of suffering. It is precisely suffering which enables man to employ his free will and select the contrasting good. It enables good to exist in a selectable context. *Bet Aharon*, p. 42.

62. Rabbi Yitzchak Isaac of Komarno, *Notzar Hesed*, 1:10. See also *Bet Aharon*, p. 74. "The more one sees darkness, etc."

63. *Kedushat Levi*, pp. 26–27.

64. *EK*, pp. 21–22, 76.

65. " 'And the Lord called to him from the bush' (Exodus 3:4). Said the Holy One, blessed be He, to Moses: 'Don't you feel that I am saturated with suffering, as are the people of Israel? Therefore, let it be known, from this very spot that I speak to you, from amidst these thorns, so to speak, I share in their suffering.' And thus it is said: 'In all their suffering does He suffer' (Isaiah 63:9)." Exodus Rabah 2.

66. Uffenheimer, *Quietistic Elements*, p. 93.

67. *Kedushat Levi*, p. 54. "Thus, we find that when Israel, God forbid, is confronted with crisis, the godly component within them sustains them, and it suffers as well. . . . That is to say, their loss is His loss, and this should be the thrust of their prayers, for God's sake."

68. *Magid Debarav Leya'akov*, p. 3.

69. *EK*, pp. 21–22, 76.

70. *Toldot Ya'akov Yosef*, p. 38.

71. Uffenheimer, *Quietistic Elements*, pp. 33, 36.

72. *EK*, pp. 5, 9, 38, 56–58, 100.

73. *Bet Aharon*, p. 3.

74. Uffenheimer, *Quietistic Elements*, p. 43.

75. A classic rabbinic statement, "If I am not for myself, who will be for me? If I am for myself only, what am I?" Mishnah Avot 1:14.

76. *If* I am, (then) not for myself. *Zava'at Harivash*, p. 19.

77. Ibid., p. 20.
78. Ibid., p. 19.
79. *EK*, p. 100.
80. Uffenheimer, *Quietistic Elements*, p. 37.
81. *EK*, p. 27.
82. *Kedushat Levi*, p. 33.
83. Ibid., p. 30.
84. Genesis 1:26–27.
85. Uffenheimer, *Quietistic Elements*, p. 124.
86. *Magid Debarav Leya'akov*, p. 3.

NOTES TO CHAPTER 6

1. These pains, not unlike the birthpangs of a woman in labor, take on various forms of suffering described in the Talmud, Pesahim 118a, Ketubot 111a, Sanhedrin 97–98; and Megilah 178. Isaiah 26:17. As a woman with child, that draweth near the time of her delivery, is in pain and crieth out in her pangs, so have we been at Thy presence, O Lord," is interpreted by Rashi: "We recognize that these [pangs] are indications of salvation and redemption." See also Talmud Sanhedrin 98b.
2. *EHS*, pp. 22–23.
3. Ibid., pp. 26–27. The Shekhinah evidently also is bound by the premessianic suffering.
4. Elimelech Elazar Ehrenberg, *Artze Levanon*, p. 171. See also Unger, *Sefer Kedoshim*, pp. 50–51.
5. Ibid.
6. Eyewitness reports recorded in Unger, *Sefer Kedoshim*, p. 110.
7. Ibid., p. 232.
8. Ibid., p. 233.
9. Ibid., p. 309. The origin of the Messiah suffering in Rome emanates from the Vilna Gaon's reading Sanhedrin 98a (Babylonian Talmud): " 'When will the Messiah come?' 'Go and ask him' was the reply. 'Where is he sitting?' 'At the entrance of Rome' [vs. 'entrance of the town']. He sits among the poor lepers."
10. *Yoman Getto Warsha*, pp. 68–69. The tragedy unfolding in the ghetto was the necessary prelude to the messianic era.
11. *EK*, pp. 106–107.
12. Talmud Sanhedrin 98a.
13. *EHS*, pp. 27–28.
14. Ibid., p. 30.
15. Probably referring to the redemption from Egypt, which was subsequently nullified by the first exile and the destruction of the First Temple (586 B.C.E.). Unilateral action by God is highlighted in the Passover Haggadah. " 'The Lord brought us out of Egypt' [Deuteronomy 26:8], not by an angel, not by a seraph, not by a messenger, but by Himself. . . . 'I will pass through the land of Egypt that night. . . . I am the Lord' [Exodus 12:12], I and no one else." Philip Birnbaum, *The Passover Haggadah*, pp. 36–37.

16. *EHS*, pp. 83–84, 102.
17. *EHS*, p. 102.
18. "Thou bringest death and restorest life and causest salvation to flourish." The term *matzmiah*, related to *tzemah*, is employed in the part of the morning service devoted to the subject of redemption. Birnbaum, *Daily Prayer Book*, pp. 83, 89.
19. *EHS*, p. 108. The unexploited seed of Peretz Gabbai serves as a symbolic backdrop to this teaching.
20. Ibid., pp. 141–143. The degree to which Holocaust events stimulated these activist motifs, so disproportionate to the Hasidic norm, becomes clear in the *EHS* responses related to the importance of settling the land of Israel as the major step toward redemption.
21. *EHS*, p. 241.
22. *EK*, p. 55.
23. *EK*, p. 58. See also ibid., pp. 101 and 114, for responses suggesting that faith enhances redemption. Huberband, however, documents the attempts of some Rebbes to predict an exact date for redemption on various days in the years 1940 and 1941, based on biblical verses and kabbalist numerology, including a reference to Rabbi Yaakov Yosef of Polnoya, *Toldot*, p. 72b. Huberband, *Kiddush Hashem*, pp. 303–305.
24. Exodus 14:15. God's urging during the Exodus from Egypt.
25. *EHS*, p. 316.
26. *EK*, p. 179. The emphasis here is on Israel's lack of *emunah*, which prompted them to cry out to God in the first place. God's impatience is reflected in "let them move!"

The quotation from Rashi is actually a paraphrase. Rashi says in full: "They need but go forward, since the sea does not stand in their way. Worthwhile is the merit of the Patriarchs. They and their *emunah* in Me will split the sea for them."

27. The parting words of the Oliker Rebbe (Rabbi Alter Yosef David) to his daughter before being transported to the death camp. Unger, *Sefer Kedoshim*, p. 15. See also *EK*, pp. vii, 101. The Piazesner Rebbe concludes a letter (which accompanied the *EK* manuscript) with the following: "And may God have mercy upon the remnant of Israel, wherever they may be, and save and redeem us, *keheref ayin*."
28. Elimelech Hacohen Schwartz, "Agudisten in Lodzer Ghetto," pp. 108–109.
29. The *kimah kimah* ("bit by bit," gradual) process of *geulah* suggests the important role of man in precipitating redemption, as opposed to the cataclysmic and instant salvation brought about by sudden divine intervention. *EHS*, p. 175. *EHS* offers numerous Kabbalah and Hasidic references documenting the gradual redemption theory. *EHS*, pp. 86, 88, 89, 91, 108.
30. "To the redemption of the land is tied our redemption, and to its subjection is tied our own subjection." Ibid., p. 178.
31. The term "Zionist" in the pre–World War II period referred to a supporter of the movement to establish a Jewish national state in Palestine. Though religious Zionism gradually assumed an active political role in Palestine and abroad, striving to establish a political Jewish state based on

biblical-rabbinic law, the waves of immigration between the world wars consisted in the main of non-Orthodox Jews. The violent opposition of the ultra-Orthodox elements (including a number of Hasidic leaders) to the Zionist movement was premised on the following arguments: (a) man should not intervene in the affairs of the divine, (b) the Zionist movement was in the hands of secularists who would defile the sanctity of the land. Salo Baron in Robinson and Friedman, *Guide to Jewish History Under Nazi Impact*, p. 424. See the statements against political Zionism by a former Lubavicher Rebbe (1903) and a Gerer Rebbe (1901) in Michael Selzer, *Zionism Reconsidered*, pp. 11–22. Rabbi Teichthal's entire thrust is directed against these two premises; hence his analysis of the "nonexpected" road to redemption.

32. *EHS*, p. 120.

33. Ibid. *Shlihe derahmana*, lit., "emissaries of the Compassionate One." Rabbi Avraham Yitzchak Hacohen Kook (1868–1935), the first Chief Rabbi of Israel, noted that, though the *haluzim* (working pioneers) in Palestine were not religious in the formal sense, "these elements which seem materialistic and lowly, because they want to partake in the rebuilding of the 'precious land,' immediately they are uplifted . . . the sanctity of Israel is apparent in them." Efraim Zoref, *Haye Harab Kook*, p. 64.

34. *EHS*, pp. 121, 127–128. "Judges and accusers" *(dayanim vehamekatregim)* likely refers to the heavenly prosecutors and satanic forces who would seek to obstruct any attempt at man's redemption. The Jobian confrontation with satanic forces (Job 1:6–12) is frequently encountered in rabbinic literature.

35. Ibid., pp. 133–134.

36. Ibid. Thus both the Komarner and the Vizhnitzer, for different reasons, see the Zionist movement as possibly a manifestation of the divine redemptive process.

37. *No'am Elimelekh*, p. 19b.

38. *EHS*, p. 121. Since unholy forces cast the Jew into Galut (exile), the redemption must be realized by identical means, e.g., the nonobservant Zionists.

39. This is obviously a reference to the "impure" pedigree of the Davidic dynasty in the instance of Perez, the son of Judah and Tamar (Genesis 38), and Ruth the Moabite, the great-grandmother of David (Ruth 4:12, 13, 18–22). By a remarkable coincidence both Judah and Tamar, as well as Ruth and Boaz, met under veiled and concealed circumstances. In each instance a non-Hebrew woman was involved (Genesis 38:2, Shua, the Canaanite wife of Judah; Ruth 1:4, Ruth of Moab), and both instances concern brothers who die prematurely as apparent punishment for sins. Thus the Davidic dynasty, the source of Jewish hopes for redemption, is clouded with the "impurity" and "stain" of mixed marriages and moral imperfections.

40. *EHS*, pp. 122–123.

41. Talmud Hulin 63a, referring to the *shrakrak*, an unknown species of the vulture family. It will herald the Messiah's coming by means of its characteristic call, fulfilling the prophecy of Zechariah 10:8: "I will whistle to them and gather them in, because I shall redeem them."

42. *EHS*, pp. 119–120.

43. Scholem, *Major Trends*, pp. 346–348.

44. Ibid., p. 10.
45. *EHS*, p. 245.
46. Ibid. "Golden ages" in the diaspora, such as the Golden Age of Spain from the tenth to the fourteenth century, were but temporary islands of tranquility in a sea of suffering. Ibid., p. 14.
47. Ibid., p. 260.
48. Ibid., p. 324. *EHS* develops the thesis that a people in its own land, not at the mercy of others, develops and enhances a sense of unity and purpose.
49. The *kelipot*, lit., "shells," are the prisons in which the holy sparks are confined against their will. In Kabbalah and Hasidism, they represent the forces of evil. The term originated in the *Zohar*, which "interprets evil as a sort of residue [the shell] or refuse of the hidden life's organic process." Scholem, *Major Trends*, pp. 238, 267.
50. *EHS*, p. 30.
51. Ibid., p. 91.
52. *EK*, p. 158. The *Galut Mitzrayim* (the exile of the Jewish people in Egypt) is defined as a delimiting experience. *Mitzrayim* has a twofold meaning: "Egypt" and "boundary" (from the term *metzar*). Similarly, the Hebrew letters in *PaROh* (Pharaoh) may be rearranged as *ORePh*, referring to the rear of the neck. This would symbolize an indirect or limited experience and confrontation. Complete self-fulfillment is, therefore, not possible in the Galut. Further, the absolute recognition of the divine in man is also not possible in the Galut.
53. Isaiah 40:1.
54. Lamentations 5:21. "Turn us unto Thee, O Lord, and we shall return; renew our days as of old."
55. *EK*, p. 110.
56. *EHS*, p. 96.
57. Aaron Sorsky, "From the Life of the Piazesner Rebbe," in *EK*, pp. 24–25 (rear pagination).
58. Ibid., p. 25.
59. Ibid. The tragedy of his people and his God, suffering in Galut, transcends his own personal tragedy.
60. *EHS*, p. 256.
61. Ibid., p. 259. *EHS* documents the manner in which Galut sharpens the narrow self-interest of the individual while eroding his fraternal and altruistic sensibilities. Ibid., pp. 245–248.
62. Ibid., p. 221.
63. Ibid.
64. Baron, "The Emergence of Israel," p. 422.
65. Ibid.
66. Ibid.
67. *EHS* cites biblical tradition for the formulation of a vow in time of crisis: "And Jacob vowed, stating, 'If God will be with me, and watch over me, etc.' " (Genesis 28:20).
68. In addition to the desirability of making a vow during crisis, the merit of Eretz Yisrael may be invoked when one is seeking a Jew's release from

mortal danger. *EHS* cites a letter of Rabbi Shneur Zalman of Liadi to Rabbi Levi Yitzchak of Berdichev, in 1802, following his release from a tsarist prison. ". . . who am I, the lowest among human beings, that God's Name should have been sanctified through me . . . but I was destined by God to enable the merit of the Holy Land to stand by us and assist us in every instant, and to rescue us from the enemy." *EHS*, p. 21.

69. Ibid., p. 23. Thus the *EHS* document incorporates the concept of the vow and the glorification of Eretz Yisrael. The obligation to fulfill the vow made in Budapest 1943 was evidently based on the assumption that Hungary would remain outside the grasp of Nazi Germany.

70. "The cause of all the suffering that has overtaken us is that we have forgotten to respect properly our true mother, namely, Eretz Yisrael." *EHS*, p. 20. Citing talmudic sources, *EHS* throughout the work refers to Eretz Yisrael as the "mother who desperately yearns for us to return to her bosom," and urges the Jew "to leave his stepmother, the countries of exile." Ibid.

71. Ibid., p. 14. "Sit back and wait," evidently for the Messiah.

72. Ibid., pp. 14–15. "Our hands did not spill this blood" is a direct quotation from Deuteronomy 21:7, in reference to the discovery of an unknown dead person in the fields. The elders of the community in closest proximity to the body are required to wash their hands over the broken neck of a heifer and declare: "Our hands did not spill this blood, our eyes did not see it."

73. Ibid., p. 16. Rabbi Shimon Huberband, a Hasid, headed the religious section of the Emanuel Ringelblum archivists documenting the Holocaust in the Warsaw Ghetto. He noted: "The Rebbe of Gur, like most of the Polish Hasidic Rebbes, adopted a negative attitude toward the building of Eretz Yisrael. Had the Rebbe of Gur ordered his Hasidim (among them thousands of wealthy Jews, owners of factories, property, and real estate) to settle in Eretz Yisrael . . . how different would have been the current state of settlement in the land [Eretz Yisrael] as well as Poland." *Kiddush Hashem*, p. 295.

74. *EHS*, p. 227. *EK*, p. 32, suggests that the original purpose of Eretz Yisrael was to serve as a protective device allowing the Jew to harness resources and energies for the higher purpose of serving God, rather than responding to the persecutions encountered in foreign lands.

75. Actually, *metaken* in this context suggests "make amends."

76. The expression for Jewish martyrdom.

77. *EHS*, p. 213. Since the martyred Jews were a factor in the rebirth of an independent Jewish land, they are in essence reborn. They perpetuate their own existence through those who rebuild the land. Their deaths assume meaning because they have become partners in the process of *tikkun*. This is indeed a remarkable observation. Some observers of the Holocaust have consistently objected to even the most casual connection, or cause-effect relationship, between the Holocaust and the rebirth of the Jewish state. "We cannot be content with the old cliches, rehearsing the 'sins' of our people and revelling in visions of Messianic Glory. Nor can we point to the 'miracle' of Israel as the counterweight to the tragedy of the Six Million. The scales do

not balance, however much we try." Jacob B. Agus, "God and the Catastrophe," p. 14. Elie Wiesel observes: "To me, the Holocaust teaches nothing. I object to Israeli politicians when they claim that 'Israel is the answer to the Holocaust.' It is not. It has no right to be. Sometimes I feel it is a disgrace to link these two events and thus diminish them both. They are two mysteries, both historic and Messianic. [Note the difference between Wiesel and Agus on the relationship between the Holocaust and messianism.] I refuse to give children in tomorrow's Israel such a burden, such a guilt. I do not want them to think: 'If we are free and independent, it is because of the Holocaust!' This would mean being, in a way, responsible for the past." Elie Wiesel, "Jewish Values in the Post-Holocaust Future," p. 287.

78. Tikkun in this context suggests *improvement*. In Kabbalah and in Hasidism, the role of man is to assist God in returning the upper and lower worlds to their original state of perfection. Scholem, *Major Trends*, pp. 265, 269, 273. The rebuilding of Eretz Yisrael to its original state is integral to the total process of *tikkun*.

79. *Tikkun hatzot*, a prayer service recited at midnight by devout Jews, commemorates the destruction of the Temple. The ritual is usually performed in privacy while sitting on the floor as if in mourning.

80. *EHS*, p. 54.

81. Ibid., pp. 34, 78.

82. Ibid., p. 147.

82a. Ibid., p. 91.

83. It is rare for a Hasid to disagree with his own Rebbe. The very relationship between them implies the Hasid's unquestioning trust in the Rebbe, especially concerning matters dealing with theological or messianic speculation.

84. *EHS*, p. 94.

85. Ibid., pp. 94–95.

86. Man is expected to direct his efforts toward redemption and help bring it about; hence, the importance of actively settling the Holy Land. *EHS*, pp. 94–95. "Heaven awaits our initiative." Ibid., p. 106.

87. A difficult passage. "Rulers of the world" (*malke eretz*) may refer to the Balfour Declaration of November 2, 1917, wherein the British Foreign Secretary, Sir Arthur James Balfour, communicated to Lord Walter Rothschild: "His Majesty's Government view with favour the establishment in Palestine of a national home for the Jewish people".

88. Ibid., pp. 95, 178, 180.

89. Ibid., p. 225. This further documents Rabbi Teichthal's contention that "nonobservant Jews must also become involved in developing Eretz Yisrael, so that a united front is realized."

90. "Yet the Orthodox, in the name of God, stood aside and shared not in this work." *EHS*, p. 14.

91. "Surely, had the God-fearing and Orthodox been involved in this project, our Holy Land would have a different appearance and shape." Ibid., pp. 14, 158.

92. "Had Orthodox Jews become involved in this task . . . and inspired

others to participate in it . . . how many thousands of Jews would have settled there and been saved from death." Ibid., pp. 14–16, 95, 214.

93. "Thus, in our own day, even rabbis, Rebbes, and Hasidim [are caught up in the search for material gain]; one has a fine rabbinic post, another has a lucrative *rebistve* [the term for leading a Hasidic rabbinic dynasty]; this one operates a successful business, a factory, or has a good position. All are concerned that departure for Eretz Yisrael would threaten their [material] status." Ibid., p. 31.

94. "Our recital of the words 'He who causes the return of Thy Divine Presence in Zion' [recited thrice daily in the liturgy], 'let us worship before His holy mountain' [from the morning service], and similar [prayers], is mere twitter of birds, recited without concentration [on their meaning]." Ibid., p. 104.

95. The term *morashah* (inheritance, possession) is applied to both Torah ("The Torah which Moses commanded us is the *morashah* of the congregation of Jacob," Deuteronomy 33:4) and Eretz Yisrael ("I will bring you into the land which I swore . . . I will give it to you for a *morashah*," Exodus 6:8). Hence, the equation, *EHS*, pp. 38, 287.

96. Ibid., p. 193. *EHS* continues to bolster his position, which justifies the rebuilding of Eretz Yisrael by every kind of Jew. Eretz Yisrael rejects all distinctions among Jews. The mere involvement in the mitzvah (commandment) of settling Eretz Yisrael raises the seemingly nonobservant Jew to the level of the fully observant. "Even without their knowledge, they fulfill the important positive commandment, 'And you shall possess it and dwell therein' [Deuteronomy 11:32] . . . and I say with full conviction that their actions are worthy before God and their reward is great indeed." *EHS*, p. 194.

97. *Sefirot*, lit. "numbers," is a mystical term employed in Kabbalah to signify the "Divine powers and emanations" manifested in the ten "spheres" or "regions" "in which God emerges from His hidden abode." Scholem, *Major Trends*, pp. 206, 213. See also Louis Ginzberg, "The Cabalah," p. 225.

98. *Malkhut*, lit. "the Kingdom [of God]," is one of the ten *sefirot*. The *Zohar* also refers to this sphere as *Knesset Yisrael* (the community of Israel), and Shekhinah (the Presence or radiance of God). Ibid., pp. 213–214. Though *EHS* designates *malkhut* as the highest order of the *sefirot*, the *sefirot* tree, a symbolic sketch of the ten *sefirot* in the form of a tree with branches (ibid., p. 214) places *malkhut* at the base or near the roots of the tree.

99. *EHS*, p. 13.

100. Ibid., p. 152.

101. Ibid., p. 206.

NOTES TO CHAPTER 7

1. Scholem, *Major Trends*, pp. 245–247.

2. S. Z. Kahane, "The Foundation of Redemption in Hassidic Thought," p. 292. Kahane contrasts the Hasidic rationale with the idea, held by many

other religious leaders, that suffering in exile was retribution for the sins of the people.

3. Menahem Brayer, "The Hasidic Rebbes of Romania, Hungary, and [their relationship to] Eretz Yisrael," pp. 214, 220.

4. *Kekadranuta dezafra,* ibid.

5. *Yeridah lezorekh aliyah.* Rabbi Nahum of Tchernibol (d. 1798) responded to disciples who complained of "darkness and depression," that their mental state was a prerequisite for the regeneration of the redemptive forces within man. Martin Buber, *Tales of the Hasidim: Early Masters,* p. 173. The descent-ascent formula operates as well in other areas of Hasidic concern, such as the "descent of the Zadik [which] means, an elevation of divine light," since he descends to the lower planes, "in order to rescue the scattered sparks of light." Scholem, *Major Trends,* p. 346.

6. *Likute Mohran,* p. 32b, 22:11.

7. *Eli Zion,* the closing hymn of the *Kinot* (Elegies) service recited by Jews in the synagogue on Tisha Be'av (the ninth day of the month of Av), when Jews commemorate the destruction of the first and second Temples (586 B.C.E. and 70 C.E.). Abraham Rosenfeld, *Kinoth for the Ninth of Ab,* p. 176.

8. *Kedushat Levi,* p. 83a.

9. Genesis 21:6, referring to Sarah's comment upon the birth of Isaac when she was clearly beyond child-bearing age. The biblical text explains her laughter thus: "Anyone who hears will laugh with me. And she added, Who would have said to Abraham that Sarah would suckle children! Yet I have born a son in his old age." Ibid. 21:7.

10. Sarah had been childless. The Berdichever paraphrases Sarah.

11. Not the laughter of ridicule, but of joy, accentuated and intensified by the contrasting pain of being childless. Note the manner in which the relationship is developed between *hevle ledah* (the pains of child-bearing), the birth of Isaac, who was to be the link in the covenantal promise to Abraham (Genesis 18:18–19), and the exegesis of Psalms 118:21 pertinent to redemption.

12. Rabbi Levi Yitzchak does not read *anitani* ("you have answered me") but *initani* ("you have oppressed me"), the *pi'el* form of the verb.

13. A symbolic reference to the people of Israel, rejected by the nations (Rashi, Psalms 118:22).

14. Psalms 118:23.

15. Ibid.

16. Ibid. 118:24. *Kedushat Levi,* p. 10d. The recognition of "The Lord has made this day," made possible by the *Hevle Geulah–Geulah* sequence is a form of *bitul hayesh* (dissolving of the ego forces). This corresponds to the relationship between *Hevle Mashiah* and *bitul hayesh,* noted earlier. A tradition in the name of Ba'al Shem Tov also relates the process of *Hevle Mashiah* to *bitul hayesh,* where the *yesh* represents the material affluence that inflates man's ego and prevents redemption. Louis Newman, *Hasidic Anthology,* p. 253. The Kotzker Rebbe notes this concept in another form. He admits that many great rabbis and scholars throughout Jewish history have consciously sought to hasten the Messiah. "It seems to me, however, that the Messiah will appear at a time when the children of Israel are completely occupied with the

struggle to make a living, and their thoughts are thoroughly distracted; then will the Messiah indeed come." *Emet Ve'emunah,* p. 22. The *yesh,* in this instance, may represent the ego forces which led the rabbis to believe that they would be instrumental in bringing the Messiah.

17. Talmud Sukkah 52a. See also Abba Hillel Silver, *History of Messianic Speculation in Israel,* pp. 43–44.

18. Ze'ev Rabinowitz, *Hahasidut Halita'it,* p. 39.

19. Ibid., pp. 38–39.

20. Buber, *Origin and Meaning of Hasidism,* pp. 202–218.

21. Israel Ba'al Shem Tov, *Igeret Hakodesh,* p. 168. This document, a letter from the Besht to his brother-in-law, Rabbi Gershon Kitover, who had settled in Palestine, was to have been delivered by a disciple of the Besht, Jacob Joseph of Polnoya, but he never reached his destination. It has been interpreted by Scholem as part of the early Hasidic effort to negate the idea of a personal Messiah following the turmoil in the wake of the Sabbatai Zvi debacle. The thrust of the letter seems to suggest the need for spiritual revival in order to bring about the redemption. Gershom Scholem, "Demuto Hahistorit Shel Habesht," p. 348.

22. Scholem, *Major Trends,* pp. 30–31.

23. Numbers 6:23. The Berdichever Rebbe employs this verse as an introduction to a teaching of the Besht.

24. Psalms 121:5.

25. *Kedushat Levi,* p. 70b.

26. Ibid., p. 59d. The Berdichever Rebbe especially points to Eretz Yisrael, the primary focus of redemption, as "benefiting [from the *hesed* of God] because of the actions of those below." Ibid., p. 60a.

27. Exodus 12:33, Deuteronomy 16:3.

28. *Bet Ahron,* p. 152a.

29. Founded by Rabbi Mordechai Yosef Leiner, the Izbitzer Rebbe (d. 1854), a disciple of Simha Bunam of Parsischa (d. 1827), in turn a disciple of Jacob Isaac of Parsischa (d. 1814), the disciple of the (Seer) of Lublin (d. 1815), a disciple of Dov Ber of Mezritch. A grandson of the last Radziner Rebbe, Rabbi Shmuel Shlomo, called for active physical resistance against the Nazis.

30. S. Z. Shragai, "Hasidut Haba'al Shem Tob Bitfisat Izbitza-Radzin," pp. 161–163. Man must initiate the redemption process. Ibid., p. 161.

31. I prefer the Hebrew original *hesed,* rather than Maurice Friedman's translation, "grace."

32. Buber, *Origin and Meaning of Hasidism,* pp. 122–123.

33. The source of the reference is not known to the writer. There are, however, numerous references to the hidden, veiled nature of the miracle. *Niddah* 31a; *Bamidbar Rabbah* 24:2; *Zohar,* Numbers 200.

34. *Hasidut Vezion,* p. 15. *Nekamot,* "acts of revenge" in this context, may refer to unnatural and violent kinds of action.

35. "Then came Amalek." Exodus 17:8.

36. According to Rabbi Israel, man's redemptive work is superior to supernatural events. The latter may be neutralized by other supernatural events, but man's redemptive acts are eternal. Aaron Pechenik, "Zadikei Rizin V'Chernibol Weyahasam Le'erez Yisrael," pp. 178–179. Alfasi's study

of the role of *moftim* (wonders, miracles) in Hasidism is not pertinent to the present discussion of miracles and *geulah*. The miracles employed by Zadikim are aimed at easing the daily burdens and concerns of the Jew in Galut, or at highlighting God's majesty. Yitzhak Alfasi, "Hasagot al Enoshiyut Umoftim Beyisrael," pp. 112–129.

37. Scholem, *Major Trends*, p. 274.

38. Ibid., pp. 273–274.

39. Ibid., p. 283.

40. Ibid., p. 284.

41. The Berdichever relates the *gilgul-tikkun* process to the equation of the 613 commandments with the numerous organs and nerves in the human body, as described in the Midrash *(Tanhuma, Ki Teze)*. "When this person violates a positive or negative commandment, he causes a blemish in the respective organ. . . . He must thus undergo the process of many *gilgulim* until he restores *(shitaken)* those commandments. In this manner all his organs shall be healed until *his* body shall be restored to its original unity. . . . The organs which were restored by way of *gilgulim* represent new organs." *Kedushat Levi*, pp. 85d–86a.

42. Scholem, *Major Trends*, p. 317. Scholem has indicated the points of contact between Sabbatianism and Hasidism (ibid., pp. 330–334), as well as the significant differences which separated these two movements; both sprung from the womb of Kabbalism. Among the similarities, in essence, though not in degree, is the concept of descending "to a lower or even dangerous plane in order to rescue the scattered sparks of light, for 'every descent of the Zaddik means an elevation of divine light.' " Ibid., p. 346.

43. Note the application of this principle in the discussion of *Hevle Mashiah*.

44. When there is no transgressor among those who pray. The talmudic variant reads: "A fast-day is not deemed worthy if it does not include sinners of Israel." Keritot 6b.

45. Elimelekh of Lizensk, *No'am Elimelekh*, p. 7d. If divorced from mundane concerns and insensitive to human imperfections, the Zadik will be unable to bring about *tikkun*, for he will be functioning in the pristine realm of holiness, out of context with human reality. By descending (or being diverted), and grappling with the unholy, he is able to bring his positive influence to bear.

46. The "unholy" so to speak, as in the *gilgul* process, must participate in its own redemption.

47. Buber, *Origin and Meaning of Hasidism*, p. 207.

48. Uffenheimer, *Quietistic Elements*, p. 170.

49. Scholem's contention that "the [Hasidic] movement as a whole had made its peace with the *Galuth*" (*Major Trends*, p. 336) may be questioned in the light of the evidence marshaled by Horodetzky, Buber, Werfel, Dinaburg, Shazar, and Federbush (see Bibliography for full citations), the *EHS* Hasidic documentation, and the sources in this research. Scholem's concern with the Hasidic-Sabbatian interaction and reaction (*Major Trends*, pp. 331–334) forces the Galut issue into a context of contrast. A radical messianic movement such as Sabbatianism, by definition, radicalizes Galut. The Hasidic Galut (outside the heated radical frame) remains, nevertheless, a significant negative ele-

ment harassing and disturbing the personal-religious-national quest for *tikkun* and *geulah*.

50. *No'am Elimelekh*, p. 16c.

51. Lamentations 1:2. The interpretation focuses upon the double use of the verb *b-k-h* (cry), *bakho tivke*.

52. Evidently based upon the *Zohar*'s "What is the aspect of night? The Galut." *Zohar*, p. 152b.

53. *Vezeh nimshakh mizeh*, a critical phrase seemingly discounted by Scholem and Uffenheimer, who emphasize the individual vs. national Galut in Hasidism (Uffenheimer, *Quietistic Elements*, p. 170). The Beshtian tradition views the former as a consequence of the latter.

54. *Toldot Ya'akov Yosef*, p. 163d.

55. Ibid., pp. 102a–102b.

56. *Likute Mohran*, p. 12b; the word *Mitzrayim* (Egypt) is related to the Hebrew root m-tz-r, meaning to set limited boundaries, and also to *tz-r-h*, signifying distress.

57. *No'am Elimelekh*, p. 16d.

58. *Hasidut Vezion*, p. 22. The spirit of the Torah is misrepresented and distorted as a consequence of exilic spiritual degeneration.

59. *EHS*, p. 245.

60. Ibid.

61. *Toldot*, p. 27d. See also, *Hasidut Vezion*, p. 15, for a summary of the teaching of Rabbi Dov Ber on the divisive nature of Galut.

62. *EHS*, p. 30.

63. *Kedushat Levi*, p. 27b.

64. Ibid., p. 71c.

65. The term *hitun*, in this context, may refer to a state of engagement prior to marriage.

66. *No'am Elimelekh*, p. 16c. In a subsequent passage, Rabbi Elimelekh actually relates *galut hashekhinah* to Galut of Israel, resulting in a fracture of the union. "The shekhinah has been in Galut a long time, and is thus not in a state of true unity [with the Jewish people], but rather in a state of *hitun*." Ibid., p. 17.

67. *Kedushat Levi*, p. 93d.

68. *No'am Elimelekh*, p. 16d. As in suffering, man is asked to assist God, thereby sustaining the man-God partnership.

69. Note the implication for the *EHS* response which questions Galut as a divine decree that could only be reversed by God.

70. See full citations in the Bibliography. Only the Horodetzky work is not entirely devoted to this subject, though a significant subsection of his fourth volume is entitled "Eretz Yisrael and Hassidism" (pp. 59–63).

71. Buber, *Origin and Meaning of Hasidism*, p. 206. Note the correlation with the *EHS* response relating Eretz Yisrael to *geulah*, clearly assumed in Hasidic literature. For a summary of contrasting interpretations, specifically highlighting the "personal and not collective [redemption], the spiritual, but not historical," see Uffenheimer, *Quietistic Elements*, pp. 168–177.

72. Horodetzky, *Hahasidut Vetoratah*, vol. IV, p. 57.

73. *Aliyah*, lit. "ascent," refers to visits to Eretz Yisrael, and especially to

permanent settlement there. The concept of Eretz Yisrael as being on a higher spiritual and physical plane is significantly evident in Hasidic literature. Note Rabbi Dov Ber of Mezritch's explanation of the purpose of the spies sent to investigate the land promised by God to Israel: "['Send men to scout the land of Canaan, which I am giving to the Israelite people' (Numbers 13:3) seems paradoxical to Rabbi Dov Ber.] He interprets the verse as follows: He [Moses] wanted to test [the Israelites] because Moses aspired to enter Eretz Yisrael, he sought to ascend in order to enter Eretz Yisrael . . . he wanted to step up to a higher plane, and, therefore, he wanted them to be tested." *Torat Hamagid*, vol. I, p. 185. Evidently the criteria for determining a higher level of existence is the process of being tested, by which one achieves the higher level. This concept may be related to the discussion in which man is urged to assume the initiative in bringing redemption closer. God may have tentatively given Israel the land, but Israel must now prove itself worthy by rising to the higher level of expectation. That level, in the context of human experience, is ultimately determined by man. Moses, seeking a higher level of experience, hoped that Israel would pass the test so that aliyah (the ascent) would indeed become a reality.

74. For the aliyah ambitions of the Ba'al Shem Tov, see *Igeret Hakodesh*, p. 168.

75. Horodetzky, *Hahasidut Vetoratah*, vol. IV, p. 63; Shazar, "Kisufe Hage'ulah," p. 103.

76. Ibid.

77. Deuteronomy 30:2–5.

78. *Hasidut Vezion*, p. 13.

79. *Kedushat Levi*, p. 8b–c. The Berdichever may be alluding to the benefits accrued to God when His People achieve completeness in Eretz Yisrael. "By way of the completeness of the children, the fathers benefited [as well]" ostensibly refers to the fathers who had left Egypt and were unable to enter the Promised Land. The supporting talmudic evidence (*Bera mezakeh aba*—"A son confers benefits upon his father,") is in the singular form, and can readily assume the Hasidic exegesis of God as the father and the people of Israel as the son, especially in the context of *galut hashekhinah*, which represents "the abnormality of Galut disturb[ing] the unity of God with His People."

80. *Likute Mohran Tanina* 116:43.

81. Rabbi Nahman (1770–1811) was the great-grandson of the Ba'al Shem Tov and one of the most ardent and active devotees of Eretz Yisrael among Hasidic leaders. He devoted an entire volume, *Zimrat Ha'aretz*, to Eretz Yisrael emphasizing its centrality for the Jewish people, Torah, and God. The centrality of the land of Israel in the life motif of Rabbi Nahman of Brazlav is clearly articulated in a special prayer he composed, probably on the eve of his departure for Palestine in 1798: "O God, merciful and compassionate God! Grant me the privilege, because of your abundant compassion, that I and all of Israel be inspired with a longing and sincere desire to come speedily to Eretz Yisrael, the Holy Land. Because of the vast distance between us [the worshiper and God], the immense mass of materialism [impeding the quest for spirituality], the confusion in my heart, and the turmoil in my mind

make it necessary that I draw close to Eretz Yisrael. There one may discover the primary source of the holy faith and the roots of all of Israel. This is the land selected by God for his chosen people. . . . Please, O God, be good to me. Grant me, with compassion and kindness, the privilege of speedily coming to Eretz Yisrael, the land inherited by our forefathers, and deeply desired by all of the true Zadikim. All who come there can restore that which is in need of restoration, accomplish that in need of realization, experience a rare privilege—all because of the sanctity of Eretz Yisrael, which exists at the very center of the world's holiness." Wertheim, *Hala'khot Vehalikhot Behasidut*, p. 221, n. 100.

82. *Likute Mohran Tanina*, 8:10, 18a.

83. *Kedushat Levi*, p. 85d.

84. *Hasidut Vezion*, p. 25. Rabbi Avraham of Kalisk, a disciple of Dov Ber, who settled in the land of Israel in 1776 together with another disciple, Rabbi Menahem Mendel of Vitebsk and three hundred others, mostly Hasidim, also perceived aliyah (settlement in Israel) as rebirth. Ibid., p. 37.

The Hasidic literature also recognizes that Eretz Yisrael, on its own, will not necessarily, reform the individual from within if he does not recognize the unique character of the land and respond inwardly to its sanctity. It is said in the name of the Berdichever: "Now some Jews have appeared to demand Palestine without Torah. And the Father in Heaven answers: 'I gave Palestine to you to enable you to respect and prize Torah. But if you do not care for the Torah, you have no claim to Palestine.' " Newman, *Hassidic Anthology*, p. 298. Rabbi Nahman of Brazlav noted: "One who goes to Palestine to attain holiness will achieve his aspiration, but one who goes there for other ends can gain no benefit." Ibid., p. 299; see also pp. 300–301. Hasidic literature is not clear on how to apply the principle of *mitokh lo lishma* (an act completed or conceived without the proper motive) to the rebuilding of Eretz Yisrael. Hasidic sources supporting those utilized by *EHS* are cited by Newman, *Hassidic Anthology*, pp. 302–303. These sources articulate the talmudic concept *mitokh shelo lishma, ata ba lishmah* (positive acts initiated for the improper motives will eventually direct the person to the proper motives). Jerusalem Talmud, Hagigah 1:6.

85. Steinman, *Sha'ar Hahasidut*, p. 89.

86. "The primary focus of prayer, which in turn affects the very lifeline of the Messiah, is in Eretz Yisrael." Rabbi Aaron of Karlin describes the "Holy Land [as the] awe-inspiring place, the gate of the heavens through which all the prayers of the heart pass." *Bet Ahron*, p. 151a.

87. "The principle form of *tikkun* is articulated through the true light that most effectively emanates from there [Eretz Yisrael]."

88. Nahman of Brazlav, *Zimrat Ha'arez*, pp. 2b, 5a. See also *Likute Mohran*, 9:5, 12b, "The essence of prayer can only be experienced in Eretz Yisrael."

89. *Kedushat Levi*, p. 5d.

90. The Flood episode described in Genesis 6–7.

91. The text in the Midrash actually reads: ". . . except for Eretz Yisrael. The flood waters did not descend upon it." *Yalkut Shimoni*, Noah 7:56.

92. *Bilah* (to decay, become worn out) is derived from the root *b-l-h*, and *mebalbel* (to confuse, to mix) from *b-l-l*. The two terms are not related

etymologically, but the alliterative relationship between them is exploited for homiletical purposes in this passage.

93. Genesis 6:11. *Vatishahet,*" [the earth] was corrupt."

94. In the name of Rabbi Dov Ber, *Torat Hamagid,* vol. I, p. 59. Elsewhere, Dov Ber notes: "Eretz Yisrael suggests an innocence and state of cleanliness of all impurities." Ibid., p. 210. The final quotation in the passage is from Talmud Baba Batra 158a.

95. *Zimrat Ha'aretz,* p. 5b.

96. Haim Yehuda Berl, *Reb Yitzhak Isaac Mekomarno,* p. 286.

97. *Kedushat Levi,* p. 83a. Only the combination of the people of Israel and Eretz Yisrael can create the vital elements of a normal and viable national existence. It represents national *tikkun* (restoration) and *shelemut* (completeness).

98. Menahem Mendel of Vitebsk, *Pri Ha'aretz,* p. 5.

99. *No'am Elimelekh,* p. 22d. For the significant use of sexual imagery in the literature of the Kabbalists, especially a description of "the relation of God to Himself, in the world of the *Sefiroth,*" see Scholem, *Major Trends,* pp. 227–230. Rabbi Elimelekh clearly implies a true unity of the Jewish people in its land, comparable to "the union of God and the Shekhinah [which] constitutes the true unity of God." Ibid., p. 230.

100. Leviticus 25:23.

101. Berl, *The Komarner Rebbe,* p. 233. The term *ki li* in the verse is interpreted as "[the land] is like myself."

NOTES TO CHAPTER 8

1. Louis Gottschalk, *Understanding History,* pp. 118–138, 139–170.

2. Controversial polemic literature has developed around the views of Hannah Arendt *(Eichmann in Jerusalem)* and Bruno Bettelheim *(The Informed Heart),* and the rejoiners of Jacob Robinson *(The Crooked Shall Be Made Straight),* Ernest Simon and Alexander Donat ("Revisionist History of the Jewish Catastrophe") concerning the propriety of Jewish responses during the Holocaust. See Bibliography for full citations.

3. Moses Maimonides, *Ma'amar Kiddush Hashem* pp. 29–65. Also, Maimonides, *Mishneh Torah,* Yesode Hatorah, vol. 1, chap. 5.

4. Huberband, *Kiddush Hashem,* pp. 23–24.

5. Hillel Seidman, *Yoman Getto Warsha,* p. 221.

6. Mordechai Lansky, *Meme Hayehudim Begetto Warsha,* p. 209. Huberband, Zemba, and Zeitlin were all close to Hasidism. Rabbi Huberband's maternal grandfather, who had much influence on him in his youth, was the Hasidic Rebbe of Chencin in Poland. *Kiddush Hashem,* p. 11. Rabbi Menahem Zemba, a key religious leader in the Warsaw Ghetto and among those who encouraged physical resistance (Seidman, *Yoman Getto Warsha,* pp. 95, 221), was significantly influenced by the Hasidic school of Kotzk, of which his grandfather was an ardent follower. The Kotzker school was known for its emphasis on intellectual depth, a disdain for ceremony, intellectual honesty, and a relentless search for new horizons in the realm of the holy. He also studied

in the yeshiva of the Rebbe of Gur. Simha Elberg, "Rabbi Menahem Zemba," pp. 38–51. Hillel Zeitlin, noted religious scholar, writer (including a number of authoritative studies on Hasidism), and mystic, spent the final days of his life in the Warsaw Ghetto studying the *Zohar* prior to his death in Treblinka. Hillel Seidman, "Hillel Zeitlin." Also a brief essay, "Hillel Zeitlin," in Seidman, *Yoman Getto Warsha*, pp. 294–298.

7. Huberband, *Kiddush Hashem*, p. 23. A search of Maimonides' works and consultation with scholars has failed to reveal any such statement. See, however, Hatam Sofer, *She'elot Utshuvot*, Yoneh De'ah 333.

8. *Ma'amar Kiddush Hashem*, p. 60. See Talmud Sanhedrin 74a, which cites Leviticus 18:5, "You shall keep My laws and My norms, by the pursuit of which man shall live." Rabbi Yishma'el interprets this as: "You shall live, and not die, by them."

9. *Ma'amar Kiddush Hashem*, p. 55.

10. Meir Dvorzeski and Yosef Gutfershten, *Jewish Resistance During the Holocaust*, pp. 129, 380.

11. Ibid., p. 119.

12. "It was then that the vaccum of the ghetto was filled with Rabbi Yitzchak Nissenbaum's profound dictum, 'This is the hour of *Kiddush Hahayim*, and not of *Kiddush Hashem* by death. The enemy demands the physical Jew, and it is incumbent upon every Jew to defend it: to guard his own life.' " Nathan Eck, *Hato'im Bedarke Hamawet*, p. 37. See also Shaul Esh, "Kiddush Hahayim Betok Hahurban."

13. Meir Dvorzeski, "Ha'amidah Behaye Yom Yom Begeta'ot U'vemahanot," p. 128.

14. Ibid.

15. A robe usually white, worn by observant Jews on Yom Kippur, the holiest day on the Jewish calendar, and by some Hasidim on Rosh Hashanah (the Jewish New Year), as well as the first two nights of Passover at the Seder table. Like the *takhrikhim* (the white shrouds in which the Jew is buried), the white kittel symbolizes purity of body and soul.

15a. Unger, *Sefer Kedoshim*, p. 36. See also "Delegat Shildert Letzte Minuten Fun Ostrovzer Rebben."

16. Unger, *Sefer Kedoshim*, p. 342.

17. Ahron Zeitlin, "A Maisse Mit A Rebben Un Zein Zuhn."

18. Y. M. Kersh, "Brief fun Churef-Gevorene Yiddishe Shtet un Shtetlech."

19. Unger, *Sefer Kedoshim*, p. 374, citing Joseph Fuchsman, an eyewitness. The legend evidently refers to attempts at forced conversions in the communities of Zaslow, Sivtovke and Danwitz, related the Ba'al Shen Tov's letter to his brother-in-law, Rabbi Gershon Kitov. *Shivhe Habesht*, pp. 168–169. Also, Horodetzky, *Hahasidut Vetoratah*, vol. 1, p. 56.

20. *EK*, pp. 97–98.

21. Moshe Prager, *Eleh Shelo Nikhne'u*, vol. 1, pp. 157–158. As recorded by eyewitness Rabbi Abraham Shmuel Binyamin Sofer.

22. The Brezner, Rabbi Nahum Yehoshua Halevi Pachenik, in an open grave in Sarne, Poland. Unger, *Sefer Kedoshim*, p. 84. The Zaloshizer, Rabbi Shem Klingberg, in the main square of Plashov, Poland. His final prayer included: "May it be Thy Will that I have the privilege of atoning for all

Jews." Ibid., p. 152. The Matislaker, Rabbi Yehezkiah Fisch, prior to entering the gas chamber of Auschwitz. Ibid., p. 233. "With a joyous clap of his hands, he exclaimed: 'Tomorrow we shall meet with our Father!' " Among his books found in the Matislaker Ghetto, a note was discovered with the inscription of the prayer to be recited prior to *Kiddush Hashem. Eleh Ezkerah*, vol. 4, p. 75. The Stoliner, Rabbi Moshe Perlow, in the Stoliner Ghetto. Unger, *Sefer Kedoshim*, p. 272.

23. Ibid., pp. 84, 101, 152.

24. Dignity in response to crisis was the theme of the Slonimer Rebbe, Rabbi Shlomo David Yehoshua Weinberg, in a message to his Hasidim delivered on Purim in 1940. Drawing upon the teaching of the Riziner Rebbe (Rabbi Israel of Rizin, d. 1850), the great-grandson of Rabbi Dov Ber, the *Solnimer* prepared his Hasidim. "The son of the king, who is an inseparable part of his father the king, does not alter his character under any condition, no matter how depressed. Though he may be degraded and despised . . . at the nadir [of life], he must yet know, and recall always, that he is the son of a king." *Zikhron Kadosh*, retold by eyewitness Moshe Weinberg.

25. The *tallit katan* is a four-cornered shirt-like garment with a set of ritual fringes *(tzitzit)* on each corner worn throughout the day by observant Jews. See Numbers 15:37–41 for the biblical commandment of *tzitzit*. The tallit is a prayer shawl with four ritual fringes on each of its four corners. Hasidim prefer long woolen shawls, praying with the tallit covering their head. In Jewish tradition a man is buried in a tallit with the fringes severed.

26. Maimonides, *Ma'amar Kiddush Hashem*, p. 58.

27. *Ani Ma'amin*, pp. 23–24.

28. The twelfth of the thirteen principles of faith articulated by Moses Maimonides and incorporated at the close of the daily liturgy. Joseph H. Herz, ed., *Daily Prayer Book*, p. 254. Unger, *Sefer Kedoshim*, pp. 103, 110.

29. M. A. Ger, "Der Dombrover Rebbe Tanzt Mit Zeine Hassidim."

30. Hertz, *Daily Prayer Book*, pp. 390, 458, 534, 578.

31. *EK*, pp. 8–9. The Rebbe supports this thesis by citing various medieval rabbinic sources on the subject of *Kiddush Hashem.*

32. Unger, *Sefer Kedoshim*, p. 280. See also *Zikhron Kadosh*, p. 5.

33. *EK*, pp. 191–192.

34. "The power of the *kelipah* is dependent upon the Galut. With the abolishment of Galut, the *kelipah* will also be abolished." *EHS*, p. 30.

35. Ibid., p. 214.

36. Ibid., p. 15. Evident here is the profound idea that *Kiddush Hashem* in death eventually leads to *Kiddush Hashem* in life, as reflected in the context of the Jewish people in its homeland. This is the form of *tikkun* already noted above. Seidman, a Hasidic Jew, quotes an anonymous Rebbe's "Torah": "Why was the Temple not built on Mount Sinai but rather on Mount Moriah? Because the place where a Jew performs the act of *Kiddush Hashem* is superior to the site of the giving of the Torah." *Yoman Getto Warsha*, p. 223. Mount Moriah was the site of the binding of Isaac (Genesis 22:2; II Chronicles 3:1) and the symbol of martyrdom in Jewish history. See J. H. Hertz, "The Binding of Isaac *(Akedah)*," in The Pentateuch and Haftorahs, p. 201.

37. The various forms of resistance are treated more fully below in chap. 12.

38. L. Feingold, "Megai Hahregah," *Ani Ma'amin*, p. 23.

39. As told to Moshe Prager by an eyewitness, Dr. Warman, the chairman of the Judenrat in Lublin.

40. Prager, "The Hasidic Movement During the Holocaust," *Sefer Habesht*, pp. 269–270.

41. *Kiddush Hahayim* was reflected in the transformation of humiliation into an elevating religious experience.

42. Unger, *Sefer Kedoshim*, p. 181.

43. Mishnah Avot 4:1.

44. *EK*, p. 169. *Kiddush Hashem* in death assumes meaning from the manner in which those who remain alive achieve *Kiddush Hahayim*. Note a similar *tikkun* theme related to *Kiddush Hashem* and Eretz Yisrael in *EHS*, p. 213.

45. Issar Frankel, *Yehide Segulah*, p. 212.

NOTES TO CHAPTER 9

1. Buber, *Origin and Meaning of Hasidism*, pp. 180–181.

2. Ibid., p. 239.

3. Leviticus 22:32 reads: "You shall not profane My holy Name, that I may be sanctified in the midst of the Israelite people, I the Lord who sanctify you." Expounding on the talmudic discussion concerning *Kiddush Hashem* (Sandedrin 74), Rashi notes: "And one must sanctify the Name, this is the meaning of *Venikdashti* [that I may be sanctified], namely, *shemoser nafsho al ahavat yotzro* [that he sacrifices his soul because he loves his Creator]." Rashi's comment on Leviticus 22:32 further defines ultimate *Kiddush Hashem* as martyrdom. "And when he sacrifices his soul, let him be prepared."

4. Psalms 44:23.

5. Berl, *Reb Yitzchak Isaac Mekomarno*, p. 190. See also *Tanhuma* Tetzaveh 5. According to *gematriya* (numerological wordplay), popular among mystics, the Hebrew letters in the phrase "Because of You, we are killed all the day" have the same numerical value as the letters in "Israel" (541).

6. Buber, *Tales of the Hasidim: Early Masters*, pp. 83–84. Compare with *Shivhe Habesht*, p. 161. Actually it was his disciple, Rabbi Pinhas of Koretz (d. 1791) who interpreted his master's offer to the Angel of Death: *Ani mohel lekha otan shte sha'ot, velo ta'aneh oti* ("I relinquish to you these two hours, and desist, pray, from further torment") as a final precious gift of life to God. "My teacher, the Ba'al Shem Tov, realizing the imminence of his death, exclaimed: 'Lord of the Universe, I make Thee a gift of the remaining hours of my life.' This is true martyrdom for the sake of the Lord." Pinhas of Koretz, *Nofet Tzufim*, p. 11.

7. *Likute Amarim: Tanya*, pt. I, chap. 18, p. 22. Tishby has documented the unique teaching of the Habad school whereby there is hidden in "the right space of the heart" of every Jew, (irrespective of his degree of Jewish observance or level of intellectual attainment) an equal amount of natural respect and love for the divine and holy. The *Kiddush Hashem*, phenomenon

prevalent among all strata and elements in Jewry, articulates this collective view of the relationship between the Jewish people and its God. I. Tishby, "Hassidut," *Haenziklopedia Ha'ibrit*, vol. 17, p. 814.

8. *Kedushat Levi*, p. 69b.

9. David Hardan, *Meolamo Shel Rabbi Nahman Mebrazlav*, pp. 62–63.

10. Mishnah Avot 4:1.

11. *Toldot*, pp. 19b, 26b.

12. *Bet Ahron*, p. 157.

13. Berl, *Rabbi Yizhak Isaac Mekomarno*, pp. 238, 308, 309. See also *Likute Amarim: Tanya*, pt. I, chap. 18.

14. Newman, *Hasidic Anthology*, p. 438.

15. Buber, *Tales of the Hasidim: Later Masters*, p. 59.

16. Ibid., p. 168.

17. The formula is usually stated as follows: *Betaruta deletata, itaruta le'elah* ("With that which has an effect below, one has an effect above"). The statement appears routinely in Kabbalah and in Hasidic thought. See *Toldot*, p. 4b; *Likute Amarim: Tanya*, p. 18b. A variant of the formula reads: *Uveubdah deletata* (With action below), *it'ar le'elah* ("one has an effect above"). *Kedushat Levi*, p. 23a. See also the discussion of Hasidic thought above in chap. 3. In this study, the concept was applied to suffering, and to the significance of man's initiative in stimulating redemption.

18. Buber, *Tales of the Hasidim: Early Masters*, p. 149.

19. Lit., "false libel," possibly a reference to the blood libel, whereby a Jew would be accused of using the blood of a Christian child to bake matzot (unleavened bread) for Passover. On the subject of blood libels, see Rudavsky, *Emancipation and Adjustment*, pp. 20–21.

20. Referring to Genesis 22:1–19 and Abraham's readiness to sacrifice his only son. This episode was subsequently transformed into the forerunner and prototype of *Kiddush Hashem*. See Shalom Spiegel's definitive treatment of the *Akedah* (Binding) theme in Jewish martyrdom, *The Last Sacrifice*.

21. *Shivhe Ba'al Shem Tov*. p. 132.

22. For a detailed analysis of the ten *sefirot* and their hierarchic system, see Scholem, *Major Trends*, pp. 212–217.

23. As a result of man's sinful pattern, the manifestation of *malkhut* had fallen from its previous higher sphere. This represents a form of *Hillul Hashem* (the desecration of God's Name), the very opposite of *Kiddush Hashem*. Only *mesirat nefesh* and *Kiddush Hashem* can restore (tikkun zeh) *malkhut* to its original position.

24. Buber, *Tales of the Hasidim: Later Masters*, p. 311.

25. Newman, *Hassidic Anthology*, pp. 67–68.

26. *Igeret Hakodesh*, in *Shivhe Habesht*, p. 169.

27. Berl, *Rabbi Yitzchak Isaac Mikomarno*, p. 238.

28. Leviticus 18:5.

29. The interpretation of "live by them but not die by them" was originally noted by Rabbi Ishmael in Talmud Sanhedrin 74a.

30. *Toldot*, p. 113. Rabbi Yaakov Yosef refers to death under normal, natural circumstances.

31. Yisrael Klapholz, *Torat Hamagid*, vol. 1. Especially significant is the

following reference: "That which is written, 'You shall be holy, [for I, the Lord your God, am holy' (Leviticus 19:2)], may be interpreted as follows: When you sustain the ideas referred to as holy, as we know, then you too will be holy—modeled after the Name of God. Thus, you will not encounter death . . . to wit, when you are alive you will not be considered like the dead, God forbid." Ibid.

32. *Me'olamo Shel Rabbi Nahman Mebrazlav*, p. 63.

33. Ibid. Implied is the following: Absolute termination of life prevents man from further sancitfying God's Name. Life is indispensable for repeated *Kiddush Hashem*. This concept is a favorite of the psalmist. "What use would my death be, if I went down to the grave? Can the dust praise You? Will it declare the truth?" (Psalms 30:10); "The dead cannot praise the Lord; nor any who descend to silence" (Psalms 115:17); "I do not wish to die, but to live, and I shall tell of the works of God" (Psalms 118:17). A simulated experience of *Kiddush Hashem*, without sacrificing one's physical existence, is also noted in the teachings of Rabbi Elimelekh of Lizensk. "Thus we deliver our souls to [sanctify] His great Name, blessed be He. Man should always imagine that he truly sacrifices his soul in order that he may achieve the unity of His great Name." *No'am Elimelekh*, p. 24d. "This is the meaning of 'And when the time approached for Israel to die' (Genesis 47:29): He [Jacob] so completely devoted his soul [to the sanctification of God] that he was indeed close to death." Ibid. Both teachings indicate a form of *Kiddush Hashem* without destroying life.

34. Newman, *Hassidic Anthology*, p. 49.

35. *Shivhe Ba'al Shem Tov*, p. 151. An implied facet of *Kiddush Hahayim*. For further treatment of the manner in which Hasidism viewed miracles as the glorious manifestation of the divine in this world, see Yitzhak Alfasi, "Hasagot al Enoshiut Umoftim Beyisra'el," *Sefer Habesht*, pp. 112–129.

36. Exodus 22:30.

37. Steinman, *Sha'ar Hahasidut*, p. 236. See also *Emet Ve'emunah*, p. 133.

38. Ibid., p. 261.

NOTES TO CHAPTER 10

1. Unger, *Sefer Kedoshim*, pp. 70, 84, 97, 178, 205, 351, 358; *Ani Ma'amin*, p. 33; *EK*, p. iv.

2. Ringelblum, *Notes from the Warsaw Ghetto*, p. 125. A similar response is reported for Hasidim in the Lodz Ghetto. Schwartz, "Agudisten in Lodzer Ghetto."

3. Yehezkel Rotenberg and Moshe Sheinfeld, *Harebi Mekotzk Veshishim Giborim Sabib Lo*, vol. 2, p. 676.

4. Eyewitness report of Mr. Alex Turner, in Unger, *Sefer Kedoshim*, p. 387.

5. Ibid., p. 405.

6. *EK*, p. 96. The quotation in the middle of the passage is from the Passover Haggadah, p. 30.

7. Ibid., p. 157.

8. Ibid., p. 158. The Slonimer Rebbe, Rabbi Shlomo David Weinberg, is

recorded as having made the same respones in Barnowich in the winter of 1940. He utilizes the *ben-melekh* (prince) parable in the name of Rabbi Israel of Rizin. See *Zikhron Kadosh*, p. 12.

9. Batya Kampinsky-Lieberman, *Stolin: Sefer Zikaron*, pp. 225–226. The biblical quotation at the end of the passage is from I Samuel 15:29.

10. Note the remarkable similarity to the ideas elaborated earlier, that the weapon utilized to combat any obstacle should be similar in character to that which is being confronted.

11. *EK*, p. 62. The last line is a paraphrase from the daily prayer service. "Blessed art thou, O Lord, who blessed Thy people Israel with peace." *Standard Prayer Book*, p. 66.

12. "Remember what Amalek did to you on your journey, after you left Egypt—how, undeterred by fear of God, he surprised you on the march when you were famished and weary, and cut down all the stragglers *(kol hanehshalim)* in your rear." Deuteronomy 25:17–18.

13. Referring to the biblical account of Amalek's defeat (Exodus 17:8–16): "Whenever Moses held up his hands, Israel prevailed." The Talmud comments on this verse, "Can the hands of Moses, indeed, make victory or defeat? However, this verse is to teach you that whenever Israel directs its gaze to heaven and declares its devotion to its Father in heaven, Israel is victorious." Mishnah Rosh Hashanah 3:8. Self-confidence and inner strength provide the physical strength by which one is sustained during crisis.

14. *EK*, p. 169.

15. Ibid., p. 179. Note again the interrelationship between man and God; in this instance, in the process of countering despair. The Gerer Rebbe, following his escape from Poland, offered a message of encouragement (in the winter of 1942 in Jerusalem), calling upon Jews to "unite ourselves in unity and good deeds; 'let us search and inquire as to our ways, and let us return to God.' We must be strong within ourselves." Yehezke'eli, *Nes Hahatzalah*, p. 114.

16. At times the Zadik's sense of responsibility for his community conflicted with his Hasidims' concern for his safety. The Belzer, Gerer, and Satmer Rebbes were among the leading Hasidic leaders secretly smuggled out of their respective communities to Palestine and Switzerland in 1943 and 1944. The Yehezke'eli volumes (see Bibliography) shed some light on the Belzer-Gerer rescue and will be utilized as source materials below in this chapter. The escape of the Satmer Rebbe from Hungary to Switzerland in 1944 has been the source of controversy since it relates to efforts by members of the Va'ad Ezrah Vahazalah (Council for Assistance and Rescue), notably Joel Brand, Dr. Rezso Kastner, and Samuel Springmann, to divert trainloads of Jews from Auschwitz to Switzerland and Spain, which involved negotiations with Adolph Eichmann. For an account of this episode, see Nora Levin, *The Holocaust*, pp. 619–666. See also Joel Brand and Hansi Brand, *Hasatan Vehanefesh*. Additional critical research is warranted in order to explore the precise relationship between the Satmer Rebbe's rescue and these negotiations.

17. At the outbreak of World War II a special emissary arrived in Komarno

from Vilna (still unoccupied by German forces) with a United States passport for him. Baruch Yashar, *Bet Komarno*, p. 129.

18. Paraphrase of *Imo anokhi betzarah* (Psalms 91:15), utilized by Midrash Rabbah, Exodus 2:5, and quoted in Rashi, Exodus 3:2. On the background of Israel's suffering in Egypt, God appears in the burning bush, "and not in another tree, because 'I am with him in suffering.' " The Rebbe shares the role with God in the suffering of his flock.

19. Yashar, *Bet Komarno*, p. 129. Unger, *Sefer Kedoshim*, p. 352, quotes the Rebbe in the Samborer Ghetto: "As long as one Jew remains in the ghetto, I shall remain." A variant response is noted by David Weisbrod Halachmi in *Artze Halevanon*, p. 209.

20. *Eleh Ezkerah*, vol. 3, p. 102.

21. Nahman Blumenthal and Meyer Kozin, *Lublin*, p. 554. Unger, *Sefer Kedoshim*, pp. 212–213.

22. Introduction to *EK*, p. iii. His devotion to his Hasidim was extraordinary. Following upon zealous efforts to assist a young Hasid, he said: "A Rebbe who is not prepared to go down to Gehinom [hell] in order to save his Hasid on the brink of destruction is not a Rebbe at all!" *Appendix* to *EK*, rear pagination, p. 11.

23. Lazer Cahane, "Der Piazesner Rebbe hot Verloiren Finf fun zein Familia in der Milchume," *Forward*, March 30, 1940, p. 8

24. Unger, *Sefer Kedoshim*, pp. 84, 88.

25. Ibid., p. 108.

26. For the Zvoliner, Rabbi Chaim Yerachmiel Taub, see ibid., p. 156. The Zabner, Rabbi Eliezer Unger, remained in Turna with his Hasidim rather than relocate to a prepared bunker in neighboring Zabne. Ibid., p. 160. The Lisker, Rabbi Zvi Hersh Friedlander, remained in the Lisker Ghetto despite the extraordinary efforts of his son Shlomo in Budapest (March 1944). The plan had succeeded in smuggling a Hungarian army officer into the ghetto to carry out the rescue. A similar second rescue effort in the Oheler Ghetto was also declined. Ibid., p. 224. For the Stoliner, Rabbi Shlomo David Yehuda Weinberg, see ibid., p. 278. M. Barzowski in *Baranowich*, p. 268, tells how the Rebbe refused to save himself from a severe beating by agreeing to beat another Jew. For the Karliner, Rabbi Avraham Elimelech Perlow, see Unger, *Sefer Kedoshim*, p. 367.

27. Ibid., pp. 393–394. Mr. Abba Bornstein, a leader of religious Zionist Jews in England, related the following to the researcher (November 27, 1971): As a Radomsker Hasid in London, he repeatedly telephoned the Rebbe in Sasnowtze, Poland, during August 1939, with an offer to fly him to England. The Rebbe's response: "Wi ahin zol ich iberlossen die Yidden?" ("And where shall I leave the Jews?"). To Mr. Bornstein this was an act of pure *Ahavat Yisrael*.

28. *Eleh Ezkerah*, vol. 3, p. 15.

29. Ibid., vol. 4, pp. 56–57. Unger, *Sefer Kedoshim*, pp. 35, 234.

30. Ibid., p. 61.

31. Ibid., pp. 70–71.

32. Talmud Makkot 10b.

33. Moshe Kushner, eyewitness, in Unger, *Sefer Kedoshim*, p. 375.

34. *Sefer Zikhron Kadosh,* p. 13.
35. *Kiddush Hashem,* pp. 296–297.
36. Unger, *Sefer Kedoshim,* p. 20.
37. Huberband cites the misjudgment of the Gerer Hasidim, involved in "business as usual" in the summer of 1939, on the advice of their Rebbe who did not believe that a major catastrophe loomed on the horizon. *Kiddush Hashem,* p. 296.
38. The Zvoliner Rebbe permitted his young Hasidim to escape to Communist Russia though this endangered their religious way of life. *Pikuah nefesh* (safeguarding of life) took precedence over all else. The Chichover Rebbe urged his Hasidim to escape from the ghetto in Cracow. See Unger, *Sefer Kedoshim,* pp. 156, 200; Alfasi, *Sefer Ha'admorim,* p. 90.
39. There is evidence that the Belzer Hasidim attempted to prevent their Rebbe from leaving Budapest for Eretz Yisrael. See *Harab Hakadosh Mebelz,* p. 128; Yehezke'eli, *Hatzalat Harebe Mebelz,* p. 80.
40. Unger, *Sefer Kedoshim,* p. 356. Yashar, *Bet Komarno,* p. 130, contains the identical material without reference to the partisan units.
41. A public communication from a Rebbe to his Hasidim is referred to as an *igeres* (lit., "letter"). Rabinowitz, *Hahasidut Halitait,* p. 16. A "Torah" is a Sabbath or festival discourse.
42. "the heifer with the broken neck," Deuteronomy 21:1–9. This portion deals with the responsibility of the community for the interim physical safety of the individual.
43. Deuteronomy 20:1–20, 21:10–14.
44. Unger, *Sefer Kedoshim,* p. 213.
45. Leviticus 19:16.
46. *EHS,* p. 249.
47. This enabled Polish refugees to enter pre-1944 Hungary as "citizens." Unger, *Sefer Kedoshim,,* p. 140. The Bobover Rebbe, Rabbi Shlomo Halberstam, reported possessing such papers. Personal interview in Brooklyn, New York, July 30, 1969.
48. Schwartz, "Agudisten in Lodzer Ghetto," pp. 108–109.
49. Eyewitness Moshe Schenfeld, in Yehezke'eli, *Hatzalat Harebbe Mebelz,* pp. 52–56.
50. *EK,* p. 329.
51. Unger, *Sefer Kedoshim,* p. 123.
52. Yehezke'eli, *Hatzalat Harebe Mebelz,* p. 12. The Belzer continued rescue operations from his temporary haven in Budapest in 1943. The Rebbe and his brother, Rabbi Mordechai Rokeach, were disappointed at the apathy of religious Jewry in Budapest who did not anticipate their own precarious position. He emphasized that the principle of "no limits" when applied to the Mitzvah of *pidyon shebuim* (the redeeming of captives). (The principle of unlimited assistance in fulfillment of *pidyon shebuim* is set forth in Maimonides, *Mishneh Torah,* Matnat Aniyim 8:10.) Ibid., pp. 82, 84.
53. Unger, *Sefer Kedoshim,* pp. 291–292.
54. Ibid., pp. 307–308. The Rebbe had a police barrier in front of his house torn down. The gate was to deny access to refugees.
55. *Eleh Ezkerah,* vol. 3, p. 81.

56. David Weisbrod Halachmi, *Artze Halevanon*, p. 209. See Yashar, *Bet Komarno*, pp. 130, 174, for a slightly different eyewitness account. In response to his family's concern for his personal welfare, the Rebbe replied: "In a time of crisis for all of Israel, we cannot respond, 'I shall look out for myself only.' If, with God's help, we survive this terrible period, we shall then purchase new valuables."

57. Unger, *Sefer Kedoshim*, pp. 357, 419.

58. *Eleh Ezkerah*, vol. 5, p. 100.

59. Ibid., p. 287.

60. Huberband, *Kiddush Hashem*, p. 282. Instead, a life-size dummy dressed in Hasidic garb was burned in effigy.

61. The Russians had prohibited assisting Polish Jewish refugees.

62. Yashar, *Bet Komarno*, p. 174.

63. *Kiddush Hashem*, pp. 296–297.

64. A temporary haven for many orthodox Jews, including the Piazesner Rebbe and the brother of the Gerer Rebbe. Seidman, *Yoman Getto Warsha*, p. 125. For account of the unsuccessful attempt to smuggle the elder Bobover Rebbe into the Warsaw Ghetto, see ibid., p. 176.

65. Unger, *Sefer Kedoshim*, p. 21.

66. Avraham Mordechai Alter, in Yehezke'eli, *Nes Hahatzalah shel Harebe Megur*.

67. Personal interview with Rabbi Shlomo Halberstam, the Bobover Rebbe, in Brooklyn, New York, July 30, 1969. The Gestapo officer was evidently deeply involved in prior bribe arrangements. The Hasid risked death in the gamble that the officer would wish to continue the lucrative relationship. The plan succeeded, and the officer used his authority to have the Rebbe released.

68. Unger, *Sefer Kedoshim*, pp. 61, 108–109.

69. Alfasi, *Sefer Ha'admorim*, p. 87.

70. Yehezke'eli, *Nes Hahatzalah shel Harebe Megur*, p. 15.

71. A gabbai, like a shamash, is a personal attendant of a Rebbe. While the shamash deals with the Rebbe's personal needs, the gabbai is concerned with the broader responsibilities of the Rebbe's household.

72. Unger, *Sefer Kedoshim*, p. 162.

73. Yehezke'eli, *Hatzalat Harebe Mebelz*, pp. 10, 23–24, 99–100.

74. Unger, *Sefer Kedoshim*, p. 358.

75. The *kiddush* (sanctification) ritual consists of a three-part blessing over a cup of wine at the beginning of the Friday eve Sabbath meal, sanctifying the Sabbath, and at the beginning of the Sabbath lunch. Wine is also utilized when the Sabbath is ushered out on Saturday evening with the *havdalah* (lit., "separation") service. According to the source, the Rebbe boarded the train on a Thursday, at which time one ordinarily completes preparations for the Sabbath.

76. Unger, *Sefer Kedoshim*, p. 225.

77. *Eleh Ezkerah*, vol. 4, p. 57; Unger, *Sefer Kedoshim*, pp. 35–36.

78. Yehezke'eli, *Hatzalat Harebe Mebelz*, p. 26. A variant version identifies the gabbai as Ahron Yehoshua Landau, without the verbal response noted above. *Harav Hakadosh Mebelz*, p. 85.

79. Yehezke'eli, *Hatzalat Harebe Mebelz*, p. 69.

80. A number of variations on the episode are cited in Unger, *Sefer Kedoshim*, pp. 408–409. While these identify the martyred gabbai as Moshe, another source makes reference to a Yehoshua Wolf. *Ani Ma'amin*, pp. 69–70. S. Z. Shragai also cites two versions, noting respectively the names of the elder Moshe and a young Hasidic martyr named Yaakov Yosef. *Sefer Habesht*, p. 187. It is possible that the versions may correspond to two different attempts to cover for the Rebbe. The episode is also noted in Yizhak Katzenelson, *Ketavim Aharonim*, p. 451. See also *Jewish Resistance During the Holocaust*, p. 130.

81. This expression is used when honoring and paying respect to the dead, since the dead person cannot possibly reciprocate.

82. Unger, *Sefer Kedoshim*, pp. 128–129.

83. Report of Pinhas Feinstatd. *Eleh Shelo Nikhne'u*, vol. 1, pp. 39–40.

84. Yehezke'eli, *Hatzalat Harebe Mebelz*, p. 13.

85. Ibid., p. 28.

86. *EK*, p. 23.

87. Exodus 32. God threatens to destroy the Jewish people. Moses' plea arouses *Rahamim* and God spares the people.

88. See Exodus 32:32.

89. *EK*, p. 23.

90. Ibid., p. 93.

91. Ibid.

92. *EK* supports the equation of *Ahavat Yisrael* and *tzelem Elohim* (the image of God within every man) in the following exegesis of Deuteronomy 6:4–5: "Hear, O Israel! The Lord is *our* God, the Lord alone. You shall love the Lord *your* God." Every Jew shall love the godly within himself (*Elohekha*—your God, the unique divine component in man), and be aware that the "Lord is our God," one God whose unity is reflected in the common bond and destiny of *kelal Yisrael*. *EK*, p. 179.

93. Ibid., pp. 180–181.

94. *Eleh Ezkerah* ("These Martyrs I Well Remember"), recited on Yom Kippur.

95. Talmud Yoma 85 is mistakenly cited by *EK*. The original source is found in Avot Derabi Natan 38:3.

96. *EK*, pp. 130–131. Once again the symbiosis of man and the divine is emphasized.

97. *EHS*, pp. 317, 324.

98. Birnbaum, *Passover Haggadah*, p. 30.

99. *EHS*, p. 228. Consistent with the *EHS* thesis; elaborated above in chap. 6; that the plight of the Jew, including the Holocaust, is partly his own doing. Lack of *Ahavat Yisrael* prevented a united effort to liquidate the Galut in Europe by means of mass settlement in Eretz Yisrael during the first four decades of this century.

100. Lit., "Sabbath perimeter," the restricted area, set by rabbinic law, within which one is permitted to walk or to carry on the Sabbath; i.e., a very confined area. Maimonides, *Mishneh Torah*, Hilkhot Shabbat, chap. 27.

101. *EHS*, p. 251.

102. Ibid., p. 329.

103. Unger, *Sefer Kedoshim*, p. 452.

104. Eyewitness Leibel Yud in *Eleh Shelo Nikhne'u*, vol. 2, p. 32. Only a sense of *Ahavat Yisrael* could have provided this rationale for the Holocaust. If the suffering inflicted by the Nazis was not the prelude to redemption, it served no purpose.

105. Robinson, *And The Crooked Shall Be Made Straight*, p. 221; *Jewish Resistance During the Holocaust*, p. 34.

106. Ibid.

107. Huberband, *Kiddush Hashem*, p. 67.

108. Ibid., pp. 67, 84–88. This also included the prohibition of the shtreimel, the fur hat worn by Hasidim on Sabbaths, festivals, and special occasions. Ibid., pp. 96–98.

109. *Ani Ma'amin*, p. 31.

110. Huberband, *Kiddush Hashem*, pp. 100–111.

111. Ibid., p. 111.

112. *EK*, p. 20 (rear pagination). Yosef Schapiro, the Rebbe's nephew, indicates that "details as to how these 'Torahs' were said are not known to us." They were related orally on the Sabbath and festival and subsequently handwritten by the Rebbe later on when writing was permitted. Yosef Schapiro, personal letter, September 13, 1970.

113. Unger, *Sefer Kedoshim*, pp. 162, 172, 351. Yehezke'eli, *Hatzalat Harebbe Mebelz*, pp. 44–45. *Eleh Ezkerah*, vol. 3, pp. 26, 139–140.

114. Yehezke'eli, *Hatzalat Harebbe Mebelz*, p. 104.

115. *Ani Ma'amin*, pp. 123–124.

116. The Hasid, with a small glass of wine or liquor, offers *lehayim* (a blessing for life) to the Rebbe, and the Rebbe acknowledges with a nod of the head or a personal blessing. At times the Hasid may personally approach the Rebbe for such a blessing. Wertheim, *Halakhot Vehalikhot Behasidut*, pp. 221–224.

117. Yehezke'eli, *Hatzalat Harebbe Mebelz*, p. 121.

118. From the Sabbath morning liturgy. Ben Zion Bokser, *The Prayer Book*, p. 126.

119. M. S. Geshuri, "Letoldot Hahasidut Vehaneginah Hahasidit B'krako," Aryeh Bauminger, in *Sefer Krako*, pp. 167–175.

120. Personal interview with Rabbi Shlomo Halberstam, the Bobover Rebbe. Brooklyn, New York, July 30, 1969.

121. Eyewitness David Applebaum, in Unger, *Sefer Kedoshim*, p. 34.

122. Yehezke'eli, *Hatzalat Harebbe Mebelz*, p. 52.

123. Ibid., p. 88.

124. Eyewitness Shlomo Waga, in *Hurban Chenstochow*, p. 24. The Rebbe is not identified.

125. Huberband, *Kiddush Hashem*, pp. 200–204.

126. Personal interview with Rabbi Shlomo Halberstam, the Bobover Rebbe. Brooklyn, New York, July 30, 1969.

127. Eyewitness Moshe Flescher, in Unger, *Sefer Kedoshim*, p. 23.

128. The concluding day of the Sukkot festival. This holiday is noted for its emphasis on joy. The Torah reading cycle is completed. Dancing and singing during the *hakafot* (procession in a circle) center about the Torah

scrolls. Because of the danger, the Rebbe and Hasidim escaped from Belz immediately following the *hakafot,* though the festival was not concluded until the following evening.

129. Eyewitness Avraham Haim Marwa, in Yehezke'eli, *Hatzalat Harebbe Mebelz,* pp. 13–14.

130. Eyewitness Z. Levinbuch, in *Baranowich,* p. 622.

131. The Yehudah Feingold documentation in Aryeh Avatihi and Yohanan ben-Zakai, *Stolin,* pp. 210–213, may be apocryphal.

132. Eyewitnesses Yisrael Zweig, Leibel Brickman, and Mendel Yoskowitz, in Moshe Prager, *Eleh Shelo Nikhne'u,* pp. 130, 133, 138. The incident inspired a dramatic work by the Holocaust poet Yitzchak Katzenelson, "Hashir Al Shlomo Zelichovsky," in *Ketavim Aharonim,* pp. 52–58.

133. David Stein, "Hassidishen Yid Hot Ungefihrt mit Untergrunt in Belgiya."

134. A series of letters discovered by the Hasid's sister in the ruins of the Lodzer Ghetto, in 1945. *Eleh Ezkerah,* vol. 2, p. 286.

135. Referring to Rabbi Simeon bar Yohai, a leading tanna (the tannaim were the teachers of the mishnaic period, 80 B.C.E.–200 C.E.). According to Jewish mystical tradition, he was the author of the *Zohar*. Scholem, *Major Trends,* pp. 157, 163.

136. Probably *Likute Mohran*. See Bibliography for full citation.

137. *Eleh Ezkerah,* vol. 2, p. 287.

138. *Eleh Shelo Nikhne'u,* vol. 1, pp. 99–101, 102–103.

NOTES TO CHAPTER 11

1. Samuel Dresner, *The Zaddik.*
2. Ibid., pp. 148–190.
3. Buber, *Origin and Meaning of Hasidism,* p. 44.
4. Dresner, *The Zaddik,* p. 155.
5. *No'am Elimelekh,* p. 8a.
6. Eliezer Steinman, *Sha'ar Hahasidut,* p. 102.
7. *No'am Elimelekh,* p. 10d.
8. Psalms 130:1.
9. *No'am Elimelekh,* p. 11a.
10. "Had the Ba'al Shem Tov redeemed only the Jewish people in his generation from *ye'ush,* it would have been sufficient." *Sha'ar Hahasidut,* p. 36.
11. Uffenheimer, *Quietistic Elements,* p. 37.
12. Ibid., p. 42. "Despair in the ability of man to achieve is an insult to the ability of God." Ibid., p. 44.
13. Nahman of Brazlav, *Likute Etzot,* p. 35; *Likute Mohran* 6:7, 7b–8a.
14. Ibid.
15. See above, p. 73.
16. *Sha'ar Hahasidut,* p. 185.
17. *Sha'ar Hahasidut,* p. 27. Though Rabbi Yisrael specifically refers to a Jew

who has fallen into the depths of sin, the principle operates as well for the Jew in despair.

18. *Hastarah*, related to *hester panim* (the eclipse of God's Presence), which is a state of *Din* (retribution).

19. Exodus 20:2.

20. Berl, *Rabbi Yitzchak Isaac of Komarno*, pp. 229–230.

21. Uffenheimer, *Quietistic Elements in 18th Century Hasidic Thought*, p. 149. As opposed to the quietistic-mystic isolate.

22. Wertheim, *Halakhot Vehalikhot Behasidut*, p. 155. Rabbi Nahman of Brazlav notes the extent of the Zadik-Hasid interrelationship: "All of man's concerns whether fiscal or health, etc., none can be resolved but through the Zadik" *Likute Etzot*, p. 149.

23. *Toldot*, p. 19b.

24. Dresner, *The Zaddik*, p. 241.

25. *Kedushat Levi*, p. 65a.

26. *Toldot*, p. 65d.

27. *No'am Elimelekh*, p. 25a. The *shelemut* (perfection) and *ihud* (unity) of the upper spheres cannot be realized when man, and especially the Zadik, functions in isolation "below." See also ibid., p. 24d. Rabbi Elimelech of Lizensk compares the two sons of Joseph, *Ephraim* with *Manasseh* (Genesis 48:1–20). Both were Zadikim. The former was concerned with Israel and this world. The latter was absorbed in the world beyond. "And [the approach of Ephraim] was more essential in the opinion of Israel [Jacob] our father, because his [Ephraim's] major objective was to draw forth benefits for Israel [the people]."

28. *Sha'ar Hahasidut*, p. 237; *Emet Ve'emunah*, p. 22.

29. Berl, *Rabbi Yitzchak Isaac of Komarno*, p. 254.

30. Ibid., p. 305.

31. Leviticus 19:17.

32. *Sha'ar Hahasidut*, p. 42. The *yeridah letzorekh aliyah* (the prerequisite descent in order to ascend) motif is noted once again. Aspects of *yeridat hazadik* (the descent of the Zadik can be achieved by any Jew who performs an ethical act that benefits a fellow human being.

33. *Likute Etzot*, pp. 160, 164.

34. *Sha'ar Hahasidut, p. 185.*

35. Ibid., p. 228.

36. *Sha'ar Hahasidut*, p. 11.

37. Steinman defines this symbiosis by comparing the Hasid to the branches of the tree, and the Zadik to the tree. "And the branch is always attached to it." Ibid., p. 14.

38. Wertheim, *Halakot Vehalikot Behasidut*, p. 155, and primary source documentation, p. 148, fn. 18, citing Rabbi Moshe Haim Efraim, the grandson of the Ba'al Shem Tov.

39. *Emet Ve'emunah*, p. 7. Yet more intense was the reaction of the Belzer Rebbe in Budapest, 1944, during the escape from Holocaust Europe. Evidently a throng of zealous Hasidim clamored to meet with him. Under great tension, losing his composure, he entered the outer waiting room and

pleaded: "What do you want from me? What can I do? I am also only flesh and blood!" *Harab Hakadosh Mebelz,* p. 123.

40. Buber, *Tales of the Hasidim: Early Masters,* p. 5.

41. "Kuntrus Meirat Enayim," *Shivhe Habesht,* pp. 4–7. These included Rabbis Gershon Kitover, Yaakov Yosef of Polnoya, Dov Ber of Mezritch, and Yisrael Harif of Satinov.

42. Rabinowitz, *Hahasidut Halita'it,* p. 28.

43. *Likute Mohran,* p. 256, 19:1.

44. Ibid., 3:6, 2b; 9:4, 12a. "The major inspiration for life emanates from the Zadik" (ibid., 8:2, 9b) implies that the attachment cannot be for its own sake but as a means to improve one's own life.

45. In the context here, *talmid hakham* (lit. "wise student") refers to the Zadik.

46. Ibid., 4:8, 4a. It is likely that the significance of the confession is limited to the opportunity for the Hasid to "unload his burdens" (*hishtapkhut hanefesh,* lit., "the outpouring of the soul"), which was in character with the Zadik-Hasid relationship. Dresner, *The Zaddik,* pp. 154–155. The confession, as Rabbi Nahman clearly implies, was not related to the classic *teshuvah* (repentance) process, of which confession is an essential ingredient, and certainly unrelated to the confessional in Catholic doctrine. In the latter, confession is part of the process of penance where the bishop or priest-penitentiary, and eventually, the priest was central to the pardoning and reconciliation of the sinner. *Encyclopaedia Britannica,* (1967), s.v. "Confession."

47. Berl, *Yitzchak Isaac of Komarno,* p. 307.

48. Rabinowitz, *Hahasidut Halita'it,* p. 73. "During these visits to the court of the Rebbe, the Hasid had the opportunity to disengage from the bitter and pathetic realities [about him] and his daily concerns. There he found refuge for his tired body and weary soul." Ibid.

49. Alfasi, *Hahasidut,* pp. 177–183.

50. *Ahavat Yisrael* is not unique to Hasidism. Leviticus 19:17 ("You shall love your neighbor as yourself") has served as the basis of numerous rabbinic laws defining a Jew's responsibility and duty to his fellow Jews. (See Maimonides, *Mishneh Torah,* Hilkhot De'ot, chapts. 6 and 7.) Hasidism injected new fervor into this concept, especially through its relating of *Ahavat Yisrael* to *Ahavat Hashem.*

51. Self-mortification, particularly fasting at regular intervals, was common among Jewish mystics. Self-inflicted punishment of the body, as a means of penance, especially among mystics in medieval Germany, is treated in Scholem, *Major Trends,* pp. 104–105.

52. Barukh of Mezibiz, *Buzina Denehora,* p. 64. See also ibid., p. 14. Altruistic acts directed toward God, fellow man, and study of Torah are a superior means of sublimating ego and material forces in man because they are outer- (or other-) directed. Self-mortification *(sigufim)* suffers from the element of self *(ani).* See also Solomon Schecter, "The Chassidim," p. 177, elaborating on Hasidism's aversion to ascetic practices.

53. Alfasi, *Hahasidut,* p. 177.

54. *Toldot*, p. 19b. Identical with "Every Jew is part of the very Shekhinah," *Rabbi Yitzchak Isaac of Komarno*, p. 293.
55. Alfasi, *Hahasidut*, p. 177.
56. Leviticus 19:18.
57. Deuteronomy 6:5
58. *Rabbi Yitzchak Isaac of Komarno*, p. 218. Hence, proof of the equation of love of God and love of man. See Steinman, *Sha'ar Hahasidut*, p. 12, for the significance of *gematriya* in Hasidic thought as a conscious effort to conserve and restrict verbiage.
59. The letters *v* and *u* are interchangeable in Hebrew wordplay since both can be designated by the letter *vav*.
60. i.e., thus removing the letter *r* from *tzibur*.
61. Ibid., p. 41. The *tzav* as an impure animal is mentioned in Leviticus 11:29. The differences in the community are blurred by Beshtian tradition because "differences" are essential ingredients in a complete and "pure" community. The *rasha* (wicked) serves a purpose. It is from the *rasha* that trapped *nitzotzot* (sparks of holy origin) are distilled and elevated to their source. *Toldot*, p. 8.
62. Ibid., pp. 72a–72b.
63. *Toldot*, pp. 27d, 28a.
64. Deuteronomy 29:9.
65. *Toldot*, p. 191c.
66. Leviticus 19:18.
67. Equivalent to the consonant *y* and also to the term "Jew," from the Yiddish *Yid* or the Hebrew *Yehudi*.
68. Among the various abbreviated spellings of "The Lord," especially in the liturgy, is the use of a double *yud*, instead of the Tetragrammaton.
69. Symbolic allusion to a Jew who considers himself above his fellow. The resultant misalignment in the spelling of God's name creates a "false" God.
70. *Sha'ar Hahasidut*, p. 261.
71. *Rabbi Yitzchah of Komarno*, p. 226.
72. *Sha'ar Hahasidut*, p. 270.
73. Ibid.
74. *Toldot*, p. 5c.
75. *Emet Ve'emunah*, p. 82.
76. Josephus, *The Jewish War*, trans. G. A. Williamson (Baltimore: Penguin Books, 1959), pp. 125–126. See also Shimon Dubnow, *Divre Yeme Olam*, pp. 104–105.
77. "Rabbi Shimon said: 'Three who ate at the same table without speaking any words of Torah, it is as if they had eaten of the sacrifices to dead idols. . . . But if three have eaten at the same table and did speak words of Torah, it is as if they had eaten at a table set before the Lord." Mishnah Avot 3:4. See also Talmud Berakhot 45a–54b for laws and traditions reflecting the sanctity of the table.
78. Wertheim, *Halakhot Vehalikhot Behasidut*, p. 165.
79. Ibid. See also Rabinowitz, *Hahasidut Halita'it*, p. 11.
80. The Hasid extends the blessing "to life!" to the Rebbe over a raised glass. The Rebbe acknowledges in kind.

81. Wertheim, *Halakhot Vehalikhot Behasidut*, p. 166.
82. *Shirayim* is a Yiddish derivative of the Hebrew *she'er* (remnant).
83. For fuller treatment of the notion of *berur Hanitzotzim* (the selection of the sparks), considered part of the process of consuming food left by a Zadik, and assuming the form of *tikkun* (restoration of lost sparks), see Wertheim, *Halakhot Vehalikhot Behasidut*, p. 168.
84. This meal, conducted at twilight on the Sabbath, is referred to in colloquial Yiddish as *shalosh sudos*, lit., "three meals." The mood created by the Hasidic melodies, the darkened, hushed room, and the Torot of the Rebbe is one of *devekut* and longing for the holy Sabbath day receding in the sunset. See Wertheim, *Halakhot Vehalikhot Behasidut*, pp. 151–153. The fraternal *Se'udah shelishit* is evident in the following early Hasidic source: "The Ba'al Shem Tov once spent a Sabbath in a village with his retinue [*minyan*, lit., group of ten men, representing a quorum for worship]. When it came time for *shalosh sudos*, the head of the town assembled a number of townspeople, [who participated in] eating, drinking, and singing *zemirot* [traditional Sabbath and *shalosh se'udot* melodies] in praise of God. When the Ba'al Shem Tov realized that this [custom] was welcomed above, he beckoned him [the town leader] after the meal and asked him why so much attention was lavished upon the 'third meal,' He replied: 'I have heard it generally acknowledged, "May my soul depart among fellow Jews." I also understand that on the Sabbath every Jew is possessed of an additional soul. At the conclusion of the Sabbath, this soul leaves us. Thus I said, "May my soul also depart among fellow Jews." Therefore, I gather Jews in this fashion!' And he [the Ba'al Shem Tov] greatly appreciated this." *Likute Keter Shem Tov*, p. 42. Note the integration of the Ahavat Yisrael nuance with the fraternal aspect of the Hasidic meal.
85. In order to expand the Sabbath experience, a fourth meal assumed prominence in Jewish mystical tradition, in which the Jew "escorts" the Sabbath Queen in a hesitant gesture of farewell. This tradition is noted in the Talmud (Shabbat 119b) and in subsequent rabbinic law, but achieves its greatest prominence in Hasidism. Wertheim, *Halakhot Vehalikhot Behasidut*, p. 153.
86. Ibid., pp. 227–228. Wertheim cites the reason for this tradition in the name of Rabbi David Moshe of Tchartkov, the son of the Riziner. "Therefore, the children and disciples of the Zadik shall celebrate on the anniversary of his death, since on that day annually, the soul of the Zadik ascends to a higher rung. This is comparable to the day on which a miracle has been realized for his forefathers." Ibid., p. 228.
87. Ibid., p. 161. Seeking out a man of God for assistance in times of personal need is noted in biblical and talmudic sources. I Samuel 9:6, II Kings 4, Talmud Berakhot 34b, Talmud Bava Batra 116a.
88. *Likute Mohran* 7:3, 8b.
89. Wertheim, *Halakhot Vehalikhot Behasidut*, p. 162. Many Rebbes eventually discarded the practice of accepting payment for assistance because it degraded the dignity of the Zadik's authority. Ibid.
90. Ibid., pp. 162–163.
91. Ibid., p. 163, esp. fn. 39.

92. Ibid.

93. Ibid., p. 164. The current practice of visitors to Jerusalem of placing written requests in the cracks of the Western Wall is related to the Hasidic tradition of the Kvittel.

94. Meir Simon Gershuri, "Letorat Hanigun Behasidut." See also his *Haniggun Veharikkud Behasidut.*

95. In order to sustain the memory of the tragedy of the *Hurban Bet Hamikdash* (destruction of the Temple). Ibid., See Lamentations Rabbah 1:59 for a description of the contrast between the joy expressed through music during the zenith of Jewish independence in Eretz Yisrael, and the depression of exile "where I come and go in tears."

96. Nahman of Brazlav, *Likute Mohran,* pp. 3, 3a. Rabbi Yisrael of Karlin viewed music as a path to God, suggesting that one cleanse one's hands prior to participating in a musical experience. Rabinowitz, *Hasidut Halita'it,* p. 87.

97. Israel Rabinowich, *Of Jewish Music,* pp. 84–85.

98. Wertheim, *Halakhot Vehalikhot Behasidut,* pp. 105–106.

99. *Me'olamo Shel Rabbi Nahman Mebrazlav,* pp. 54–55. Thus involvement in the art of music may lead to *bittul hayesh* (the dissovling of the ego), a Hasidic objective.

100. Steinman, *Sha'ar Hahasidut,* p. 261. For a comparative analysis of various musical styles and traditions in Hasidism, see the works of Gershuri cited above in n. 94.

NOTES TO CHAPTER 12

1. *Jewish Resistance During the Holocaust,* pp. 47, 57, and the reinforcing comments of Sarah Nashmit, pp. 52–53.

2. Ibid., p. 35.

3. Unger, *Sefer Kedoshim,* p. 88.

4. Ibid., p. 281.

5. Shragai, *Sefer Habesht,* pp. 152–201. *Hasidut Vezion,* p. 89. *Eleh Ezkerah,* vol. 5, p. 287. Frankel, *Yehide Segulah,* pp. 203–206.

6. Seidman, *Yoman Getto Warsha,* pp. 153, 221. Frankel, *Yehide Segulah,* p. 210.

7. David Weinsklad, "Brief fun Churef-Geworene Yiddishe Shtet un Shtetlech." See also Unger, *Sefer Kedoshim,* p. 397.

8. Ibid., pp. 412–413.

9. David Stein, "Hassidishen Yid hot Ungefihrt mit Untergrunt in Belgia."

10. M. Y. Nurenberger, " 'Z'il, 'Yiddisher Fihrer fun Franzoizishen Untergrunt."

11. Unger, *Sefer Kedoshim,* p. 274.

12. Huberband, *Kiddush Hashem,* pp. 27–28.

13. Unger, *Sefer Kedoshim,* p. 279.

14. Ibid., p. 205.

15. *Ani Ma'amin,* pp. 73–74. Anilewitz was the commander of all resistance

activities during the uprising in Warsaw (August 21, 1942–May 16, 1943). Hilberg, *Destruction of the European Jews*, pp. 322–327.

16. Seidman, *Yoman Getto Warsha*, p. 173.

17. *Eleh Ezkerah*, vol. 3, p. 16. Seidman (*Yoman Getto Warsha*, p. 257) reports on a group of Gerer Hasidim who fought in the uprising. It is not certain whether they can be identified with the remnants of Weinberg's study group.

18. *Eleh Shelo Nikhne'u*, vol. 2, p. 17. Report of eyewitness Leibel Pinkoswitz.

19. Cries of *nekamah* at the moment of execution or etched into the walls of the camps and ghettos are routinely depicted in the Holocaust literature. Robinson, *And The Crooked Shall Be Made Straight*, p. 216. *Eleh Shelo Nikhne'u*, p. 138. Yisrael Tabaksblat, *Hurban Lodz*, p. 137.

20. Unger, *Sefer Kedoshim*, p. 233.

21. S. Z. Cahane, "Hitkomemut Be'em Hageta'ot," in Sh. Niger, *Kiddush Hashem*, p. 684.

22. See above, p. 82. Also, Robinson, *And the Crooked Shall Be Made Straight*, p. 221; Huberband, *Kiddush Hashem*, p. 79.

23. As per Unger, *Sefer Kedoshim*, pp. 166–167.

24. See Wertheim, *Halakhot Vehalikhot Behasidut*, pp. 195–199, for a detailed description and analysis of various facets of Hasidic dress and the wearing of beard and *pe'ot*.

Eyewitness Yaakov Leib Manila cites the death penalty for the wearing of beard and *pe'ot* in the Michov Ghetto. Prager, *Eleh Shelo Nikhne'u*, vol. 1, p. 55. See also Huberband, *Kiddush Hashem*, pp. 84–88, and Robinson, *And the Crooked Shall Be Made Straight*, p. 221.

25. Unger, *Sefer Kedoshim*, pp. 101, 160, 172, 187. *Eleh Ezkerah*, vol. 4, p. 96; vol. 5, pp. 232–233. *Ani Ma'amin*, p. 21. In the instance of the Tomashover Rebbe, he agreed to be smuggled from Lodz to Warsaw on the condition that his beard not be removed for purposes of disguise.

26. Unger, *Sefer Kedoshim*, p. 205.

27. *Kiddush Hashem*, p. 79. Photos nos. 17, 18, 20, 21, 22, 23, 24, 25, 29, 30, 35, and 36, in the rear of the volume illustrate the manner in which Hasidim were apprehended and harassed. Photos nos. 21, 22, 24, 25, 36 depict the forced removal of beards and *pe'ot* as described in the detailed narrative, ibid., p. 84. The danger of being caught with beard and *pe'ot* is documented in ibid., p. 67.

28. *Ani Ma'amin*, pp. 146–147; *Eleh Shelo Nikhne'u*, vol. 1, p. 40. For similar behavior in the Cracow Ghetto, see Seidman, *Yoman Getto Warsha*, pp. 179, 335; *Eleh Shelo Nikhne'u*, vol. 1, pp. 48–50.

29. *Ani Ma'amin*, pp. 150–151; Robinson, *And The Crooked Shall Be Made Straight*, p. 221.

30. *Eleh Shelo Nikhne'u*, vol. 1, pp. 43–45. Ozer Grundman also cites evidence related to the Shidlowitz Hasidic cell. Following Mati Gelman's departure for Cracow, Naftali Lokover assumed the leadership of this group. Ibid., pp. 46, 57.

31. Elimelech Schwartz, "Agudisten in Lodzer Ghetto," p. 108.

32. Eyewitnesses Leibel Yutzanka and Yaakov Manila report a Hasidic cell meeting on Chashnizka Street in the Michov Ghetto. Shaul Harmetz, Feivel

Ulman, and his younger brother were active in the cell. *Eleh Shelo Nikhne'u*, pp. 42, 54–56. Yehoshua Kustman directed the illegal group in the Willizkah Ghetto. This cell included two young Hasidim named Klein and Stern, and Itchie Abalis. Ibid., pp. 52–53.

33. The round fur hat traditionally worn by some Hasidic groups on Sabbaths, festivals, and special occasions. Wertheim, *Halakhot Vehalikhot Behasidut*, p. 196.

34. Ehrenberg, *Artze Levanon*, p. 171.

35. Yehezke'eli, *Hatzalat Harebe Mebelz*, p. 44.

36. *Eleh Ezkerah*, vol. 6, p. 113.

37. Unger, *Sefer Kedoshim*, pp. 164–165.

38. Rectangular undergarment with ritual fringes *(tzitzit)* worn by observant Jews.

39. Unger, *Sefer Kedoshim*, p. 324.

40. Huberband (*Kiddush Hashem*, p. 113) cites the prohibition posted at the entrance to every mikveh in the Warsaw Ghetto: "For unlocking the ritual pool, or its use, the resulting penalty will be equal to that of sabotage—from ten years [imprisonment] to death."

41. *Eleh Ezkerah*, vol. 5, pp. 232–233.

42. See above, p. 12.

43. *Ani Ma'amin*, p. 204.

44. *Eleh Shelo Nikhne'u*, p. 108.

45. Aaron Friedenthal in *Bet Ya'akov* 46 (March 1963): 8–9; *Eleh Ezkerah*, vol. 4, p. 57.

46. Unger, *Sefer Kedoshim*, p. 409.

47. Huberband, *Kiddush Hashem*, pp. 111–113. The incident probably took place at the mikveh on Zirov Street in the Warsaw Ghetto; it probably occurred after October 1941. See ibid., p. 91.

Many Jews who do not normally utilize the mikveh during the course of the year do so on the day prior to Yom Kippur. Mikveh has assumed a special relationship with Yom Kippur in accordance with Leviticus 16:30 ("For on this day, atonement shall be made for you to cleanse you of all your sins; you shall be clean before the Lord") and Talmud Yoma 85b: "*Mikveh Yisrael Adonai* ['God is the hope of Israel' (Jeremiah 17:13)]—like the mikveh [Rabbi Akiva reads *mikveh* (ritual pool) rather than *mikve* (hope)] which purifies the impure, so does the Holy One, blessed be He, purify Israel."

48. Upon the death of Rabbi Mendele Hager, the Vishiver Rebbe, in 1941, his sons Rabbi Baruch and Rabbi Meir were appointed as Rebbe for the Vishiver and Bizkiver communities respectively. When the Zichliner Rebbe, Rabbi Menahem Yedidya, died in the Zichliner Ghetto in 1940, his son, Rabbi Avraham Abba, was "crowned" in his stead. Unger, *Sefer Kedoshim*, pp. 137–138, 171–172.

49. Ibid., p. 126.

50. Ibid., p. 250.

51. Ibid., p. 278.

52. *Eleh Shelo Nikhne'u*, vol. 2, p. 175.

53. Unger, *Sefer Kedoshim*, p. 358.

54. Ibid., pp. 376–379.

55. Ibid., p. 387.
56. *Eleh Ezkerah,* vol. 6, p. 73.
57. *Eleh Shelo Nikhne'u.*
58. Ibid., p. 141. The Germans frequently ordered lengthy mass outdoor reviews of the prisoners, often under adverse weather conditions.
59. *Ani Ma'amin,* p. 109.
60. Avraham Weissbrod, *Es Shtarbt a Shtetel: Megilas Skalat,* p. 123.
61. Unger, *Sefer Kedoshim,* pp. 125–126.
62. *Eleh Ezkerah,* vol. 4, p. 96.
63. Eyewitness Avraham Hendel in *Eleh Shelo Nikhne'u,* vol. 2, p. 177.
64. Ibid., p. 178.
65. Ibid. Also involved were the Rebbes of Strikov and Sosnov, the two brothers of the Alexander Rebbe, and the brother of the Radomsker. The laws of Passover allow for the sale of *hametz* to, and its subsequent repurchase from, a non-Jew. This procedure enables the Jew to temporarily renounce ownership of the *hametz* during the Passover period. The risk involved in negotiating with a non-Jew outside the ghetto was extreme. The Krimilover endangered his life in order to draw water from a deep well for the baking of matzah. See also Unger, *Sefer Kedoshim,* p. 384.
66. Ibid., p. 387.
67. Yosef Weiss, "Oshviz Ha'aheret: Seder Hashai im Zemer 'Had Gadya,' " pp. 6–7. The Seder was conducted without the traditional foods and ritual objects, and was built around Hasidic Passover melodies.
68. Weissbrod, *Es Shtarbt a Shtetel,* pp. 124–125.
69. *Eleh Shelo Nikhne'u,* vol. 2, pp. 152–153.
70. Kaplan, *Scroll of Agony,* p. 214.
71. *Ani Ma'amin,* p. 204.
72. *Eleh Shelo Nikhne'u,* vol. 2, p. 29. The exclamation is taken directly from the Purim liturgy. Haman traditionally symbolizes the archenemy of the Jew. *Standard Prayer Book,* p. 423.
73. Yoel Frankenthal, "Nerot Hanukah Shehe'iru et Ofel Ha'abdut."
74. *Eleh Shelo Nikhne'u,* vol. 2, pp. 165–167. Remnants of discarded Nazi newspapers, cement sacks, and official record slips were utilized for this purpose.
75. *Eleh Ezkerah,* vol. 5, p. 95; *Eleh Shelo Nikhne'u,* vol. 2, pp. 29–30. Compare the simulated Friday eve Sabbath meal of the Bobover Rebbe and his son in the Gestapo jail, symbolized by a hard crust of bread. Personal interview with Rabbi Shlomo Halberstam, the Bobover Rebbe, Brooklyn, New York, July 30, 1969.
76. Hilberg, *Destruction of the European Jews,* p. 318. This was the central assembly point in the ghetto for deportation.
77. Seidman, *Yoman Getto Warsha,* p. 215.
78. See Huberband, *Kiddush Hashem,* pp. 100–111, for a comprehensive description of the illegal underground *shehitah* activities in Warsaw and elsewhere.
79. *Scroll of Agony,* p. 276.
80. *Eleh Ezkerah,* vol. 6, p. 124.
81. *Eleh Shelo Nikhne'u,* vol. 2, p. 121.

82. Ibid., pp. 182–183.
83. Eyewitness Leibel Yud, in ibid., vol. 1, p. 71.
84. According to Matityahu, the most effective counter to the satanic forces, who thrived on suffering and death, was marriage, representing life and joy. Ibid., p. 62.
85. *Ani Ma'amin*, p. 60.
86. *Eleh Shelo Nikhne'u*, vol. 2, p. 20.
87. Sternberg, "Hahavai Hayehudi Bime Hashoah," p. 412.
88. *Ani Ma'amin*, pp. 150–151, 204. Based on evidence from various eyewitness reports (*Eleh Shelo Nikhne'u*, vol. 1, pp. 28–30, 32, 34, 39–40, 48, 61, 62, 64–66, 70–71, 76–78, 97–99, 102; *Sefer Kraka*, p. 412; *Eleh Ezkerah*, vol. 3, p. 51; *Ani Ma'amin*, pp. 146, 150–151, 204), the Cracow Hasidic cells included Avraham Leib Horowitz, Moshe Sheinfeld, Yaakov Gefen, Leibel Hendles, Getzel Sluftzer, Elimelech Klein, Moshe Rosenwasser, Shmuel Lifshitz, Naftali Plutzker, Haim Shomo Klein, Avraham Kleinerer, Yisrael Eisenberg, a younger brother of Pinhas Feinstat, a Hasid named Meitner (first name unknown), and their leader, Yaakov Shapiro. The legendary Mati Gelman frequently joined the Cracow group in order to organize liaison missions to similar Hasidic cells in the ghettos of Stofnitz, Ziyaloshiz, Pinzev, Michov, Welbrum, and Chashnizah. Yaakov Gefen made unsuccessful attempts to contact Polish resistance groups in the forest outside of Cracow. Shmuel Lifshitz ran assistance missions to the ghettos of Michov, Proshowitz, Vzisko, Kushitza, and Neishtat. The Gerer Hasidic shtiebel on Esther Street served as one of the meeting places for the illegal groups. Some of the cells were exclusively Gerer Hasidim, others consisted of mixed Hasidic traditions and schools.
89. Prager, *Eleh Shelo Nikhne'u*, vol. 1, pp. 48, 71, 88–89. *Ani Ma'amin*, p. 146.
90. *Eleh Ezkerah*, vol. 3, p. 51.
91. He gives the respective addresses of seven illegal Gerer study circles and one each of Lubavicher, Brazlaver, Novhordoker, Alexander, Chentchiner, Sochochover, and Piazesner study circles. *Kiddush Hashem*, p. 79.
92. *Eleh Ezkerah*, vol. 3, p. 16.
93. *Yoman Getto Warsha*, pp. 84, 179, 335. Seidman notes at least ten locales where these groups met regularly, including 14 Mila Street and 35 Nowalki Street. Mordechai Pinskowich was the commander of a Hasidic group meeting in a fortified bunker at 37 Novolipye Street in the Warsaw Ghetto. The group included Shlomo Rosenberg, Leibel Rotbard, Avraham the son of Rabbi Mendel of Pavnitz, Fishel Pinskowich, and Meir Schein. Other Gerer Hasidic groups in the Warsaw Ghetto met at 11a Faviah Street, 18 Twarda Street, and Ganshe Street. *Eleh Shelo Nikhne'u*, vol. 1, pp. 72–76; vol. 2, pp. 16–33.
94. *Dafim Leheker Hashoah Vehamered*, vol. 1, p. 130. Approximately fifteen young Hasidim met in the Gerer "shtiebel" on Marinska Street and ten Alexander Hasidim used the "shtiebel" on Yakova Street.
95. *Eleh Ezkerah*, vol. 6, p. 124.
96. Prager, *Eleh Shelo Nikhne'u*, vol. 2, pp. 129–130, 166. Study of any sort

was considerably more difficult in the death camps and was often accomplished by memory, without texts.

97. Ibid., vol. 1, pp. 13–71.

98. *Eleh Shelo Nikhne'u*, vol. 2, p. 122; *Ani Ma'amin*, p. 158.

99. Seidman, *Yoman Getto Warsha*, pp. 63–64, 127.

100. *EK*, p. 20.

101. *Eleh Shelo Nikhne'u*, vol. 1, p. 146.

102. Ibid.

103. *Kiddush Hashem*, pp. 79–82. This group seems not to have been related to the network under the leadership of Matityahu Gelman with headquarters in Cracow.

104. Ibid., p. 81. The Rebbe had already left Poland for Palestine.

105. Because of this opposition, the group was forced to vacate their quarters at 9 Mila and transfer to 30 Muranowska Street.

106. For the full text of the letter, see Huberband, *Kiddush Hashem*, pp. 81–82.

107. The plea of Rabbi Moshe Bezalel did not improve matters. Ibid. Though the motives of such behavior are not explained, it appears to have been unacceptable to the Hasidic elements. By disengaging from the community under the guise of noncooperation with the enemy, they lashed out at friend and foe alike, displaying little sensitivity to fellow victims of the Holocaust. Perhaps they took the ideal of *hishtavut* (indifference to external realities) and *hafkarah atzmit* (personal abandonment) to its negative extreme, and in the process sacrificed the ideals of *Ahavat Yisrael* (love for a fellow Jew) and *Kiddush Hahayim* (the sanctification of God's Name in life).

In contrast, Huberband lauds a group of young men, in the main tradesmen and evidently Hasidim, who devoted themselves to assisting the poor and to studying Talmud each night after putting in a full day's work, *Kiddush Hashem*, pp. 83–84.

108. Unger, *Sefer Kedoshim*, pp. 389–390.

109. Huberband, *Kiddush Hashem*, p. 264.

110. Unger, *Sefer Kedoshim*, pp. 339–340. Not surprisingly, in view of their special interest in music, some Hasidic Rebbes were proficient musicians.

111. *Eleh Ezkerah*, vol. 6, p. 73.

112. Huberband, *Kiddush Hashem*, p. 28.

113. Yehezke'eli, *Hatzalat Harebe Mebelz*, p. 121.

114. Shmuel Rotstein, *Rabbi Menahem Zemba*.

NOTES TO CHAPTER 13

1. Arendt, *Eichmann in Jerusalem*, p. 9.

2. Robinson, *And the Crooked Shall Be Made Straight*, pp. 142–226.

3. Robinson accuses Arendt of the following: (1) Conveying unreliable information, (2) misreading pertinent documents, (3) not having "equipped herself with the necessary background for an understanding and analysis of the [Eichmann] trial." Ibid., p. viii. Another researcher has noted the special context in which the Holocaust unfolded and in which resistance of any sort

must be evaluated: "The struggle from its very inception was uneven. A seemingly unlimited power and authority imposed a death sentence upon a dispersed people without any means of a civil and military regime, at a time when many nations, large and small, who had all these means at their disposal could not withstand the strength of the conqueror. Only within this factual framework can we raise the question as to the character of the resistance and the response of the Jewish people." Leni Yahil, "Ha'amidah Hayeduhit-Aspaklarya Lekiyum Hayehudi Letzuroteha Hape'ilot Wehasebilot Bitkufat Hashoah," p. 27.

4. Robinson, *And the Crooked Shall Be Made Straight*, pp. 224–225.

5. Hilberg, *Destruction of the European Jews*, pp. 14–17.

6. Ibid., pp. 16–17.

7. Prior to Hitler, the Jew who sought to escape from anti-Semitism and was solely concerned with his own physical survival could exercise the option of rejecting Jewish identity.

8. "We see, therefore, that both perpetrators and victims drew upon their age-old experience in dealing with each other." *Destruction of the European Jews*, p. 17.

9. Exodus 17:14–16, Deuteronomy 25:17–19.

10. The "enemy" Amalek present in every human being is the factor that enables man to exercise freedom of choice. The *yetzer hara* was created in order that it might be vanquished by means of man's initiative. *Toldot*, p. 59b. The refrence to "the prince of Amalek" suggests that Amalek generally refers to all negative manifestations with which man must battle. The *yetzer hara*, though significant, is but a portion of the Amalek hierarchy.

11. *No'am Elimelekh*, p. 25b, referring to Genesis 33:18–34:31. In reprisal for Shechem's rape of Dinah, their sister, the two sons of Jacob slew all the males in the city.

12. Genesis 49:5. In his final testament to his sons, Jacob makes reference to this act of violence which he had originally abhorred (Genesis 34:30).

13. Talmud Berakhot 5a, referring to the statement of Rabbi Shimon ben Lakish: "One should always incite the *yetzer hatov* against the *yetzer hara*."

14. The act was therefore considered more courageous because the *yetzer hara* was in its most advanced and entrenched state.*No'am Elimelekh*, p. 25b.

15. Genesis 47:28.

16. *No'am Elimelekh*, p. 23d.

17. By means of prayer the Zadik battles on behalf of God or struggles to resist the evil decress against man. Ibid., p. 22a.

18. Deuteronomy 21:10.

19. Ibid.

20. *Likute Mohran*, 98b:107. Rabbi Nahman suggests that vanity opens the door to other negative influences which in turn endanger the divine component in man. When one focuses on the ego and ceases to be conscious of the divine image, the outcome of the struggle against the negative forces is in jeopardy. Evident once again is the idea previously noted: "If ever someone wishes to break the power of a particular substance he must do so by employing an identical substance."

21. This is a brilliant allusion to the concluding portion of Deuteronomy

21:11. The soldier falls in love with his captive and desires to marry her. In Hebrew *lekadesh* (to marry) also connotes to bring into the realm of sanctity (*Kiddushin*). This is consistent with the Hasidic doctrine of *tikkun* (rehabilitation) of the *nitzotzot zarot* (estranged sparks) and their return to the Holy Source. See also Uffenheimber, *Quietistic elements* p. 16.

22. *Emet Ve'emunah,* p. 14.

23. *Kedushat Levi,* pp. 131–132. Since vengeance is placed in the divine and not in the human context, it is characterized as an extension of love and not of hate, consistent with Hasidic thought. In any event the concept of vengeance is removed from human initiative.

24. Numbers 31:3. The biblical commandment urges vengeance against the Midianites for provoking the Israelites to engage in idolatry. See Numbers 25:1–9.

25. Yehiel Meir Lipshitz of Gastinin, *Sefer Me Hayam.*

26. Uffenheimber, *Quietistic Elements,* pp. 23, 85, 168–177. Uffenheimer's theory of Hasidism's spiritualization of Jewish national and messianic aspirations may be challenged, as documented by the works of Ben Zion Dinaburg and Zalman Shazar (fully cited in the Bibliography). If indeed the emphasis in Hasidism is on individual redemption, i.e., the spiritual variation of national redemption, it likely was intended as a prelude, rather a substitute for, national redemption.

27. The study did not reveal any evidence of any formal manifesto issued by groups of Hasidim involved in forms of spiritual resistance, in contrast to the publication by other resistance groups of underground press materials verbalizing the resistance struggle.

28. Lebel Eisner, a survivor of the Piyotrakov and Warsaw Ghettos, where he participated in the underground Gerer Hasidic cells, employed the terms *bitahon, emunah, hashgahah pratit,* and *mesirat nefesh* to characterize the critical stimulus and rationale behind the activities of the illegal Hasidic groups. *Eleh Shelo Nikhne'u,* vol. 1, pp. 125–126. The primacy of God's Will is articulated in the resistance response of Yaakov Gefen, one of the leaders of the Hasidic underground in Cracow. When urged to register for work in the Plashow labor camp, he said: "I was not created to work for the Germans, but rather for God. *That* is my job." Ibid., p. 98.

29. In a rare explanation of the motives of the Hasidic underground cells, Moshe Sheinfeld, a survivor of the Cracow group, recalls the significant lesson of *hishtavut* (the expression was used by Sheinfeld) taught by Yaakov Gefen, the leader of the cell. When Haim Shlomo Klein, a young member of the group, panicked in near hysteria during a search by German forces immediately outside the hidden bunker, Geffen asserted: "What did you attempt to accomplish! Didn't we know who they were? Didn't we hear them approach? So what of it? Who really cares? Isn't this actually what they want—for us to disintegrate before them? This is why they make all the noise and confusion. They want to break us and subdue us! Let them proceed with their business and we shall proceed with ours. That is why we shall not run away or retreat from them! This is the meaning of the verse 'How happy and fortunate is the man who trusts in God so that God becomes his source of confidence' (Jeremiah 17:7)." *Eleh Shelo Nikhne'u,* vol. 1, p.79. Eyewitness

Yisrael Mordechai Pinskowich relates the *hishtavut* attitude of his nephew, Leibel Pinskowich, who was one of the "commandanten" in the underground Gerer Hasidic cell at 37 Novolipye Street in the Warsaw Ghetto. "We do not recognize the enemy regime. For us they do not exist! We shall not reckon with them. To us they are nothing!" Ibid., vol. 2, p. 17.

30. *Zava'at Haribash*, p. 5.

31. In the name of Rabbi Asher of Karlin. Rabinowitz, *Hahasidut Halita'it*, p. 86. The mikveh is thus related to the pattern defining the centrality of the divine holiness in life and the unique potential *within* man to be realized in life.

32. Buber, *Origin and Meaning of Hasidism*, p. 133.

33. Alfasi, *Hahasidut*, pp. 87–88. The waters of the mikveh symbolically dissolve the material. Buber (*Origin and Meaning of Hasidism*, p. 133) cites Hasidic tradition observing that a true spiritual act of *bittul atzmi* (dissolution of the self) "could substitute for the immersion bath [mikveh]." In this instance the mikveh is related to the second pattern noted previously; namely, man's limitations when he focuses only on the material aspects of existence.

34. Avraham Malach, *Hesed Le'abraham*, front page.

35. Alfasi, *Hahasidut*, pp. 87–88.

36. Buber, *Origin and Meaning of Hasidism*, p. 132. Huberband cites the attempt of Hasidim to use the Vistula River near Warsaw as a mikveh in the summer of 1940. Due to the cold temperature of the water and a case of drowning caused by the swift currents (a young Gerer Hasid, Beyrish Filger or Forlger, was the victim), the experiment was terminated. *Kiddush Hashem*, pp. 82, 91.

37. *Eleh Shelo Nikhne'u*, vol. 2, pp. 14–15.

38. Buber, *Tales of the Hasidim: Early Masters*, p. 4.

NOTES TO CHAPTER 14

1. Referring to Genesis 18:25, where Abraham pleads with God to spare Sodom from impending destruction.

2. Those *Rebbes* who did not abandon their communities and continued to guide and comfort their Hasidim.

3. Bettelheim, "Individual and Mass Behavior in Extreme Situations." Also, idem, *The Informed Heart*, chaps. 4 and 5.

4. Bettelheim's term, *Informed Heart*, pp. 112–113, referring to responses of the victims related to "former [pre-Holocaust] main interests" and removed from and counter to the. mass behavior imposed by extreme Holocaust conditions.

5. Ibid., p. 120.

6. Ibid., pp. 122–123.

7. Deuteronomy 26:6, referring to Israel's bondage in Egypt.

8. The prepositional phrase *lanu* (were harsh "to us") would seem more appropriate than the biblical use of the pronoun *otanu* ("[with] us").

9. The depraved environment transformed the victims into depraved indi-

viduals. The victim is therefore the potential object of the personality transformation. Hence the pronoun *otanu* is appropriate.

10. The Germans utilized Jews for police actions in the ghettos. Robinson, *And the Crooked Shall Be Made Straight*, pp. 151, 162, 188. But see ibid., pp. 172, 241, 281, 331, for evidence of noncooperation by the Jewish police.

11. During the subsequent stages of the ghetto annihilation, the decent elements refused to serve in the Jewish police force when they realized they would be participants in the Nazi plan of genocide. Ibid., p. 331, fn. 113.

12. Alienated youth or members of street gangs.

13. Seidman, *Yoman Getto Warsha*, pp. 138–139. Also ibid., pp. 214–215. Seidman's allegation that Jewish policemen were willing collaborators with the Germans in the Warsaw Ghetto seems to have some support from Hilberg's account of the Warsaw Ghetto uprising. "The first blow of the resistance movement was struck at Jewish collaborators of the *Judenrat* machinery. On August 21, 1942, when the deportations were at their peak, one Israel Kanal fired the first shot in the struggle; the bullet felled the Jewish police chief, Jozef Szerynski. His successor, Jacob Laikin, was also shot. Assassins' bullets struck down policemen, informers and collaborators. Hilberg, *Destruction of the European Jews*, p. 322. Had the Jewish police indeed assisted fellow Jews and not collaborated with the enemy (as reported by Robinson, *And the Crooked Shall Be Made Straight*, p. 171, in the communities of Mlawa, Rohatyn, and Kovno), the resistance movement in Warsaw would not have reacted against the Jewish police force with such vehemence.

Eyewitness Nathan Pick in the Gerlitz work camp describes an exceptional Kapo (supervisor of a forced-labor party; normally noted for curelty), who was unusually good-natured to the workers assigned to him. The man's origin it turns out, was of Hasidic stock. His name was Sandrowich, and he came from the city of Sadonshoh-Valliah. *Eleh Shelo Nikhne'u*, vol. 2, p. 120. See also Hilberg, *Destruction of the European Jews*, p. 583, for a description of the inmate bureaucracy in the concentration camps, including the role of the Kapo.

14. Baruch Kurzweil, "Job and the Possiblity of Biblical Tragedy," p. 330.

15. Steinman, *Sha'ar Hahasidut*, p. 26.

Index

Names

Places

Subject